# Political Extremism

Political extremism is widely consider
behavior. The distinguishing feature
economists and political scientists fr
Australia is to propose a variety of e
rationality of the phenomenon. C
approach to shed light on subjects such as the conditions under
which democratic parties take extremist positions, the relationship
between extremism and conformism, the strategies adopted by revolutionary movements, and the reasons why extremism often leads to
violence. The authors identify four core issues in the study of extremism: the nature (definition) of extremism and its origins in both democratic and authoritarian settings, the capacity of democratic political
systems to accommodate extremist positions, the strategies (civil disobedience, assassination, lynching) chosen by extremist groups, and the
circumstances under which extremism becomes a threat to democracy.

**Albert Breton** is Professor of Economics Emeritus at the University of
Toronto. He is the author of *Competitive Governments* (Cambridge
University Press, 1996; paperback edition, 1998) and *The Economic
Theory of Representative Government* and coauthor or coeditor of
eight other books (*The Economic Constitution of Federal States*, *The
Design of Federation*, *Why Disunity?*, *The Logic of Bureaucratic
Conduct*, besides the ones mentioned below). Professor Breton has
served as president of the Canadian Economic Association and is an
officer of the Order of Canada.

**Gianluigi Galeotti** is Professor of Public Finance at the University of
Rome (La Sapienza), the author of numerous articles in professional
and scholarly journals, and has previously taught at the Universities of
Pisa and Perugia.

**Pierre Salmon** is Professor of Economics at the University of Burgundy.
He is the author of numerous articles and coauthor of *Méthodologie
Economique* (1985). He formerly taught at the Universities of Rennes
and Paris and at the European University Institute in France.

**Ronald Wintrobe** is Professor of Economics at the University of
Western Ontario. He coauthored with Albert Breton *The Logic of
Bureaucratic Conduct* (Cambridge University Press, 1982), and he is
the author of *The Political Economy of Dictatorship* (Cambridge
University Press, 1998; paperback edition, 2000).

**Professors Galeotti**, **Salmon**, and **Wintrobe** previously coedited with
**Albert Breton** *The Competitive State* (1991), *Preferences and
Democracy* (1993), *Nationalism and Rationality* (Cambridge
University Press, 1995), and *Understanding Democracy* (Cambridge
University Press, 1997). Professors Galeotti, Salmon, and Wintrobe
also coedited *Competition and Structure: The Political Economy of
Collective Decisions: Essays in Honor of Albert Breton* (Cambridge
University Press, 2000).

# Political Extremism and Rationality

*Edited by*

**ALBERT BRETON**
*University of Toronto*

**GIANLUIGI GALEOTTI**
*University of Rome*

**PIERRE SALMON**
*University of Burgundy*

**RONALD WINTROBE**
*University of Western Ontario*

CAMBRIDGE
UNIVERSITY PRESS

CAMBRIDGE UNIVERSITY PRESS
Cambridge, New York, Melbourne, Madrid, Cape Town, Singapore,
São Paulo, Delhi, Dubai, Tokyo, Mexico City

Cambridge University Press
The Edinburgh Building, Cambridge CB2 8RU, UK

Published in the United States of America by Cambridge University Press, New York

www.cambridge.org
Information on this title: www.cambridge.org/9780521168618

First published 2002
First paperback edition 2010

*A catalogue record for this publication is available from the British Library*

*Library of Congress Cataloguing in Publication Data*
Political extremism and rationality / edited by Albert Breton ... [et al.].
    p. cm.
Includes bibliographical references and index.
ISBN 0-521-80441-8
1. Radicalism.   2. Rationalism.   3. Democracy.   I. Breton, Albert.
HN49.R33 P65 2001
320. 53-dc21                                    2001022305

ISBN 978-0-521-80441-7 Hardback
ISBN 978-0-521-16861-8 Paperback

# Contents

# List of Figures and Tables

## FIGURES

## TABLES

# Contributors and Discussants

**Nachman Ben-Yehuda**,
Hebrew University, Israel ·

**Vani Borooah**,
University of Ulster, UK

**Giorgio Brosio**,
Università di Torino, Italy

**Geoffrey Brennan**,
The Australian National University, Canberra, Australia

**Albert Breton**,
Department of Economics, University of Toronto, Canada

**Silvana Dalmazzone**,
Department of Economics, Università di Torino, Italy

**Mario Ferrero**,
Università del Piemonte Orientale, Alessandria, Italy

**Gianluigi Galeotti**,
Università di Roma "La Sapienza," Italy

**Luisa Giuriato**,
Università di Parma, Italy

**Amihai Glazer**,
Department of Economics, University of California, Irvine, USA

**Russell Hardin**,
New York University, USA

**Harold M. Hochman**,
Department of Economics and Business, Lafayette College, Easton, PA, USA

**Jean-Dominique Lafay**,
University of Paris I, France

**Louis Lévy-Garboua**,
University of Paris I, France

**Isidoro Mazza**,
Università di Catania, Italy

**Maria Cristina Molinari**,
Università di Venezia, Italy

**Guido Ortona**,
Università del Piemonte Orientale, Alessandria, Italy

**Francesco Parisi**,
George Mason University, USA

**Pierre Salmon**,
Université de Bourgogne, Dijon, France

**Janez Sustersic**,
Institute of Macroeconomic Analysis and Development, Ljubljana,
Slovenia

**Ronald Wintrobe**,
University of Western Ontario, Canada

# Introduction

Political extremism is a complex and difficult subject. Indeed, the very concept "extremist" sometimes makes people uncomfortable. Is not extremism always relative to some set of values, whose rightness is open to debate? As citizens of democratic countries, we often find extremism inside our polities distressing. On the other hand, when extremism occurs in non-democratic settings it often appears to many of us as liberating. Thus, we are often forced to distinguish between the "decent" extremism of those "fighting for political liberation" and the "indecent political brutality" of domestic extremists. And even when we are sympathetic to the aims of the latter, we are often led to wonder why human rationality is unable to eliminate the social waste implicit in the violence and disruption often associated with extremist activities.

As is widely acknowledged, we owe our political liberties today to some extremists of the past and too much conformity is a danger to our intellectual life and to social progress. At the same time, the conformity often observed within extremist movements is sometimes even more remarkable and disconcerting than the conformity within the wider society to which such movements sometimes set themselves up in opposition. Thus, another contraposition is that, in some ways, extremism and conformity are opposites; in other ways they are simply different aspects of the same phenomenon.

Extremism might not appear to be an easy topic for a science like economics, built on individual rationality, "well-behaved" utility functions, and the invisible hand and welfare maximization. Corner solutions – often thought to be implicit in any extremist choice – are not easily handled by the standard marginal calculus. But the economic way of thinking has in recent years been extended to encompass "tipping," irreversibility, bandwagon effects, hysteresis and so forth. Extremism has also been much studied using other methodologies, and the Villa Colombella Group has always invited scholars from the various social

sciences to its conferences. Having reflected in previous books on nationalism and on the working of democratic decision-making, we thought
that a reflection on the politics of extremism could usefully complement
our understanding of the reality of political life in many countries.
Therefore, we invited a number of scholars to France – in Vichy, evoca-
tively – to formulate consistent explanations of what appears to be a
pervasive yet heterogeneous phenomenon.

The initial questions we asked ourselves concerned a number of issues.
First, among the many forms of extremism, we chose to concentrate on
its political expression. As for the kind of political systems to be considered – democratic versus totalitarian settings – we thought of them as
posing different challenges. The presence of at least some kinds of extremists inside a democratic polity can be particularly puzzling. Why is it
that some people in democratic societies who can freely access information come to believe propositions that on standard canons of proof are
simply not credible? How is it, for example, that a number of Americans,
mostly members of paramilitary groups, would come to believe the view
expounded in Mark Koernke's 1993 video, *America in Peril*, that "elements within the US government are working with foreign leaders to turn
the United States into a dictatorship under the leadership of the United
Nations" (Karl 1995, p. 69)?

Another set of questions pertained to the social and economic causes
of extremism as well as to whether extremism is always or even typically
destructive, or whether it can contribute positively to society, for example
by posing the right questions, or by dampening what could otherwise be
even more extreme reactions, or by stimulating positive kinds of change.
We were also concerned with the relationship between extremism and
democracy: does extremism pose a threat to the survival of democracy,
and if so, how and under what circumstances? To what extent are the
sources of extremism and related phenomena to be found in the failings
of democracy to represent or accommodate "fringe" viewpoints?

Most of those questions did, as it turned out, play a large role in the
contributions and in the discussion at the Seminar. But we got more, as
the reader will discover in the following chapters. Before summarizing
them, however, it may be worthwhile to make a few general remarks on
some of the traits that characterize and differentiate the contributions. As
well, it seems useful to elaborate on what appear to us, after the Seminar
and after rereading the contributions, some of the core issues of political
extremism.

Consider first the matter of defining extremism. The definitions used
by most authors are, it would appear, influenced by the cultural traditions from which they emerged as well as by the cases of extremism that
were prominent in the authors' mind. Though no more than a *curiosum*

but one that illustrates the impact of cultural backgrounds, we note that in defining extremism the French, German, and Italian dictionaries emphasize the radicalism of ideas while the English dictionaries stress the violence of the instruments that are adopted.

If the definition of extremism is one of the core issues to which the chapters that follow draw attention, we must acknowledge that little consensus was reached on the topic. What is extremism? What are the kinds of behavior which it is appropriate to consider extremist, that is, what is the domain of extremism? The definitions used in this book portray extremism variously in terms of

1. location at a corner rather than in the interior on some dimension of an individual's preferences. Sometimes, relatedly, extremism is defined as a move away from the center towards the extreme rather than an equilibrium position;
2. a characteristic of the way beliefs are held rather than their location along some dimension; for example, if they are held rigidly or the person holding them displays a small capacity or willingness to compromise;
3. a shrinking of the range, or a limitation of the number of options and choices which are considered;
4. the salience or importance of a belief or set of beliefs; that is, an extremist is someone who is fixated on some idea or belief;
5. the means used; for example, a political extremist is one who resorts to terror or violence to further political ends.

Some will find this diversity more inviting than disconcerting. Others may wish to note that the definitions are not mutually exclusive. One possible synthesis of the various approaches is that, rather than alternative definitions, the different concepts may be thought of as representing different dimensions along which it is possible to be more or less extreme. Combining the different dimensions into a single concept, one might say that a movement in any of these directions would constitute an increase in extremism. Thus, in this way of thinking, a person is more extreme, the further away her views are from the mainstream or center view, the less willing she is to compromise about them, the fewer alternatives to them she is willing to contemplate, the more salient they are to her, and the more willing she is to use violent methods in support of those views. Of course, not all would agree with this synthesis, and in any case a person can be more or less extreme in each of these five senses as well.

A second core issue is the origins of extremism. Are the origins of extremism primarily due to the activities of extremist leaders, to the psychological propensities of followers, to the workings of the political system, or to economic and social change? The chapters in Part I focus more on the first and second of these possibilities. Parts II and III look at the workings of, respectively, democratic and non-democratic systems in terms of stimulating or dampening extremism. The chapters in Part II in particular show how extremism can be stimulated, quite easily, it would appear, by political party competition, a somewhat surprising finding for those who are used to the focus on convergence and the median voter model in standard public choice.

A third core issue is the capacity of the political system to accommodate extremist pressures. Why do some societies appear to be capable of absorbing extremist groups better than others? Both Parts II and III address this question. Democracy appears to be less of an antidote, and more of a stimulus, to extremism than we had thought previously. Even in non-democratic environments, it appears that fundamentalism and extremism can both be stimulated by political competition.

A fourth core issue is the nature of the strategies adopted by extremist groups: why are different strategies (civil disobedience, assassination, lynching) chosen by different groups under different circumstances? Part of the answer to this question is that it depends on the environment in which the extremist group is operating. Many of the chapters in Part II, for example those by Glazer, Hochman, and Salmon focus on the strategies adopted by political parties in an environment of electoral competition. Here, the question is: what makes political parties choose an extremist strategy over a more centrist one? Other chapters focus on different environments. For example, Ferrero looks at the strategies adopted by revolutionary movements along their life cycle, Ortona at mass ethnic violence, and Giuriato and Molinari at the strategies adopted by religious leaders, such as the fundamentalists of Islam, who pursue political objectives.

Finally, there is the question of the limits of the rational choice approach. For example, as Hardin points out, no theory successfully explains why some extremists are willing to commit suicide for a cause. Indeed, some people have wondered whether the subject is even "suitable" for scientific investigation. We believe that the conflicts in places like Northern Ireland, Sri Lanka, and a number of African countries and the importance of extremist phenomena in even the securest of democracies are too significant to be ignored by social scientists who, we also believe, are capable of investigating the origins and dynamics of these problems and of proposing solutions when warranted. We think that this volume demonstrates that the rational choice approach has much to contribute.

In terms of methods, two chapters develop the argument in terms of game, but in all chapters empirical testing is confined to historical or contemporary examples. In part, this no doubt reflects the underdeveloped nature of the theory, although one nice feature of many of the chapters is their focus on relating their theories to real-world illustrations and examples of extremism. The reader will find references, for example, to totalitarianism in the former USSR and China, to the dictatorial regime of Vichy, to ethnic hatred in Rwanda and Bosnia-Herzegovina, to the historical divisions in Northern Ireland, and to political oppression by the Iranian Ayatollahs, the Khmer Rouge, and the Taliban. The reader will also discover that extremist groups and extremist political behavior appear not only in socially precarious situations and in human societies which look primitive to our progress-centric eyes, but also in culturally and democratically developed settings. Indeed, extremism as it occurs in many contemporary democracies is discussed in a number of chapters (an admittedly not all-inclusive list of extremist movements is presented in the third chapter by Breton and Dalmazzone, encompassing 26 groups, half of which are in Western countries).

The chapters are assembled in three parts. Part I deals with the origins of extremism, and the vexed relationship between extremism and conformist behavior. The five chapters of Part II are all concerned with the way extremism affects and is molded by the workings of democratic politics. Part III is devoted to non-democratic settings.

In the first chapter, Russell Hardin reinterprets Jeremy Bentham's fanaticism as a group-based phenomenon. Virtually all individual knowledge comes from society, but most of that knowledge comes from groups that are open and inclusive. Instead, fanaticism requires an exclusionary group because it needs isolation to protect spurious beliefs from critical challenges. Two main factors are behind the formation and stability of those exclusive groups: a perverse working of incentives and the impact of interests on motivations. With a normal distribution of preferences, most citizens tend to believe that they are well served by median policies, whilst those in the tails of the distribution who find themselves permanent losers hive off into groups whose intent is to oppose normal politics. The tendency to interact with those who share the same beliefs makes the extremists leave moderate groups and the moderates leave the extremist groups. The second factor is the nexus between knowledge and interests which strengthens fanatical attitudes, since it requires coordination on a limited set of views, and coordination brings power, often to a small leadership within the group. Finally, it is especially through gaining control of a state that a fanatical group can defeat contrary views and thereby maintain the crippled epistemology of its followers. Here, Hardin mentions the Islamic political leaders who blocked the open discussion that would moderate religious extremism by undercutting its epistemology.

Ronald Wintrobe shows that extremism can often be interpreted as part of a process of rent seeking in which leaders seek to arouse the passions of their followers. Leaders do this when the groups their followers belong to are excluded from the distribution of rents implicit in the kind of long-term political contracts that politicians find most convenient and typically impose. The rationality of passion is that it demonstrates that outsiders are not willing to live with this situation (being excluded). According to Wintrobe, for this kind of "extremist rent seeking" to emerge, one must observe (1) an actual or perceived asymmetry in the distribution of rents, (2) political leadership to act on this, (3) conformity, and (4) the presence of a social hole or gap in trust between the center and the potential extremist movement. Given the presence of those four elements, the leadership of those who are not allowed to bid (the "outsiders") may seek either to bridge the gap or social hole between the potentially extremist group and the centrist majority, or to mobilize or inflame the passions of the group in an extremist fashion. The key point is that extremism requires mobilization whereas compromise does not. It follows that the greater the control a leader has over his followers, the more likely an extremist action is to be chosen. Some other implications of this approach are that extremism is more likely when some exogenous change deepens the social hole or trust gap; when there is an increase in conformity at the center; and when there is an increase in the perception of dominance or exploitation.

In the third chapter, Albert Breton and Silvana Dalmazzone focus on a particular dimension of extremism, namely the intolerance, the unwillingness to compromise, and the rejection of evidence contradicting one's beliefs that are often associated with the phenomenon and are incompatible with the dialectic of an open civil society. They look at the forces, within a social environment, that can contribute to the development of these attitudes. They then examine mechanisms that help reinforce and diffuse extreme positions and beliefs. Because extremism mostly becomes a socially relevant phenomenon when extremists are mobilized into groups, the authors examine the role of political entrepreneurs and leaders in the formation of these groups and in the emergence and manifestations of political extremism. Breton and Dalmazzone propose a hypothesis based on motives such as signaling and destabilization to account for the fact that extremist groups often engage in different activities such as terrorism, violence, hatred, and the promotion of resentment. It is shown that the behavior of extremist groupings in the pursuit of their objectives can be interpreted as making a rational use of the scarce resources at their disposal.

The chapters of Part II discuss how extremism emerges in democratic settings, for the most part, somewhat surprisingly, as a result of the workings of ordinary democratic party competition. For example, in Chapter 4, by Pierre Salmon, extremism is engendered by the ordinary working of a representative democracy, when a number of single issues are packaged together in an electorally profitable way by some politicians. Salmon draws a distinction between views and their saliency for the view-holders. The former feature captures the conventional spatial notion of centrist versus extreme views, the latter the weight that a voter assigns to her preference. A high saliency is identified as "monomania." This gives four polar combinations: the traditional moderate voter (characterized by a moderately held centrist position), the truly extremist voter now redefined as monomaniacal extremist (strongly held extreme position), the inconsequential extremist (moderately held extreme position), and the monomaniacal centrist, who strongly holds a centrist position. The distinction is used to explain how political leaders can arrange coalitions of voters of a rather odd nature. True extremists of completely different natures can be combined together. Or an extremist coalition can win the support of monomaniacal centrists, as happened with early Nazis' electoral success. That occurrence illustrates another implication of the suggested taxonomy. Even if voters' preferences in terms of ideas remain relatively stable in time, it is of consequence that the saliency of the issues involved may change with the ups and downs of the economic situation, the occurrence of transitory emergency, or in a context of reassessment of past behaviors.

In Chapter 5, Geoffrey Brennan starts by restating the standard normative appraisal of the superiority of centrist outcomes once given a distribution of the ideal points of a group of people and the convexity of their preferences. Then he asks which institutional arrangements promote centrism and with which sources of extremism those arrangements have to deal. When the median voter theorem applies, the presence of extremist preferences may not be a problem: the electoral competition would achieve a centrist outcome whatever the variance of the individual ideal points. However, the literature discusses a number of reasons that can vitiate that convergence. Some examples include the possibility of global cycling, the threat of entry of third parties, and uncertainty on where the median preference lies. These appear to make the outcome dependent on institutional "details," and candidates' stances become less instrumental than otherwise. It can happen that the presence of political rents and the candidates' search for an ideological identity combine with the presence of expressive voting, where citizens – differently from consumers in the market – care for self-identification, public-regardingness, moral values and the like. It is therefore the combination of those motivations on the side of voters and the rational behavior of political agents that may bring about policy outcomes more extreme than the nature of expressive preferences might lead one to think.

In Chapter 6, Amihai Glazer starts with the observation that in the history of the U.S. presidential elections most third parties have taken extreme positions rather than positions between those of the major parties, a fact that would seem to confine them to political irrelevance. Glazer shows that when parties choose their platform, they are concerned not only with positions, but also with the choice of which voters to campaign among. For that purpose a Small party may prefer the immunity from attack that Big parties grant to small-size parties only. A Small party does better when its position reduces a Big party's incentive to campaign in its direction, and when its extreme position reduces the effects of any such campaigning. Therefore, a Small party may choose an extreme position to reduce the effectiveness of campaigns against it, and to induce a Big party to campaign against another Big party, rather than against itself. If campaigning by that Big party against the Small party is particularly effective, this may drive the Small party even further to the extreme.

In Chapter 7, Gianluigi Galeotti looks at the virtues of extremism and considers not the extremism of bizarre minorities, but the circumstances in which popularly supported leaders behave in an uncompromising way. He starts by making a distinction between extremism of goals (interests) and extremism of methods (political actions). This provides four combinations: one "normal politics" case made of accepted goals and accepted methods; one "pure extremism" case of controversial goals and unaccepted methods, and two mixed cases (extremist goals pursued by accepted actions, and vice versa). Galeotti looks at the dynamics of movement among those cases, and he examines the circumstances in which political leaders face a limited set of choices. This can happen at the early stages of democratic evolution, where people can be rallied only in terms of radical signals; when representative democracy is unable to settle radical conflicts and falls in a decisional deadlock; when de-franchised groups pursuing their political empowerment are pushed towards extremist actions because of a combination of internal factors and external pressures (manufactured extremism).

In the last chapter of Part II, Harold Hochman justifies his attempt at a "non-radical deconstruction" of political extremism by the observation that the concept is exceedingly relativistic and in need of some contextual bounds prior to positive analysis. Adopting a public choice perspective, he discusses the relevance of extremist positions to political outcomes, particularly in democratic systems. Hochman raises many issues (political extremism as an artifact of collective choice; the distinction between extremes and politically relevant extremes; the role of a common enemy in reconciling opposite extremists) and puts a number of critical questions: can bounded rationality explain political extremist behavior? What is the place of political extremes in a participatory democracy? What is the influence exerted by electoral systems? His attempt to deconstruct the notion of political extremism is based on its relevance to political outcomes, as driven by the logic of the median voter model, in both static and dynamic settings. Among other questions, the chapter considers the circumstances in which such extremes are likely to fade away or to endorse terrorism.

The chapters of Part III model three instances of the origins of anti-democratic, revolutionary or non-democratic extremism. As might be expected, we are talking about what we might say are extreme forms of extremism.

Chapter 9 deals with the life cycle of extremist political organizations. There, Mario Ferrero distinguishes new political organizations from successful (mature) and declining ones. For an emergent organization, the choice of a future-oriented platform both enhances potential support and reduces the supply of labor to the organization. By balancing out those two effects, it has to find an equilibrium level of extremism, given market parameters. The organization is interpreted as a volunteer enterprise whose members engage in unpaid work in the expectation of future returns, and for reasons of incentives and asymmetric information it typically takes the form of a producer cooperative. As happens with those organizations, an increase in expected revenues decreases the optimal membership and increases actual employment. The radicalization of successful revolutions is then explained by the fact that the adoption of more extreme policies drives many members to exit "voluntarily," thus leaving the remaining ones with a higher expected income. As for senile organizations, they try to buy time by adopting more extreme policies that appeal to younger militants. The model is illustrated by the discussion of the vicissitudes of a number of totalitarian regimes.

Luisa Giuriato and Maria Cristina Molinari examine extremism in the Arab countries where fundamentalist movements of Islamic revival have recently spread. According to the authors, fundamentalism and extremism are not synonyms: the outbreak of violence featuring the rise of Islamic fundamentalism in some countries is a strategy of political struggle "adopted" when democratic compromises are not found expedient. The confrontation between the Islamic movements and the incumbent governments is modeled as an incomplete information game, in line with the literature on the escalation of conflicts. Popular support and the level of radicalism are the key variables that influence extremist reactions and the probability of a civil war. Extremism is not the only possible outcome: weak support to the Islamic groups and a low level of radicalism lead to the maintenance of the status quo; moderate radicalism and the possibility of positive gains for all make a compromise solution convenient. The results of the game are then used to interpret the extremism of a number of countries. The situation of Jordan, Morocco and Tunisia corresponds to the status quo outcome: authoritarian and relatively popular regimes manage to exclude the Islamic movement from the political competition without triggering any extremist reaction. In Lebanon and Turkey, a compromise outcome prevails, with widespread secular attitudes helping the Islamic political integration. Extremism and violence, however, ravage Algeria and, to a smaller extent, Egypt, where strong authoritarian governments do not accept the political integration of the Islamic opposition.

In the last chapter, Guido Ortona purports to provide a theoretical interpretation of generalized violence that is applicable both to settings in which the level of xenophobia is low and to settings in which it is high. For that purpose, he combines what he calls an economic interpretation of nationalism and xenophobia (in which some ethnic elite stand to gain from the presence or increased relevance of "ethnic" capital) with assumptions pertaining to the theory of social conventions. This leads him to claim that mass ethnic violence may develop among fully rational subjects – without appealing to any ancestral feature of mass psychology – when five conditions hold: (a) an initial divide of the population along ethnic or other lines not easily absorbed by market forces; (b) the collapse of the state (private violence is not sanctioned); (c) a first-shot advantage in case of aggression (making rational a preemptive attack, in the presence of what Ortona defines as "a mass greed for self-defence"); (d) the presence of agitators (individuals who do not play the ethnic game but who gain when those who do, the members of the ethnic groups, are assaulted); and (e) an expected payoff for these agitators greater than a threshold level.

We hope that this book provides a useful systematic starting point for understanding a very complex phenomenon in rational choice terms. And we also think the study of extremism reflects back on our understanding of democracy itself. On that account, it is easy to agree with Geoffrey Brennan's observation that "public choice theorists have interpreted the requirements of rationality in the political arena too simple-mindedly . . . the theory paints a picture of democracy that is much less accommodating to extremism and eccentricity in political outcomes than democracy actually is, and that the logic of rational actor analysis . . . faithfully applied, admits." Finally, despite the diversity of the approaches taken in the chapters that follow, we do hope the reader discerns a fundamental unity in the concept of rational political extremism: a counterintuitive, thought-provoking idea which has implications of great intellectual and practical interest and at the same time is simple and understandable.

We wish to thank Nachman Ben-Yehuda, Vani Borooah, Giorgio Brosio, Jean-Dominique Lafay, Louis Lévy-Garboua, Isidoro Mazza, Francesco Parisi, and Janez Sustersic for having contributed to the discussion at Vichy. Finally, the Seminar would not have been possible without the financial assistance provided by the Lynde and Harry Bradley Foundation and the Italian Ministry for the University and Technological Research (National Research Project on the Economic Analysis of Institutional Innovations, 1996). We are deeply grateful to these organizations for their support of our scholarly endeavors.

Albert Breton<br>
Gianluigi Galeotti<br>
Pierre Salmon<br>
Ronald Wintrobe

### REFERENCE

Karl, Jonathan. 1995. *The Right to Bear Arms. The Rise of America's New Militias* (New York: HarperPaperbacks).

# PART I

# EXTREMISM AND CONFORMITY

# 1

# The Crippled Epistemology of Extremism

*Russell Hardin\**

## 1. INTRODUCTION

Jeremy Bentham remarked that religious motivations are among the most constant of all motivations. And, although such a motivation need not be especially powerful, it can be among the most powerful. Because of the constancy of the motivation, "A pernicious act, therefore, when committed through the motive of religion, is more mischievous than when committed through the motive of ill-will" (Bentham 1970: 156). He explains this conclusion from fanaticism, which, of course, need not be religiously motivated and in the twentieth century has been as destructively motivated by ideological and nationalist sentiments as by religious sentiments. This is Bentham's explanation:

If a man happen to take it into his head to assassinate with his own hands, or with the sword of justice, those whom he calls heretics, that is, people who think, or perhaps only speak, differently upon a subject which neither party understands, he will be as inclined to do this [at] one time as at another. Fanaticism never sleeps: it is never glutted: it is never stopped by philanthropy; for it makes a merit

\* This chapter was prepared for and presented at the biannual meeting of the Villa Colombella Group at its conference, "Political Extremism," Vichy, France, 24–27 June, 1998. I thank the organizers of that meeting and the participants for engaging discussions. Much of the chapter was written while I was a visitor at the Universidad Torcuato di Tella in Buenos Aires, whose people recently escaped from an era of dreadful, murderous extremism to achieve a remarkable air of decency, prosperity, and tranquility. Indeed, at the time of writing, the chief political issue was largely one of the character of political leaders. That such character issues are the talk of the day and the press is a reassuring sign that politics is not pervasively destructive. I thank Julio Saguir and the Universidad Torcuato di Tella for that visit. The chapter was also presented to the UCLA workshop in political economy in March 1999. I thank Kathleen Bawm and Miriam Golden for organizing that session and I thank them and their colleagues for a spirited and insightful discussion. I also thank Jack Hirschleifer for his sharp written comments. Finally, I thank New York University for generous general support.

of trampling on philanthropy: it is never stopped by conscience; for it has pressed conscience into service. Avarice, lust, and vengeance, have piety, benevolence, honour; fanaticism has nothing to oppose it. (Bentham 1970: 156n)

Note especially the cruelty of his observation: "which neither party understands."

Bentham's remark is about the individual fanatic. My concern here will be, primarily, with groups of such individuals. Seeing the nature of a group of fanatics may help to understand why the fanatic never sleeps. When the fanatic is in a group of like-minded people, and especially when the group isolates itself from others, either by separating itself or by excluding others, that group reinforces the individual's "conscience," indeed, reinforces the individual's beliefs, both factual and normative. A fanatic who must live among others who do not share the fanatic's views may finally at least nod. It is generally the group that produces and sustains fanaticism.

Fanaticism is inherently, therefore, a sociological and not merely a psychological matter. A focus on the individual fanatic might lead one to suppose the issue is the nature of the belief, how it is different from other beliefs. This might typically be the fanatics' own account: that it is the content of the belief that justifies the fanaticism. Focus on the group leads us to ask how the belief gets inculcated and maintained. The latter focus suggests that fanaticism is less likely to be defined by its substantive content than by the way it is socially constructed. This suggests why Bentham's focus on religious fanatics was partly misplaced. In what follows, I will lay out a very short version of an economic theory of knowledge from which to attempt an understanding of fanatically held knowledge or beliefs. I will linger over the characterization of knowledge by authority, which is an especially important element of such an economic epistemology for fanatical, group-based beliefs. I will then turn to the nature of normal politics, in particular noting how it sets up fanatical politics. I will bring these discussions together in an account of the epistemology of extremism, and I will relate this to nationalism. Finally, I will discuss connections between fanatical beliefs and actions and the relationship between interests and knowledge, and I will suggest how crippled epistemology leads to fanaticism, which may in turn lead to fanatical nationalism.

## 2.  AN ECONOMIC THEORY OF KNOWLEDGE

What we need foremost to understand fanatical commitment is an adequate theory of belief – a theory of knowledge or an epistemology. One might suppose that, whatever it is, a theory of knowledge must be generally applicable to all knowledge. Hence, the explanation of extremist political belief is merely a part of the explanation of beliefs more generally, although it might exhibit special characteristics, in part because of differing incentives on offer from the larger society of the believer. An ordinary person's knowledge must depend in general on the costs and benefits of discovering bits of it and of putting it to use. Once discovered, however, a bit of knowledge, X, will be counted as true to the extent it comes from a credible authority, it fits coherently with other beliefs, it corresponds with the world, or it once seemed to meet one of these conditions. One's belief in the truth of X might also depend on the rewards of counting it as true. I wish especially to address this last possibility as applied to fanatical beliefs.

In standard philosophy of knowledge or epistemology, knowledge is "justified true belief." It is specific pieces of knowledge whose belief is justified. Often, what is meant by justified is something well beyond what any individual is in a position to know or do. The reason for this way of conceiving the problem of knowledge is that philosophers have primarily been concerned with understanding and evaluating knowledge as in the content of a science – especially, of course, the content of physics. It is not *my knowledge* of physics that is at issue, but rather *the truth* of physics. The philosophical theory of knowledge applies to *the objects of belief*, not to the believers. It is typically about the criteria for counting something as knowledge. These criteria can be about the objects themselves or about the procedures followed in assessing the objects. On this kind of theory, fanatical political belief or knowledge is highly problematic. One could not give the criteria that make such belief justified to count as knowledge. Or, if one proposed criteria, they would almost surely be different from the criteria for other knowledge.

Philosophical epistemology is therefore largely about a kind of public, not personal, knowledge. What must interest a social scientist who wishes to explain behavior is the knowledge or beliefs of actual people. An *economic* theory of knowledge would address this question. Such a theory would not focus on the objects of belief but on the ways people come to hold their beliefs. By an economic theory, I mean merely a theory that focuses on the costs and benefits of having and coming to have knowledge or to correct what knowledge one has. An economic theory of knowledge would be grounded in three quite distinct facts that matter to anyone whose knowledge we wish to explain.

First, knowledge has value as a resource and is therefore an economic good; hence, people will seek it. Sometimes we seek it at a very general level, as when we get a general education. In this case, we may have little idea of how we are ever going to use the knowledge and we may not know in advance much about the range of the knowledge we will acquire. Sometimes we seek it for a very specific matter, as when we seek mortgage rates when buying a home. In this case, we know exactly what we want the knowledge for and we know reasonably well where to get it and when we have enough of it.

Second, its acquisition often entails costs, so that the value of knowledge trades off against the values of other things, such as resources, time, and consumptions. Moreover, these costs are often very high. For example, the costs of gaining enough information to judge political candidates in an election are thought commonly to be far too high for most voters in the United States to be able to justify the expenditure, especially given that they have little to gain from voting anyway. Instead, they vote on the strength of relatively vague signals about issues they do not adequately comprehend.

And third, a lot of our knowledge, which we may call "happenstance knowledge," is in various ways fortuitously available when we use it. Some knowledge comes to us more or less as a byproduct of activities undertaken for purposes other than acquiring the knowledge, so that in a meaningful sense we gain that knowledge without investing in it – we do not trade off other opportunities for the sake of that knowledge. For example, you know a language because you grew up in human society. Much of what is loosely called social capital is such byproduct knowledge. Byproduct knowledge may simply be available to us essentially without cost when we face choices. Some knowledge may even come to us as virtually a consumption good. For example, your love of gossip may lead to knowledge that is quite valuable to you. Finally, the knowledge in which I deliberately invested yesterday for making a specific choice then may still be available to me today when I face some other choice to which it might be relevant. Fanatical political belief is very much a matter of happenstance knowledge (as is almost everything we know at any given moment).

## 3. KNOWLEDGE BY AUTHORITY

Because of the high costs of acquiring all knowledge on our own, we typically rely on authority for most of the knowledge we actually have (Hardin 1992). We could all say, with Wittgenstein (1969: 44), "My life consists in my being content to accept many things" – indeed, most things that matter. I rely on the authoritative knowledge of many people. Notoriously, most of us rely on the authoritative knowledge of professionals such as doctors, lawyers, and many others. But we all essentially rely on the authority of various historians for the bulk of what we claim to know about the world's past history and we rely on the authority of numerous writers and people in the media for the knowledge we claim to have about our own contemporary world. In all substantial areas of our lives, we necessarily accept much of what we know from authorities of various kinds, some of them quite reliable, some of them not.

A very large part of our knowledge, which at this moment is essentially happenstance knowledge, is the residue of past acceptances of authoritative assertions. Yet, at the moment when we invoke any of that knowledge now, we may no longer even remember much about its acquisition, so that we may be in no position to question it by first questioning its authoritative source. As of now, I just do know that Caesar was a Roman. I cannot say how I first came to know this fact, although I can tell you of books that I read, mostly long ago, that discussed Caesar and his life and that, in a sense, reinforced or confirmed my knowledge of him as a Roman.

Even if I revise core beliefs from my early years, I may have great trouble revising all of the bits of understanding in my mind that were influenced by my prior beliefs and my upbringing in them, so that I may still have strong ties to my earlier beliefs. For example, I may continue to have a strong commitment to the golden rule of doing unto others what I would have them do unto me. But I may never again accept on dead authority the core of my previous beliefs that led to this commitment. Indeed, I may even come to view many of the commitments I still have as deeply contrary to those that I now question.

Of course, it makes eminently good sense to rely on knowledge by authority. The costs of checking out everything one knows even by hearsay would be catastrophic for actually living instead of merely deciding how to live. If we insisted on checking out every bit of putative knowledge, we would be virtually catatonic. Even checking out a single bit of knowledge might make little sense because the costs of having it wrong would seem to be less than the costs of being surer of getting it right. We can commonly rely on others to check some facts and to benefit from their judgment of the validity and usefulness of those facts.

These characteristics of ordinary knowledge in general are exacerbated for knowledge of moral and ideological matters, because the latter are not even well tested by anyone and because it would be difficult to imagine relevant tests of them. Moreover, such facts are not subject to being discovered from experience or by application of any kind of scientific method; rather, they are almost always invented. But the person who relies on authority for acceptance of various facts need not have any particular qualification to judge which facts are more likely to be authoritatively correctly held and which are merely invented, perhaps by some fanatic. Indeed, for the ordinary person, moral, ideological, and religious beliefs might well be indistinguishable in their sources from most objective beliefs. To cite standard examples, the beliefs that the earth is round or that men have walked on the moon are no more solidly objective for many people than are their beliefs about God or the rightness of not telling a lie. The latter beliefs might get much stronger support from others in one's society, especially from others whom one knows and respects. And the benefits of believing them might be considerably greater than the benefits of believing that the earth is round or that men have walked on the moon.

That our beliefs depend in part on the larger society's assessments and reinforcements means that they can also be manipulated by that society. Or, even more significantly for ideological beliefs, they can be manipulated within small segments of that society so long as the larger society and its views are held at bay. If I am in a small community with beliefs that others would think very odd, I may find those beliefs not at all odd because, after all, they are held by everyone I know. They may be merely part of the vast catalog of beliefs that I hold from dependence on authority.

## 4. NORMAL POLITICS

Turn now to the context in which extreme politics may be played out. The median voter or Downsian model suggests that most voters must see themselves as relative losers at each election (Downs 1957). Some must always be losers. This follows for all views that display a roughly normal distribution of preferences over political outcomes.[1] Winning candidates or policies must be close to the views of some, but farther from the views of most voters. With multiple dimensions of issues, a typical voter might be close to the winner on one or a few issues but still must be far from the winner on most issues. A major trick of normal, non-extreme politics is to get people to think they do relatively well politically even though this superficially dismal implication of the median voter model is correct. In relatively prosperous times, it might reasonably seem true to most citizens that their interests are either relatively well served by politics or that those interests are not substantially affected by politics. Hence, that their preferences might not be those of the elected governors does not matter fundamentally or grievously.

Those in the tails of the distribution of preferences over major issues, however, cannot generally think they do well in normal politics. At best they can think they have done better this time than last time than usually. For example, citizens on the far right in the United States must

---

[1] Preferences over many issues, such as those that are essentially yes–no, are not likely to be even roughly normal. For example, preferences on abortion in the United States are fundamentally bimodal, with a majority of the populace evidently in favor of a liberal regime on abortion and a majority of legislators prepared to vote great restrictions on abortion.

have thought the election of Ronald Reagan as president in 1980 was a clear improvement over the previous half century.

For those who are always big losers in normal politics, exit from such politics might be a common response. In Albert Hirschman's (1970) account, they have three options: exit, voice, or loyalty. Loyalty seems incredible and self-denying. Voice has completely failed. Only exit is left. Exit can take at least two quite different forms. First, it might simply involve withdrawal in the form of reduced participation in normal politics with no other form of activity to replace it for its main functions. More worrisome for normal politics is that the permanent losers might hive off into groups whose intent is to oppose normal politics. Such groups are typically viewed as extremist by those committed to normal politics. As I will argue below, a group that hives off faces its members with epistemological constraints that may heighten the intensity of their beliefs in the wrongness of their nation's politics and strengthen their motivations to do something outside normal politics.

In the brief passage quoted above, Bentham concluded that, unlike other vices, fanaticism has no opposing virtue. Indeed, it has only normalcy to oppose it. Unfortunately, normalcy is merely a condition for living reasonably and it does not greatly motivate us unless, perhaps, we do not have it. Mere normalcy therefore may not be enough to stop overwrought fanaticism, especially when the fanatics exit from normal politics and even from normal society.

## 5. THE EPISTEMOLOGY OF EXTREMISM

A politically extreme view is likely to be a norm of exclusion that is self-enforcing, even self-strengthening. Norms of exclusion define groups to which those with the right views or with the right characteristics are admitted and from which others are excluded. Under the force of such norms of exclusion, the less intensely committed members of a group depart while extremists remain (Hardin 1995: Ch. 4). Daniel P. Moynihan (1993: 22) supposes that ethnicity is a new social aggregate and that the clear point to be made about the so-called melting pot in the United States is that it did not happen. Clearly, he is wrong if he means that there has been no or even no substantial intermarriage across ethnic lines with consequent loss of identification with such groups. But if some melt, those who are left are likely to be the more intensely committed. Hence, there may be both a lot of melting and a lot of residual ethnicity, as, for example, in the case of orthodox Jews such as the Lubavitch Jews of Brooklyn. As such residual ethnically defined groups shrink, they may become extreme in their beliefs and actions.

The logic of incentives here is the opposite of that in the account above of citizens in normal politics. In normal politics it is the extremists who depart and the less intense who remain behind. In fringe politics, the moderates exit, leaving the most intense behind. The outmigration of the less committed from an exclusionary group leaves the hard core in control (Hardin 1995: 101). But the exclusionary practices of an extreme group do more than this. *They affect the knowledge of the group's members.*

Recall Bentham's cruel remark about the fanaticism that flows from beliefs in heresies, "which neither party understands." He perhaps implicitly supposes there might be a truth of the matter and that neither of the opponents over the beliefs knows that truth. One might rather say that, those who assert the truth of some particular view have inadequate ground for their own assertions. But this is a claim from standard philosophical epistemology. In their own epistemology, they may genuinely suppose that they do have grounds or merely even that they do know the truth of what they assert (see further, Hardin 1997).

Argument from philosophical epistemology is unlikely to motivate a change in beliefs for anyone other than, perhaps, a deeply committed philosopher or scientist. Physicists have, for example, been convinced of the truth of quantum mechanics, biologists of the truth of the system of DNA structuring of life, and some philosophers of the relevance and correctness of Kantian ethics. All of these beliefs must sound incongruous and incredible to ordinary people, for whom the beliefs are dreamlike nonsense. Most of us do not have the time or incentive to be deeply committed philosophers or scientists and we need not even suspect that there is anything questionable about our beliefs.

It might seem astonishing that one could know that others generally believe differently and that one nevertheless insists strongly on the truth of one's own particular beliefs. But this capacity seems less astonishing if one's particular beliefs are those of a group or society in which one spends one's life and that those who believe otherwise are outside that group or society. In these conditions, my beliefs may get reinforced constantly by those around me even though those beliefs might be shared by at most a tiny fraction of the world's population.

If, however, we have beliefs that are contrary to widespread beliefs in our own society, we can partially protect our beliefs, whether intentionally or unintentionally, by keeping ourselves in the company only of others who share our beliefs. In our isolation, we may even begin to think those outside our group are hostile to us. We may therefore have openly hostile relations with those outside our group and we may harden our judgment of other groups over time. As an example of this self-reinforcing trend, consider the so-called ethnic hatred that was blamed by many for the recent collapse of Yugoslavia. Such group hatred seems more likely to have followed than to have preceded the grisly violence in Yugoslavia. The hostility led to the destruction of longstanding friendships and to the break-up of marriages across ethnic lines. The fact of such friendships and marriages does not fit the brutal assertion of many observers that the hatred was prior and therefore was the fundamental cause of the civil strife (see, for example, Kaplan 1993). The supposed hatred followed the politics of hostility (Hardin 1995: 155–63).

Isolation of people in a group with relatively limited contact with the larger society generates paranoid cognition, in which individuals begin to suppose the worst from those they do not know or even from those with whom they are not immediately in communication. As Roderick Kramer (1994) describes this psychological phenomenon: when people feel that they are under scrutiny they tend to exaggerate the extent to which they are the target of attention. They therefore attribute unduly personalistic motivations to others and become increasingly distrustful of those others. Kramer calls this the sinister attribution error. Although his studies are of intra-organizational contexts, one might suppose this phenomenon would color relations between relatively separatist, isolated groups and the larger society. If so, it would clearly affect the beliefs of the isolated group members.

While psychologists might suppose that such phenomena as paranoid cognition and the sinister attribution error are the result of complex psychological motors, they may primarily be simple matters of the skewed epistemology that comes from lack of contact with and, hence, lack of accurate knowledge of relevant others. Separation in order to sustain a group's beliefs might go much further and actually reinforce or even partially determine those beliefs. The hostility of an isolated extremist group may flow more from this skewing of its members' beliefs than from genuine opposition to the larger society or some other group.

In a study of the ultra-orthodox Jews of Israel, Eli Berman notes that political demands by the group to restrict the activities of others, for example, by prohibiting commerce and motor traffic on the Sabbath, may cause antagonism from the others. He notes that such "secular antagonism toward the ultra-orthodox could be desirable and efficient from the point of view of the latter community if it discourages secular activity by [the ultra-orthodox]" (Berman 1998: 24). It may be beneficial to those strongly committed to the ultra position in other ways as well. In particular, it might strengthen the norm of exclusion of the ultras and it might strengthen commitments by members in reaction to the heightened hostility of the outside community. Hence, indirectly, the politics of imposing their views on others' actions may contribute to the crippling of the epistemology of the ultras, although their intent might merely be to

cripple the epistemology of secular Israelis in the hope of leading them to
orthodox views.

## 6.  NATIONALISM

Consider the views of nationalists, views that are sometimes but not
always or even typically fanatic. As many observers of nationalism
note, the nationalist vision is perplexing for its epistemological vacuity,
even when it is far from fanatical. Benedict Anderson (1991: 5) notes
three general oddities of the vision:

1.  The objective modernity of nations to analysts vs. their antiquity
    [supposedly even primordial] to nationalists;
2.  The formal universality of nationality as a sociocultural concept vs.
    the irremediable particularity of its concrete manifestations; and
3.  The political power of nationalisms vs. their philosophical poverty
    and incoherence.

Anderson concludes that a nation is an imagined political community.
E. J. Hobsbawm (1992: 46) asks how a concept so remote from the real
experience of most humans as "national patriotism" could become such a
powerful political force so quickly. On the account of the epistemology of
nationalism, one must suppose it requires either an illogical imagination
or an imagination grounded in woeful ignorance. Illogic is not impossible
but the more likely account must be woeful ignorance.

As an example of the philosophical poverty of the nationalist vision,
consider the frequent assertion by nationalists of a common national will
(Anderson 1991: 108). Historically, the idea of a common will or sovereignty of a people may simply be a transformation of the idea of the
sovereignty of the single willed monarch. Yet, the very fact of a nationalist movement that is not universally supported implies the lack of a
common will. Moreover, in virtually every context that matters in practice, there can be no common will of a people numerous enough to
constitute a nation. It is a fallacy of composition to suppose that there
is a common will.

Hence, nationalist views share with fanatical views that they are commonly grounded in ignorance that evidently gets sanctioned by groups.
Unless it is accompanied by a creed, however, nationalism is not typically
fanatical. The ignorance that underlies commonplace nationalist views is
a relatively general kind of ignorance that can seemingly survive open
discussion in a broad society. As Hobsbawm (1992: 169) notes, vagueness
and the lack of programmatic content gives nationalism potentially universal support within its own community. For example, ethnic and lin-
guistic nationalism provide no general guidance for the future (168). Such

vagueness often underlies negative programs, such as the nationalism that is opposed to a colonial regime or the movement to overthrow the Shah. Indeed, because these views fit a quasi-utilitarian assessment of what would benefit the relevant national group, they can be supported by a relatively open society.

But when the views turn fanatic, the ignorance that underlies them must be protected from the intrusions of the broader society. For example, ideological or religious fundamentalism typically provides "a detailed and concrete program for both the individual and the society." Such fundamentalism draws strength from the claim to universal truth, applicable to all (Hobsbawm 1992: 168). Just because it does, however, it can be questioned in detail and with specificity. Such questioning could be the death of fanatical beliefs. Fanaticism is not a kind of belief; rather it is a characteristic of the way beliefs can be held, including obstinate ignorance of alternative views. Fanaticism requires exclusionary group practices for its maintenance because it requires the isolation that allows spurious beliefs to escape challenge.

Yet it is often directed at the promulgation of a universalist program, which, again, would be inclusive rather than exclusive. This peculiar divergence between the inclusive substance and the exclusionary maintenance of many fanatical views is merely a result of the economic epistemology of holding views against those of a larger society. The views require protection against corrosive contrary knowledge. This is even true to some extent of milder nationalist views. Nationalism, however powerful the emotion of being in an imagined community, is nothing without the creation of nation-states (Hobsbawm 1992: 177). That is, with neither the plausible, but vague, goal of creating a national state nor maintenance by an organized state to keep it alive, nationalism as a very general urge falters. For example, as Yael Tamir (1993: 140) notes, when a population is diverse and intermingled, we have no choice but to reconcile ourselves to living together.

Michael Walzer argues that ethnic pluralism is evidently compatible with the idea of a unified republic (Walzer 1980: 785). But, as he notes, a modern liberal pluralist state is a very different kind of republic from that envisioned by Montesquieu and Rousseau. It lacks the intense political fellowship and pervasive commitment to public affairs that they praised and advocated. Rousseau supposed that the better the constitution of the state is, the more do public affairs encroach on private in the minds of citizens. Rousseau's claim might fit a small city state, such as the Geneva of his time, but it is entirely wrong for large, complex states. It is Nazi, Soviet, and Maoist states that most push public affairs to encroach on private affairs. Large states with good constitutions typically leave citizens almost entirely alone to lead their own lives. In good times, there should be little political participation in a well organized liberal state. Such states might offer assistance to some and must generally offer coordination of many activities to enable citizens to live with each other despite their varied purposes (Hardin 1999: chap. 1). It is states such as those led by extremists that attempt to go much further in forcing public affairs onto citizens, largely by enforcing values that many citizens might not share. This is one of the reasons that Rousseau, no doubt unfairly, is sometimes seen as an early source of totalitarian thought.

As Tamir (1993: 79) notes, the idea of nationalism tends to be associated with its most fanatical versions, which assume, in a variant of the Rousseauean vision, that the identity of individuals is wholly constituted by their national membership and that personal will is only free when submerged in the national one. The liberal nationalism for which Tamir argues is, rather, the descendant of the cultural pluralism of Johann Gottfried von Herder and G. Mazzini. Their German and Italian nationalisms of the eighteenth and nineteenth centuries aimed at creating supranations out of multitudes of diverse communities. The popular idea of nationalism is, however, commonly associated with such problem cases as the later, twentieth-century German and Italian nationalisms that were radically illiberal.

One might ask of cases of fanatical nationalism, which comes first – the fanaticism or the nationalism? Below I will suggest that fanaticism often seems to require nationalism for its fulfillment or security. Fanaticism is therefore not inherent in nationalism, although nationalism may often be born out of fanaticism, in which case it is likely to be fanatical nationalism. Yet, the fanaticism might actually be diverted by the demands of a nationalism that cannot readily be exclusive and that might soon become, if not quite liberal, at least more inclusive. Hence, in principle at least, nationalism might be a counter or even an antidote to fanatical movements, not least because it might offer greater rewards to leaders of any factional group. There is, for example, a strand of Israeli nationalism that has this strong, liberal bent, but it may lose to the fanatical bent of the more prolific, rigidly exclusionary, and epistemologically crippled ultra-orthodox Israelis.

On the issue of ethnic and other pluralisms in a large society, recall Moynihan's overstatement on the failure of the melting pot in the United States (noted above). Edward Said supposes that minority immigrant groups no longer need assimilate because "the simple accessibility of the entire world makes . . . forgetfulness all but unattainable" (quoted in Tamir 1993: 86). But assimilation is primarily a generational effect; hence, this supposition seems unlikely to be true. Members of later generations will commonly succumb to the blandishments of the society in which they grow up and live and they will find life both easier and generally more rewarding if they adopt the local language and manners. Many will therefore attain "forgetfulness." But those who sustain memories and identifications may well constitute a potentially extreme group. Against the prospects of their doing so, however, is Said's "simple accessibility of the entire world," which undercuts the possibility of sustaining the crippled epistemology of extremism. Sustaining such an epistemology requires exclusion of knowledge of, and therefore traffic with, most of the rest of the entire world.

Writers on nationalism commonly ask why individuals are willing to die (or at least to put themselves at great risk of dying) for mere nations. Anderson (1991: 7 and 141) asks the question twice and, symptomatically, he fails to answer it. He says only that "It is as a community that nations lead so many to die for them despite the relative recency of nationalism (scarcely more than two centuries)." All the other major writers on nationalism, many of whom frame Anderson's question more or less explicitly, also fail to answer it, although some of them seem to think it easy to understand that people become so radically committed to a nationalist cause. The answer must turn on the fact that nationalist views do not entail fanaticism but that fanaticism can be directed at nationalist goals. To explain fanatical nationalism, therefore, requires more than merely the explanation of nationalism. Most Americans might well be nationalist but few of them are fanatically nationalist.

## 7. FANATICAL ACTION WITHOUT FANATICAL BELIEF

Members of isolated extremist groups can do things that seem extraordinary to others, as though they were audacious beyond measure. But the individuals in an isolated group are not so clearly audacious in their actual context. They merely do what people in their groups do. Such action, if undertaken by an ordinary person whose life is wholly within the larger community, would be audacious.

Although the beliefs that would lead an individual to be profoundly committed to a nation or ethnic group are surely socially instilled and defined, action is finally taken at the individual level of the person and not at the aggregate level. Knowledge can depend on a group's impact on an individual. In part, the effect of the group is through its authority as a source of knowledge. It might also turn on the incentives the group has to influence members' actions in ways that lead them to particular beliefs. Indeed, rewarding or sanctioning members for their apparently right or wrong knowledge might directly affect what the members know by making their knowledge fit more nearly with their interests.

I might come to adopt some important belief, X, of my group in a more complex causal way as a result of my interest in being in the group. As a result of my participation in the life of the group, I hear many things that actually support belief X. After some time, I may begin to have difficulty separating various things I seemingly know from the belief X, which begins to be reinforced by this growing body of related knowledge. Eventually it might even happen that the best way to make sense of a lot of related things is actually to suppose X is true, and I might therefore come to believe it as an almost necessary or deductively entailed part of this coherent larger body of beliefs. It follows then that I am led to my belief in X by the incentive for having it, or at least for credibly expressing it. I do not directly believe merely because it is in my interest to do so, but I do other things that are in my interest and in doing these things I come to believe X. The belief may be an unintended consequence of various activities and other beliefs.

As a member of a group one might recognize the force of the group's impositions without finally believing what seems to define and unite the group. Because one's interests in membership are at stake, however, one might act in ways that fit the group's beliefs. In a sense then, we might say that actions may be fanatical even when beliefs are not. For example, one of the so-called killers of Mostar during the Bosnian war explained his actions not as a result of beliefs about the evil nature of the people he was murdering, many of whom were, after all, formerly his friends. Rather, he explained it as a result of his interest in remaining a part of his Serbian community. If he wished to remain, he had to join actively in its horrors (Hardin 1995: 148–9).

At the extreme, one might suppose that some group has no genuine believers in its fanatical views but that all members are coordinated on acting fanatically by the false sense that everyone else or most others do believe. A near-cousin of this possibility is the claim by John Howard Griffin (1976: 153; see further, Hardin 1995: 90) that many, perhaps a majority of, southern whites favored the end of Jim Crow segregation policies but thought themselves a tiny minority and therefore never acted against white hegemony. Instead, they acquiesced in the prevalent racism.

## 8.  INTERESTS AND KNOWLEDGE

In general, note that the focus here is almost entirely on knowledge and not on interests. James Coleman's account of zealotry is based on interests in the individual's costs and benefits of acting for collective benefit (Coleman 1987). One must generally suppose that, if action is to be explained, we must finally deal not only with knowledge but also with motivations. Hence, to complete the story of fanatical political commitments, we need not only an epistemology of fanatical beliefs but also a motivational account of why such beliefs produce the extraordinary actions we often see.

Sometimes, as in the case of the killers of Mostar, the motivation for relevant actions is to be structurally explained as part of an imposed system of incentives, so that fanatical beliefs and fanatical actions need not be joined. We might be able in some contexts to argue convincingly that some beliefs virtually entail actions, so that believing is tantamount to acting. For various reasons, including usual concerns with akrasia or weakness of will, this easy step is not prima facie compelling in general, although it might be in some cases. In particular, it might fit the behavior of very young terrorists who have been indoctrinated in secluded terrorist camps, so that their epistemology is particularly constrained and crippled, enough so as to convince them that their interests are served by undertaking suicidal actions.

Albert Hirschman (1977) argues that the rise of capitalism helped to displace religious zealotry because passions were trumped by interests. At least part of the story even of this change is merely that people began to learn the costs of zealotry, costs that rose as the economy was depressed by turmoil, as in seventeenth-century England. Hobbes and Locke essentially wished to push religious conflict out of politics in order to allow greater material prosperity – and greater personal safety. Hobbes supposed this could be done by imposing some – any – particular variant of Protestant Christianity. Locke supposed it could be done by merely keeping religious issues out of politics and consigning them to the realm of personal conscience (a very Protestant view).

People commonly do not know their interests or do not know how to effect their interests. The constrained epistemology of extremism can exacerbate both of these failings. Part of the impact of economic progress is to make clearer to people what their interests are or how their interests can be served. Fanaticism seems to decrease with general prosperity – this is a generalization of the Marxist worry about the eventual embourgeoisement of increasingly prosperous workers. Those with a large stake in the present state of affairs are less likely to attack it.

Religious zealotry in our time has been the wreck of the economic prospects of many Islamic nations, which have generally performed far less well than comparable non-Islamic nations. The complaint of Islamic fundamentalists is an analog of that of Marxists: materialism saps religious commitment. They therefore wish to gain control of governments and laws in order to suppress material concerns and to impose their religious values. As is true of many extremist groups, therefore, their goal is inherently illiberal. It is a claim for the unquestioned rightness of particular ideas. But they seem fairly clearly to understand that their ideas can prevail only by keeping people ignorant of alternatives. Hence, they seem to have a relatively clear sense of the epistemological bases of liberalism and illiberalism. That is to say, they recognize that their problem is not merely one of motivation but, more urgently, of epistemology.

It is instructive that most of the Islamic states also fail to become democratic. John Mueller argues that this is a matter of deliberate choice on the part of the autocratic national leaders (Mueller 1999: chap. 3), although that explanation leaves open the question why those nations so typically have autocratic leadership. Because many of these leaders are not themselves religious fundamentalists, it is perhaps an unintended consequence of their anti-democratic stance that they block open discussion that would undercut religious extremism by undercutting its epistemology. Had they allowed democratic choice, they might well have lost power fairly early. But the cost of maintaining their rigidly anti-democratic stance is the creation of an opposition that could not have flourished as well in an open society.

## 9.  EPISTEMOLOGY, FANATICISM, AND NATIONALISM

In the end it is arguably the nexus between knowledge and interests that explains fanatical nationalism. This causal connection is important negatively in that, if knowledge were not radically crippled for many fanatical nationalists, they could not sustain their fanatical commitments. But it may also be important positively. Perhaps it is not so much that nationalists become fanatics, although this path is sometimes followed. Rather, it is fanatics who become nationalists. The causal story is that a crippled epistemology leads to fanaticism, which then leads to the urge for governmental control or nationalism.

It is only through gaining control of a state in the modern era that a fanatical group could expect to exclude contrary views and thereby maintain the crippled epistemology of their followers. With the power of a state behind them, they can coerce. If knowledge then tends to follow interests, as argued immediately above, coercion will work to convert some to the fanatical beliefs. We can probably safely suppose, for example, that religious belief in Iran a decade after the Ayatollahs came to power was firmer than it was before they had begun to coerce people who dared to show disbelief.

It would be false to suppose that people merely believe what is in their interest, especially when acting as though they believed might serve their interest just as well. The killer of Mostar did not even need to do this much. He could act as one might have acted if one had the fanatical belief in Serbian righteousness, and that was sufficient to maintain his status in his Serbian society. Belief is not a matter of choice or decision. Commonly, it happens to us because the facts compel us, although many beliefs are not grounded in demonstrable facts at all, as religious beliefs are not. Still, there can be a causal connection between our interests and what we see to be the facts. Moreover, among the facts that compel us are the testimony of others around us and, perhaps especially, those over us. At some level, fanatics understand this and they therefore often want to couple their fanatical beliefs with the power to coerce and influence others whose beliefs are weaker. In the twentieth century, this commonly means to connect their beliefs with the power of national control.

There may have been instances of pure nationalism that were fanatical. Hitler's Nazi program was at least partly a matter of pure nationalism. But most nationalisms that are fanatical seem to be connected with a program that is not specifically nationalist, that is merely opportunistic in seeking control of the nation. Because national independence has seemed to be a worthy goal to many who were not fanatics on any cause, fanatics may have sometimes gained from the support at least of their nationalism. Moreover, as noted earlier, fanatical movements have benefited from the enforced ignorance that authoritarian governments have imposed for reasons of their own interest rather than as part of any program of fanaticism. Hampering open discussion cripples the epistemology of a populace and makes it more readily susceptible to the blandishments of fanatics. Counter to the slogan, Knowledge is power, very nearly the opposite is true for fanatics. Suppressing knowledge is the route to power, strangely even to the power of an idea, albeit a crippled and crippling idea.

## 10. CONCLUDING REMARKS

Explanations of individual and group fanaticism pose different problems, but they are both matters of epistemological constraint. For the most part, individuals become fanatics through the backing of groups, although some individuals manage to become fanatics essentially on their own. By more or less living within a fanatical group, the individual's knowledge becomes massively distorted. This is a peculiar result in some ways because we all live to some large extent within groups, but most of us are not monomaniacally fanatic. Moreover, virtually all of our knowledge comes from our larger society, not from our own discovery. Hence, it is fundamentally group based in large part. Most of our knowledge comes, however, from groups that are open and inclusive. The knowledge of the fanatic comes from a group that is generally exclusive, although often such groups wish to include others eventually, but only by converting the others rather than merely being open to them with whatever differences they might have.

Hence, again, the fundamental problem is to explain the fanaticism of certain groups. Fanatical groups may arise in many ways, through any way that cripples the epistemology of the groups' members. A single fanatical individual might preach to others and sequester them from the larger society. Or a group that is isolated, perhaps by exclusion from other groups in the society, might become epistemologically constrained and begin to have extremist views. Group formation cannot, in general, have a single explanatory story. Rather, it must be essentially a phenomenon of coordination on a limited set of views. Coordinations get started in many and varied ways. In any particular group, it might be virtually impossible even to tell the story of how the coordination got under way, because the vast number of facts in that story may be unrecorded and not coherently remembered.

Coordination of a group of people brings power, often power to a small leadership within the group (Hardin 1995: chap. 2). Such a leadership may then see its interest as tied to the cohesion of the group that elevates them to power. They need not even hold the beliefs of the group members to want such power. Leaders often see the benefits to the group of keeping members ignorant and they impose the crippled epistemology on their members. Leaders of the Old Order Amish in Wisconsin, for example, pushed for an exception to their state's requirement that their children be educated through the tenth grade (or age 16), as all children by state law had to be. Their case went to the U.S. Supreme Court, which, in essence, sided with church leaders against the next generation of their children.

The Court noted the view of the Amish that secondary school education (beyond eighth grade or age 14) was "an impermissible exposure of their children to a 'worldly' influence in conflict with their beliefs" (*Wisconsin v. Yoder*: 211). But the Court decided that it is permissible to cripple their children's epistemology and their capacity for eventually choosing their own lives. Its decision is as merciless to these children as the church leaders are:

It is one thing to say that compulsory education for a year or two beyond the eighth grade may be necessary when its goal is the preparation of the child for *life in modern society* as the majority live, but it is quite another if the goal of education be viewed as the *preparation of the child for life in the separated agrarian community that is the keystone of the Amish faith*. (222, emphases added)

The sad fact of an education that is merely adequate for the latter life is that it is likely crippling for any alternative life these woefully undereducated people might choose later.

Once a group is under way, its fanaticism may be intensified through the exit of more moderate members. They might exit of their own accord because, say, the group is stultifying or because they have better opportunities outside it. Or they might exit because they are de facto shunned and excluded by others in the group, which is guided by its strong norm of exclusion. A group's fanaticism might also be intensified intergenerationally through blinkered education, as in the case of the Amish children of Wisconsin, or of the children governed by the Taliban in Afghanistan, the Ayatollahs in Iran, or the ultra-orthodox rabbis of Israel.

Winston Churchill reputedly quipped that fanatics are people who cannot change their minds and will not change the subject. He got their epistemology just right in his first point. But perhaps he got them wrong in his second point. It is not so much that they will not change the subject. Rather, they cannot change it, because they have no other subject. That is the nature of their crippled epistemology, without which they would not be fanatics.

### REFERENCES

Anderson, Benedict. [1983] 1991. *Imagined Communities* (London: Verso, revised edition).

Bentham, Jeremy. [1789] 1970. *An Introduction to the Principles of Morals and Legislation*, ed. J. H. Burns and H. L. A. Hart (London: Methuen).

Berman, Eli. 1998. "Sect, Subsidy, and Sacrifice: An Economist's View of Ultra-Orthodox Jews." Jerusalem: Maurice Falk Institute for Economic Research in Israel, Discussion Paper number 98.08.

Coleman, James S. 1987. "Free Riders and Zealots." Karen S. Cook, ed., *Social Exchange Theory* (Newbury Park, CA: Sage), pp. 59–82.

Downs, Anthony. 1957. *An Economic Theory of Democracy* (New York: Harper).

Griffin, John Howard. [1961] 1976. *Black Like Me* (New York: New American Library).

——. 1995. *One for All: The Logic of Group Conflict* (Princeton, NJ: Princeton University Press).

Hardin, Russell. 1992. "Commonsense at the Foundations." Bart Schultz, ed., *Essays on Henry Sidgwick* (Cambridge: Cambridge University Press), pp. 143–60.

——. 1997. "The Economics of Religious Belief," *Journal of Institutional and Theoretical Economics* **153** (March): 259–78.

——. 1999. *Liberalism, Constitutionalism, and Democracy* (Oxford: Oxford University Press).

Hirschman, Albert O. 1970. *Exit, Voice, and Loyalty: Responses to Decline in Firms, Organizations, and States* (Cambridge, MA: Harvard University Press).

——. 1977. *The Passions and the Interests: Political Arguments for Capitalism before Its Triumph* (Princeton, NJ: Princeton University Press).

Hobsbawm, E. J. 1992. *Nations and Nationalism since 1870* (Cambridge: Cambridge University Press), 2nd edition.

Kaplan, Robert D. 1993. "A Reader's Guide to the Balkans." *New York Times Book Review* (18 April): 1, 30–33.

Kramer, Roderick M. 1994. "The Sinister Attribution Error: Paranoid Cognition and Collective Distrust in Organizations." *Motivation and Emotion* **18**: 199–230.

Moynihan, Daniel Patrick. 1993. *Pandaemonium: Ethnicity in International Politics* (Oxford: Oxford University Press).

Mueller, John. 1999. *Democracy, Capitalism, and Ralph's Pretty Good Grocery* (Princeton, NJ: Princeton University Press).

Tamir, Yael. 1993. *Liberal Nationalism* (Princeton, NJ: Princeton University Press).

Walzer, Michael. 1980. "Pluralism: A Political Perspective," in Stephen A. Thernstrom, ed., *Harvard Encyclopedia of American Ethnic Groups* (Cambridge, MA: Harvard University Press), pp. 781–7.

*Wisconsin v. Yoder et al.*, 406 U. S., pp. 205–49.

Wittgenstein, Ludwig. 1969. *On Certainty.* New York: Harper, transl. Denis Paul and G. E. M. Anscombe.

# 2

# Leadership and Passion in Extremist Politics

*Ronald Wintrobe**

## 1. INTRODUCTION

Extremist acts and extremist movements often appear mysterious, frightening, and irrational. One reason for this is the apparently single-minded passion of their leaders. The examples of the contemporary militias in the United States, of Japanese religious cults, or of the radical right in France, Germany and other European countries come readily to mind. And while the leaders of these movements often appear dogmatic, perhaps even more frightening is the oft-observed fanatical loyalty of their followers.

As these examples illustrate, one of the most important sources of extremism is conformity. De Tocqueville in particular observed that the United States was the most conformist society he had ever seen (quoted in Kuran 1995). Yet Americans are typically thought of as the most rational of peoples. Another feature of many extremist movements is the phenomenon of charismatic leadership. This was particularly emphasized in the studies edited by Appleby (1997) on extremist fundamentalism in the Middle East.

In this chapter I will argue that extremist behaviour can be understood using a rational choice approach, and that all of the aspects of extremism just listed – passion, conformity, the importance of leadership and loyalty to it – are in fact perfectly consistent with rational choice. Moreover, although extremist preferences play a role in generating extremist behaviour, they do not, in the model to be described, play the main role, and in fact are not necessary to explain such behaviour. So the approach to explaining political behaviour taken in what follows is very different from that of Downs (1957), who essentially used the preferences of the population to explain political behaviour in different political systems.

* I am grateful to R. Morris Coats, Gordon Tullock, and to the participants in the Villa Colombella Seminar for helpful comments and suggestions. Any remaining errors are my responsibility.

I also suggest in this chapter that one of the keys to understanding extremism is to understand its mirror image, conformist behaviour. This is true in two different senses. The first of these is that extremist groups only succeed when their leaders successfully induce conformity among followers. More precisely, I show that the greater or "tighter" the control a leader has over her followers, the more likely an extremist action is to be chosen. The second sense in which conformism and extremism are mirror images is that conformist pressures *induce* extremism. More precisely, I will try to show that an increase in the pressure to conform within some group tends to increase extremist behaviour. Thus, in some ways, conformity and extremism are opposites; in other ways, they are simply different aspects of the same phenomenon.

While the analysis in this chapter can be applied to any form of extremism, including scientific, social or religious extremism, the focus here is on political extremism. Previous literature on political extremism is reviewed by Knoke (1990). He points out that explanations of political extremism in the past were often dominated by psychological explanations. Thus, for example, individuals were held to experience intolerable psychological stresses in their daily lives, and their joining in mob actions was interpreted as a safety valve that let off steam, but accomplished little in the way of solving their problems. In the same vein, participants in extremist movements were often held to be those who were marginal to society, or who were dispossessed by economic change.

Empirical evidence has now accumulated which contradicts these explanations, at least as applied to social movements in general. The evidence drawn from such classic social movements as the Southern Black civil rights movement, the women's movement and Three Mile Island protests, poor peoples' movements, and social protest under Weimar consistently suggests that, rather than marginal and anomic persons, collective actions generally attracted participants of higher social economic status who were more integrated and better connected to societal institutions than were the non-participants.

Instead, the modern approach tends to see social movements, including extremist movements, as the main vehicle for excluded people to gain access to and influence within an established political system. It follows that extremism can be modelled as a form of political competition. In economics, the standard model of political competition is the rent seeking model, and this is the context used here. However, the standard model of rent seeking is flawed, as will be discussed later in the chapter. This new understanding of rent seeking, based on work published elsewhere (Wintrobe 1998) provides, in my view, the second key to understanding why political behaviour sometimes takes an extreme form.

The outline of this chapter is as follows: The next section explains the definition of extremism. Section 3 discusses the elements which are necessary to produce it. Section 4 puts these elements in the context of the analysis of rent seeking, and develops a simple model of rational political extremism. Section 4 then goes on to develop some implications of this model, that is, it shows some circumstances which tend to produce extremist behaviour.

## 2.   THE DEFINITION OF EXTREMISM

A number of different definitions of extremism can be given:

1.   An extremist person or group can be defined as one whose equilibrium position is located at a "corner" rather than in the interior on some dimension (for example, the left–right dimension in political space).
2.   An extremist "move" could be defined as a move away from the centre and towards the extreme in some dimension. In this sense, an extremist *move* can be distinguished from an extremist *equilibrium*, as defined in number 1.
3.   Alternatively, a political extremist could be defined as one who uses extremist methods, for example, bombings, inflammatory language, terrorist activity, and so forth, but whose platform is or may be centrist rather than extremist in political (left–right) space.

In this chapter, I wish to cast as broad a net as possible, and do not wish to exclude any of these aspects of extremism from consideration. For the most part, I will focus on definition number 2, and therefore will be concerned with extremist moves – "bursts" or "upsurges" of extremism. However, I also discuss the extremist acts and methods which are central to definition number 3. Finally, it seems reasonable to assume that if the burst or upsurge of extremism is sufficiently large, it can lead to an extremist equilibrium, as in number 1. So I do not exclude any of the aspects of extremist behaviour discussed in these definitions. However, the formal model focuses on number 2, and therefore, I hope, captures one of the most important aspects of extremism, which is its dynamic quality. The methodology used, however, is that of comparative statics. Thus an exogenous change which leads to a comparative static displacement away from the centre of political space will be referred to as an "increase in extremism."

### 3.  THE ELEMENTS OF EXTREMISM

Four elements are central to the production of political extremism. They are:

1.  Some asymmetry in the distribution of political rents, either actual or potential.
2.  Political leadership.
3.  Conformity.
4.  The presence of a "social hole" or gap in trust between groups.

The argument to be developed is particularly simple, and can be outlined as follows. The first condition – the asymmetry of rents – means that there is an issue which people might be passionate about, and the second condition – the presence of leadership – means that the collectivity is capable of acting on it. Conformity guarantees that there is a "pooling" of opinion behind the leadership, in the sense used by Bernheim and discussed further below: two people with different opinions nevertheless take the same (the leader's) position. Given the presence of the fourth element – a gap or social hole between the potentially extremist group and the centrist majority – the leadership may act in one of two ways: it could try to bridge the gap, or it could seek to mobilize or inflame the passions of the group in an extremist fashion. The greater the distrust between the potentially extremist group and the centre (the deeper the social hole or gap), the more likely the leadership will choose the extremism over the bridging or moderate course. In the same way, an increase in any one of the other three conditions leads to an increase in extremist behaviour, that is, a movement away from the centre of political space, or a larger movement, "burst" or "upsurge" of extremism.

### 4.  THE ELEMENTS OF EXTREMISM IN DETAIL

#### 4.1.  Leadership

Group leadership was introduced into models of voting behaviour by Carol Uhlaner (1989) and Rebecca Morton (1991). Both papers propose models to deal with the vexed question of the rationality of political participation. Rationality is achieved in these models via the introduction of groups or leadership into a model of political behaviour. The way this works is that the group leader facilitates an exchange: he or she promises greater turnout at elections in a candidate's favour if the candidate or party slants the policies of the party towards the preferences of the group. Individuals are motivated to vote by the leader in various ways. The leader may give promises of direct, individualized consumption benefits from the policies provided as a result of the increase in turnout.

Alternatively, the leader may provide some sort of psychic or emotional support to the members in exchange for their participation. Thus, as Uhlaner puts it, "While individuals still vote because of consumption benefits arising from the act of voting, some of these consumption benefits are provided by group leaders out of collective benefits received by the group in return for its votes. The collective benefit comes from a candidate adopting policy positions closer to those of the group" (Uhlaner 1989, p. 390).

Two conditions are necessary for the model to work (Morton 1991): (1) candidates must choose distinct positions in electoral equilibrium (if they have the same position, groups have no more incentive to vote from a rational perspective than individual voters); (2) groups must be large enough relative to the electorate to affect the turnout of other groups, and hence the probability of the preferred candidate winning. Under these conditions, each group calculates that, if others do not turn out, its own turnout may be decisive, just the way an individual would behave in a small group.

The importance of leadership is often emphasized in works on extremist movements. In Appleby's collection *Spokesmen for the Despised* (1997), on Middle East extremism, the main theoretical message extracted is the presence of charismatic leadership. Thus, Appleby concludes the volume with the observation that

the various profiles confirm the centrality of strong male charismatic leadership in the formation and growth of the most powerful fundamentalist movements of the Middle East . . . In each of these cases [radical Jews, Islamic fundamentalists, and the Protestant fundamentalist movements] the charismatic fundamentalist preacher is the catalyst for the hardening of resentment into organized opposition. (Appleby 1997, p. 398)

Of course, leadership is important to all political movements, not just extremist ones. For example, Chong (1991) also emphasizes the leadership factor in his study of the American civil rights movement (discussed further below). In general, the existence of leadership, charismatic or otherwise, implies that *opportunities* will be filled. One way a leader can do this is to act as a broker between groups on either side of an issue. However, as we shall see, there is another way of responding to opportunity: leadership which lowers trust between groups or "inflames passions". But first let us outline the other elements of our story.

### 4.2.  Conformity

A number of different models of conformity have been developed in the literature. For example, Jones (1984) has modelled the utility function of employees deciding on the level of effort. He argues that, because of workplace pressures, workers dislike supplying a level of effort that is far from the output levels of other members of the working group (Jones 1984, p. 42). Consequently, in his model, the utility of a worker depends, in addition to the standard arguments, on the argument $d(Q_i - Q_j)$, where $d$ is the distance between individual $i$'s output and the output of levels of the other ($j$) members of the group.

In his well-known paper on social interactions, Gary Becker (1974) suggested that the effects of others' behaviour on an individual's utility could be captured by the concept of the "social environment." Later, Becker (1996), following Coleman (1990) and others, used the concept of *social capital* to refer to the dependence of an individual's consumption ($C_i$) on that of another individual ($C_j$). He also introduces the concept of habit or "personal capital": an individual $i$'s consumption in period $t(C_{it})$ depends on his consumption in a previous period ($C_{it-1}$). Becker showed that these two variables, especially in combination, can generate very large elasticities of demand and instability. One nice illustration is the consumption of addictive drugs. Suppose that the price of an addictive consumption good, $C$, rises. Then $i$'s consumption $C_i$ falls; so does that of $j$ ($C_j$). In the next period, $C_i$ falls further both because $C_{it-1}$ has fallen and because $C_j$ has fallen. These falls generate further diminutions and so on, until a "corner" solution (for example, zero consumption) has been reached. At the other extreme, something which triggers an increase in the consumption of the good by one or more individuals can lead, by the reverse process, to the opposite corner, that is, addiction. The relevance of these insights to extremist behaviour is obvious.

In politics, the most important modelling of conformist equilibria has been on the issue of participation in social movements. Again, the standard calculus is that participation is irrational, yet participation in these movements is not uncommon. In a model related to the models of leadership by Uhlaner and Morton discussed above, Chong (1991) suggested a solution to this paradox, and applied it to the American civil rights movement. Chong suggested that people benefit from the act of participation in a social movement itself, *when that movement is successful*, as well as from the outcome (the provision of the public good which is the goal of the movement). This is an interesting and highly plausible assumption. Analytically, it converts the problem of the provision of the public good which is the goal of the movement from a "prisoner's dilemma" game into an "assurance" game. In the assurance game, the more others participate, the greater the incentive to each individual to participate. At some point (when enough others participate), there is a threshold or tipping point, beyond which participation is rational. In this model, then, the problem facing leaders of social movements who are trying to motivate participation is not, as Olson (1965) suggested, that of providing selective private incentives to individuals to participate, but the "coordination" problem of creating a belief that enough others will in fact participate to make it in each individual's interest to do so.

In this respect, a group's social ties or networks can be important in successful mobilization, as stressed by Opp and Hartmann (1989) and by Knoke (1990). Knoke cites a number of studies which show that friendship, kinship, and joint organizational membership were among the most important factors promoting solidarity ties and participation in movements such as the Ku Klux Klan and the Irish Republican Army (1990, pp. 69, 72, 73). Stark and Bainbridge suggested that research on conversion to religious social movements showed that "rather than being drawn to the group because of its ideology, people were drawn to the ideology because of their ties to the group" (quoted in Knoke: 71). Similarly, the success or failure of revolutionary movements is explained in this "resource mobilization" perspective by the presence or absence of ties to local communities (p. 81).

A particularly insightful model of conformity is that of Bernheim (1994). In his model, individuals care about esteem (status, popularity), and this is, in turn, determined by public perceptions of an individual's type. However, an individual's type is not directly observable, and so others must infer his type from his choice of an action X. Hence, the key variable in his model is the effect of an individual's actions on esteem versus their effect on direct utility. The larger the first (status) relative to the second (direct utility), the more likely it is that an individual's behaviour will be governed by a norm of behaviour.

It is important to note that, in this model, concern over popularity does not explain conformity by itself. More precisely, one can get the result that the distribution of agents is more concentrated as a result of this concern, but no *clustering* at any point, that is, no two distinct types of agents make the same choice. The pooling equilibrium (conformity) arises whenever status is sufficiently important relative to direct utility. The key assumption which generates this result is that the esteem function is a discontinuous function of action. So agents are penalized significantly for *any* deviation from the social norm, no matter how small, because an observed deviation is assumed to mean the individual is the "extreme" type. Moreover, in this model, agents with sufficiently extreme preferences will refuse to conform; that is, there are no non-trivial non-conformists.

In the model that follows, we will use the concepts of leadership and conformity to develop a related analysis, where the leader controls rewards and punishments, and can control the distribution of esteem. So the analysis includes esteem, but is not limited to it. I define the levels of the variables under the leader's control as the level of *conformist pressure*.

Finally, it is worth pausing to note some psychological evidence on the importance of conformity in generating extremism. I refer to the Right Wing Authoritarianism scale developed by Bob Altemeyer (1981). The term "right wing" is not used in the political or economic sense, but in a psychological one: the right wing authoritarian is one who aggressively defends the *established* authorities in his or her life. So, for example, defenders of Communism in the former Soviet Union in the late 1980s would tend to score highly on the scale. The scale is a unidimensional measure of three attitude clusters: (1) submission to established authority; (2) authoritarian aggression, that is, aggression which is believed to be sanctioned by established authorities and which is directed at various persons whose activities are frowned upon; and (3) conventionalism, that is, a high degree of adherence to the social conventions which are perceived to be endorsed by society and its established authorities. High scores on the scale tend to accept government injustices such as illegal wiretapping, believe that "strong medicine" is necessary to straighten out troublemakers, criminals, and perverts, believe in traditional family structures, obedience and respect for authority and so on. And they are highly prejudiced against minority groups.

The findings of Altemeyer which are of particular interest here are that right wing authoritarians, one important type of extremist personality, were conformists (they exhibited what Altemeyer labels "conventionalism") and they had an exaggerated need to obey authority ("authoritarian aggression"). Authoritarianism on the left can be explained the same way, according to Altemeyer. In other words, the scales provided strong psychological evidence of a connection between conformity and extremism.

The existence of a collective action problem, leadership and conformity generate participation, but they do not necessarily generate extremist participation. For that, we need the next element.

### 4.3.  Social holes

A "social hole" can be defined as a communications gap or a lack of trust between two persons or groups in society. The most obvious examples are the gap between blacks and whites in the United States, between the Serbs and Croatians in Bosnia, between Protestants and Catholics in Northern Ireland or between (some would say) French and English Canadians. As these examples illustrate, the gap is often spurred by ethnic differences, but it need not be. It could exist between rich and poor, between social classes or between the political left and right. The term "social hole" is related to the phrase "structural hole" coined by Burt (1992), who uses this term in the context of organizations such as business corporations. For Burt, structural holes provide "entrepreneurial opportunities". That is true of the social holes discussed here as well, as will be discussed shortly. The essence of the concept of a social hole is that parties on either side of it *distrust* each other to a considerable extent. Alternatively, a social hole is a place where social capital is relatively low, so that a society with one or more social holes has a bad or malformed distribution of trust. The crucial emphasis here on the distribution of trust distinguishes the present approach from that of Fukuyama (1995), Knack and Keefer (1997), and others who emphasize the average level of some sort of generalized "trustworthiness" as the variable which is fundamental to the explanation of economic or social questions.

The reasons for the break or divide in trust denoted by the social hole can be several. The most obvious reason why there might be a social hole between group A and group B is their behaviour in the past towards each other, as in the case of Irish Catholics and Protestants, the Jews and the Arabs, and so forth. Another obvious reason is fear, which seems to underlie the behaviour of religious Jews in Israel, or that of the Serbs and the Croats in Bosnia. In each case, one group fears domination by the other.

A third possibility is that the operation of the economic or political system generates the social hole. Perhaps the classic analysis of the creation of social holes in this manner was that of Marx, although, of course, he did not use this term. In Marx's analysis, capitalism was a system in which capital exploited labour. By the "law of increasing immiserization of the proletariat," he suggested, the working class would become poorer and poorer until ultimately it would become conscious of its exploitation and the Socialist revolution would ensue. In our terms, this means that the gap or social hole is naturally amplified as the result of the actions of the dominant group, or at least, by the workings of the economic mechanism (in Marx's view, capital was as "driven" by the economic system as labour was).

In other words, according to Marx, the natural working of competition in the economic sphere opened up a social hole between capitalists and workers, and this ultimately created political forces which would bring down the capitalist economic system itself. Of course, Marx was wrong: capitalism did not widen the gap between rich and poor; it made both the poor and the rich richer, in absolute terms, in most Western countries. Some contemporary analysts, while not subscribing to Marx or Marxism, suggest that recent trends are not so sanguine: Rodrik (1997), for example, sees the operation of globalized capitalism as undoing the historic bargain between capital and labour, and increasing inequality. William Julius Wilson (1987), in a celebrated contribution, observes what is essentially a social hole in the United States between the underclass in big American cities, which is seen as a group with its own values and norms, and the rest of society.

Of course, it is also possible that fissures in the social system are generated by political, rather than economic, forces. For example, a social hole can be generated by the exercise of power. As I have suggested elsewhere (Wintrobe 1998) in the context of the analysis of dictatorial rule, the more one individual or group rules another by command or force alone, the less trust there is between them. For obvious reasons, I called this quandary the "Dictator's Dilemma," but its occurrence is not restricted to the case of authoritarian rulers and their subjects, and appears at a less severe level in many other contexts.

Larry Iannaccone (1988, 1992, 1997) analyses religious sects or cults in analogous terms. Iannaccone analyses religious behaviour or norms with a variable denoting *conduct* according to some norm, which may be far away or close to the norm governing society's conduct. The further away the religious norm of conduct from the secular norm, and the greater the intolerance of deviation from the norm on the part of either group, the deeper the social hole, in our terms. Iannaccone defines a *sectarian religion* in terms of the degree to which the religious group demands sacrifice and stigma, or the degree to which it limits and therefore increases the cost of non-group activities to its members (1997, p. 104). In his analysis, the membership benefits from these demands, because the utility of collective religious belief depends positively on the average level of participation in group activities. Thus, the social hole or gap between the membership of the sect and the rest of society is deliberately created. The purpose is to control free riding. Of course, it has frequently been noted that religious sects and cults have to limit the information available to members in order to successfully control them, and that they control association with outsiders in order to do this as well. (See for example Knoke's *Political Networks* [1990], p. 71.) What Iannaccone adds to this is the idea that they must provide an unusually high level of satisfaction as well, and that, in the end, the membership of the sect actually benefits from these restrictions.

In sum, the concept of a social hole seems to have wide applicability in explaining how the operation of political, economic, or social forces can generate social tensions. However, from the standpoint of neoclassical economic theory, there would appear to be a flaw in all of these arguments. Thus, as Ronald Burt points out (1992) with respect to the social structure of business corporations, the existence of what he calls "structural holes" and what I call social holes simply provides an opportunity for entrepreneurship, that is, for brokerage between the groups who are separated. Thus, if "connections" or ties between groups are a form of social capital, social holes will often be placed where the rate of return to this form of capital is highest. To the extent that this is true, the gaps will not persist in equilibrium. Following this logic, it could be argued that representatives of capital would get together with the proletariat (in Marx's analysis), global capitalists would get together with labour (Rodrik), representatives of "normal" society could meet with those from the underclass (Wilson), and secular leaders would chat with religious ones (Iannaccone). In each case, the representatives of the different groups could act as political or social entrepreneurs and bridge the divide between the groups, possibly meliorating the forces generating the hole. The result is that competition (in the sense of entrepreneurship) would eliminate the problem. So the problems of the immiserization of the proletariat, the adverse consequences of globalization, the persistence of the underclass, and the religious–secular divide would all be eliminated through political competition.

One way to explain the persistence of conflicts in any of these forms is to suggest that, given the existence of a gap, *entrepreneurship could seek to exploit or magnify it*, as well as to fill it. With respect to ethnic conflict, for example, the classic contemporary examples are Slobodan Milosevic, Le Pen in France, Ian Paisley in Ireland, and Hamas in Palestine. In each of these cases, there was a social hole or gap in trust, leadership arose, and the way leaders apparently profited was by enlarging the social hole or distrust: they inflamed passions and magnified the separation between groups, rather than acting as a broker to mediate between them. I suggest that this form of behaviour is the essence of political extremism.[1] And this explains why competition does not eliminate social holes: *sowing distrust under many circumstances is more profitable than acting as a broker*.

From these two points it appears that the central question in analysing extremist behaviour is the following: under what conditions does entrepreneurship tend to magnify the differences between groups rather than making them smaller?[2] The next section turns to this question.

---

[1] Of course, this form of entrepreneurship also occurs in other contexts, where it is not associated with political extremism. To take a homely example, lawyers in divorce cases often seek to promote distrust between their respective clients. The reason is simple: the more distrust there is between the clients, the more the lawyer can earn on the case.

[2] The question is obviously related to the issue of the convergence or divergence of preferences at the median of the distribution of political preferences, extensively analysed in the public choice literature (see Mueller 1989 for an overview). However, the question is not the same, because we are talking here about bursts or movements towards the centre or towards the extreme and not equilibrium convergence or divergence.

## 5. RATIONAL EXTREMIST PASSION

In this section, I develop a simple model which demonstrates how the four elements – leadership, conformity, an asymmetric distribution of rents, and social holes – interact to produce extremism. The key is to understand the circumstances under which leadership tends to lower trust or "inflame passions." In turn, to understand this, one has to first understand a flaw in the traditional analysis of rent seeking. The problem is that the rent seeking model is irrational from the point of view of politicians. The standard model makes two crucial assumptions:

A  *The resources used in bidding are completely wasted.* In the classic formula, money is spent hiring lawyers to lobby politicians to give their client the rent. The activities of lawyers, while usually thought of as pure waste in economics, could in principle be put to productive use. However, the second assumption guarantees that this is not the case with rent seeking.

B  *It makes no difference who gets the rent.* That is, no public benefit will accrue, in any form, if one of the contestants wins; the contest does not sort out the good from the bad. Nor does the necessity of competing for rents induce greater efficiency on the part of the contestants, nor cause them to modify what they would do in any way that might affect the public.

   In the standard formulation it follows that if there are ten firms bidding for a prize of $100,000, each firm will spend $10,000 on lawyers, leading, in the simplest version, to economic waste equal to the size of the rent.

Now, one problem with this formulation of a rent-seeking contest is that it is *irrational* from the point of view of *politicians.*[3] A total of $100,000 is spent trying to influence politicians, but the politicians get nothing out these expenditures: it is all wasted. Why would politicians organize the contest this way? Why wouldn't they attempt instead to profit from the bidding process? One way to do this would be to suggest to the competitors that they offer cash payments or political support instead of wasting the time of politicians through their lobbying activities. In this way the politicians could themselves collect all the rents, eliminate the waste and profit directly from it. But if bribes (in money or votes) instead of lobbying were used, the money which is received in bribes by the politicians is not waste, but a pure transfer to politicians from interest groups which represents no *social* waste or deadweight loss at all.

---

[3] This problem is discussed in more detail in Wintrobe (1998).

I argued elsewhere that this solution (bribery) is often characteristic of dictatorships (Wintrobe 1998). However, in democracies, bribery is proscribed, and in strong democracies, these proscriptions are effectively enforced. Moreover, even in dictatorships and especially in democracies there is a second problem with bribes. How is the "contract" of money or political support in exchange for rents enforced? Since the courts cannot be asked to prosecute "cheating" (for example, an interest group promises political support in exchange for rents but then reneges), the only type of contracts which will be entered into must be self-enforcing. In general, to be self-enforcing, contracts must have three properties, as originally pointed out by Klein and Leffler (1981) and Shapiro (1983): (1) they must be long-term contracts; (2) the parties must have established that they are trustworthy to begin with. For example, they may have earned a reputation for not cheating in the past; (3) there must be a premium to compensate each party for not taking advantage of opportunities to cheat. For political contracts to meet these conditions, it follows that the equilibrium distribution of rents has to be stable and long-lasting. Moreover, parties must have a means of signalling the types of groups with whom they are willing to enter into such contracts. Perhaps this is one of the main functions of a political party's ideology: it provides a codified set of "promises" against which cheating can be measured, and it signals the type of interest groups with which that party is willing to engage in exchange. To illustrate, right-wing parties seldom entertain bids for rents on the part of labour unions; left-wing parties do not do so with business groups. Of course, it is not impossible for a party to change its ideology, but a party's platform is not "up for grabs" at every moment to the group which is willing to bid the most. This would entail wasteful rent seeking which rational politicians seek to minimize, and the party would not be able to trust the winner of such a rent-seeking contest to live up to its part of the bargain in any case. For these reasons, rational politicians have settled constituencies or equilibrium long-term contracts.

To summarize, the central point is that equilibrium political contracts are characterized by long-term arrangements made with certain groups. Others are not allowed to bid; that is, they are frozen out of the possibility of bidding for a contract. The reasons are twofold: (1) if rents were opened up for bids every period, much would be wasted in rent seeking, and rational politicians dislike waste; (2) with short-term contracts, politicians would not be able to trust the recipients of rents to carry out their part of the bargain in any case.

What happens to those who are not allowed to bid and are therefore left out in the equilibrium? They will be logically susceptible to leadership which emphasizes the necessity of taking other forms of action in order to demonstrate that they are not willing to live with this situation. Normal bidding being closed, their leaders will have to resort to theatre, to shock, to radical positions, and to violation of existing norms, in order to be "heard." Hence the proclivity for demonstrations, riots, provocative and shocking statements, terrorist activity, and so forth. While these outbursts of political theatre may appear irrational, they serve a purpose: they "demonstrate" that those who are frozen out of the distribution of rents are not willing to live with the status quo and that the equilibrium situation must be "opened up" to new bids.[4] In short, the use of passion or the threat of violence is necessary to disturb the equilibrium distribution of rents. In this sense, extremist passion is "rational"; that is, if it can be mobilized, it will serve the self-interest of the passionate.

However, there is still a free-rider problem: while the opening up of the equilibrium can be expected to be of benefit, the benefits are often collective or purely public. Our survey of the literature on this question suggested four ways in which leadership can solve this problem: (1) as in the resource mobilization perspective, participation may be motivated through network ties and network pressure; (2) as in the analysis of Uhlaner and Roberts, leaders can motivate participants with the prospect of individualized rewards from success; (3) as Chong suggests, leaders can emphasize the pleasure of identification with a winning movement, and attempt to foster this belief in the prospect of success in participants; (4) passion is collective: the greater the average level of participation, the greater the utility to each from participation, just as in Iannaccone's analysis of collective religions; leaders will tend to demand sacrifices from participants and to stigmatize association with the centrists or with their policies.

To make a more precise argument, and to show how this rational extremist passion responds to economic forces, let us develop a simple formal analysis with the help of Figure 2.1. The assumptions behind the figure are as follows:

1.   Assume no extremist preferences per se; that is, we may simply assume either a normal or a uniform distribution of basic preferences. The horizontal axis of Figure 2.1 defines the level of a policy,

---

[4] Moreover, to the extent that these outbursts are orchestrated by the leaders, they also demonstrate their power; indeed, the more radical the action, the greater their control over their followers will appear to be. Radical actions on the part of the leaders may also motivate followers who are too timid to state their position openly. Breaching the norm encourages others to do so. Finally, the analysis also shows why the young are typically disproportionately involved in extremist movements: apart from the well-known point that the cost of time is lower to them, the benefits also differ. Changing the equilibrium distribution of political rents is difficult and costly, and the young have the most to gain from a long-term improvement of the situation.

Preferences

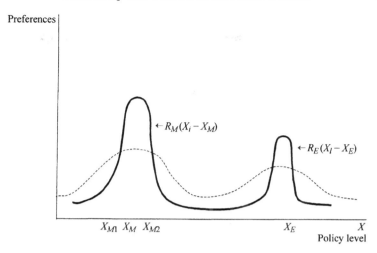

$\leftarrow R_M(X_i - X_M)$

$\leftarrow R_E(X_l - X_E)$

$X_{M1}$ $X_M$ $X_{M2}$          $X_E$          $X$

Policy level

Figure 2.1 The distribution of political preferences before and after
leaders inflame passions

$X$, and the vertical axis shows the distribution of preferences over
this policy. For example, the level of $X$ could refer to the extremity
of political "conduct," where higher values of $X$ denote more
extreme methods of political action, for example, $X = 0 =$ voting;
$X = 1 =$ political assassination. Or the dimension could refer to the
level of authoritarianism–libertarianism, as in the scale used in the
analysis of Kitschelt (1997). Or the figure could be used to analyse a
particular conflict. For example, it may be used to represent the
conflict of Israeli public opinion over the issue of peace with the
Palestinians: in that case, the level of $X$ could be taken to represent
the degree of cooperation of Israelis with the Palestinians.

2. There is a social hole. I do not model the origin of this hole here.
As discussed above, there can be many causes of this phenomenon.
Here we just assume that a hole exists, as depicted by the gap
between the two dotted distributions of initial preferences in
Figure 2.1. To illustrate with the Israeli example again, if the
level of $X$ refers to "the degree of cooperation of Israelis with
the Palestinians," the distribution depicted represents Israeli public
opinion on this issue. Note that Palestinian public opinion does not
appear on the axis. That is, the cleavage or social hole depicted in
Figure 2.1 is *not* the gap in understanding between Arabs and Jews,
but between those Israelis who believe in cooperation with the
Palestinians (for example, the Peace Now movement) and those
(for example, the Israeli settlers or the religious parties) who do
not. In a similar way, the distribution of preferences in Figure 2.1

    could be used to depict the social hole between Irish Catholics and
    Irish Protestants.

3. There is a centrist party or possibly two centrist parties, centre-left
   and centre-right. If there is one centrist party, its position is $X_M$. If
   there are two centrist parties, their policy positions are depicted by
   $X_{M1}$ and $X_{M2}$.
4. The leadership, both at the centre and at the extreme, distributes
   rewards to followers. The rewards may take the form of rents or
   esteem, according to the position (level of $X$) chosen by the followers. So the reward function takes the form $R(X_i - X_c)$ where $X_c$
   is the level chosen by the leader and $R$ is the level of rents given out
   or the esteem in which a person selecting $X$ is held, with $R' < 0$. In
   other words, the leaders exert "conformist pressure" on the members. The result of this pressure is that the distribution of policy
   positions among the membership changes from the dotted line to
   the solid line. That is, the leadership at the centre $(X_M)$ induces
   some conformity, and the same is true for leadership at the extreme
   $(X_E)$, which again changes the selection of $X$ from the distribution
   shown by the dotted line to that of the solid line.
5. The distribution of rents is an equilibrium long-term (implicit or
   explicit) contract and bidding is closed.

Now suppose the situation depicted by the dotted line in Figure 2.1 is
an initial equilibrium.[5] The analysis suggests that this equilibrium is the
result of five variables:

1. the initial distribution of preferences
2. the size of the rents or the esteem distributed by the leaders
3. the rate at which these rents fall away as an individual deviates
   from the leader's preferred policy, as summarized by the functions
   $R(X_i - X_c)$, where $X_c = X_M$ or $X_E$
4. the responsiveness of the membership to these rent/esteem distributions
5. the positions chosen by the leaders.

Suppose now that a disturbance (some change in the initial conditions)
arises. The question to which we would like the answer is: will the non-
centrist leadership, whose leader's initial position is at $X_E$, become more
or less extremist than before?

---

[5] I do not inquire in this chapter how this equilibrium is determined. One way to visualize it
is to assume, following Alesina (1988), that the two positions chosen by the leaders satisfy
the conditions of Nash equilibrium; that is, they maximize expected utility given the
position of the other party.

The leader of the non-centrist group has two choices: (1) she can attempt to fulfil a *brokerage* function. This would mean shifting her position towards the centre in order to claim some of the rents being distributed there. Presumably this would be done in exchange for movement by the centre group towards the policies (that is, a higher level of $X$) desired by the relatively extreme group; (2) she can attempt to *mobilize* the group's members in order to demonstrate their unwillingness to accept the level of $X$ chosen by the centre. It seems reasonable to suppose that this course will more likely be chosen, the smaller the probability of successful bargaining with the centre, the greater the probability of successful mobilization, and the greater the relative rewards to mobilization. With only one dimension, as in the model summarized in Figure 2.1, we will assume that mobilization means a movement to the right in Figure 2.1, that is, a "burst" of extremism. If there is a movement to the right, it further increases the social hole between the centre and the extreme, and therefore "inflames passions" among the outsiders at the extreme. In other words, the movement to the right makes the social hole larger between the centre and the extreme, hence making communication between the two groups more difficult than before. The movement could be accompanied by exhortations by the leader on the lack of trustworthiness of those at the centre, and possibly by a "tighter" distribution of rewards meted out (that is, in Figure 2.1, a smaller variance in the distribution around $X_E$). At the same time as it demonstrates the differences between the centre and the extreme, the leader may highlight the similarities among those at the extreme, their sense of solidarity, and so forth.

This leads to our first proposition, which may be stated as follows: *the easier it is for a leader to mobilize her followers, the greater the likelihood of extremist action.* The reason is simple: extremism, to be effective, requires mobilization, while compromise does not. Thus, to revert to the example of the Israeli–Palestinian question once again, the compromise involved in the striking of the Wye agreement required, if anything, the *demobilization* of extremist elements on both sides. The presence of extremists may (or may not) have been useful in getting the two sides to come to the table in the first place. But now they certainly have to be cooled off if the agreement is not to come unstuck as a result of further and untimely provocations.

To see what other factors might motivate this latter (extremist) course, consider the following exogenous changes.

Suppose first that there are, initially, two centrist parties, whose policy positions are initially depicted by $X_{M1}$ and $X_{M2}$. Now suppose the leadership of the two centrist parties converges more at the centre. In an interesting recent analysis, Kitschelt (1997) hypothesized that the contemporary European radical right arose as a result of the convergence in the 1970s of the mainstream left and right towards the centre. Our model shows that such a convergence alone would not necessarily produce this result: with constant conformist pressure, extremism would increase in our analysis if the social hole between the centre and the extreme gets larger than before as a result of convergence. The move to the left by the centre-right party increases the gap between the extreme right and the centre, but the gap between the centre-left and the extreme right has narrowed as a result of convergence. With two parties, it seems reasonable to define the social hole as the gap between the average position of the two centrist parties and the extremist party. If this gap increases, then the extremist group can be expected to become more extreme, but the opposite will hold if the gap decreases.

A second condition is related to the strength of the pressures for conformity. An increase in this pressure at the centre (that is, a larger $R$ in the function $R(X_i - X_c)$) increases the social hole between the centre and the extreme, making it more likely that the extreme group will choose the mobilization option and shift to the right. Put another way, greater conformist pressure at the centre effectively makes the centrist group more intolerant. This result is related to the idea that an individual's *intolerance* of others is produced by conformist pressures. This idea is discussed in a paper by Gibson (1992), where it is suggested that, because of conformist pressure, an individual may feel he has no freedom to express his own opinions. The more pressure on an individual to conform, the less freedom he may feel he has, and the less tolerant he is of deviance in other people. Our analysis shows how a mechanism like this could be the result of a rational process. In terms of Figure 2.1, an increase in the pressure for conformity at the centre produces more intolerance of outsiders (the extreme) because it enlarges the social hole between insiders and outsiders. Hence it pushes the extremist group towards more extremist behaviour. This provides a simple explanation of how conformist pressure produces extremist behaviour.

Suppose next that there is an increase in the perception of *dominance* by the centrist group of the outside group. Alternatively, this could be the result of an increase in the perception of *exploitation*, or in the perception that the dominance or exploitation which is already experienced appears likely to get worse in the future. Any of these changes reduces the possibility of the extremist leader's fulfilling a brokerage function, and makes it more likely that the leader will choose the mobilization or extremist option.

Finally, suppose that the centrist position is discredited in some way. This could be the result of a failure of the policies of the centre, or new information showing that these policies didn't work, or that they were designed to self-servingly benefit the leadership (corruption). Alternatively, and equivalently, suppose the capacity of the leader at the centre to distribute esteem falls, or suppose any change which decreases trust in the centre. The distribution of policy positions at the centre will "flatten out" in Figure 2.1; that is, the post-rent or esteem distribution around the centre $X_M$ will move back in the direction of the original (dotted) distribution. Which way does this tempt the leader at the extreme to move? On the one hand, those at the centre are more tolerant than before; that is, in part the change is exactly the reverse of that just analysed of an increase in conformity. So, on that count, the extremist leader can be expected to become less extreme, that is, to shift towards the centre. This is reinforced in that the extremist can be expected to move towards the centre to pick up disillusioned centrist support. On the other hand, the discredit of the centre also creates an "extremist opportunity" – it raises the possibility that extremist policies could eventually become dominant. Thus, the discredit of the Weimar regime provided an opening for the extremist opportunism of Hitler. Another example could be the situation after the fall of the USSR, where the destruction of the Communist Party created opportunities for extremist and nationalist leaders to exploit the situation and inflame the passions of nationalism. In any of these cases, the analysis shows that one cannot predict what will happen to the potential extremist group; one set of forces implies greater extremism, while other forces stimulate leaders of the potential extreme towards moderation.

## 6. CONCLUSION

In this chapter I have attempted to develop a simple model of political extremism and to suggest some of its implications, that is, to indicate the circumstances under which "bursts" of extremism tend to arise. In one sense, extremism is a form of rent seeking. However, contrary to the standard theory of rent seeking, the distribution of rents is here assumed to be fixed in long-term implicit political contracts, in part according to a party's ideology. That is, politicians are not "open" to bids from those groups who are left out. Consequently, other forms of action besides rent-seeking bids may be necessary in order for outsiders to demonstrate that they are not willing to live with this situation. Normal bidding being closed, their leaders may emphasize that they have to resort to theatre, to shock, to radical positions and to violation of existing norms, in order to be "heard."

Four elements are central to the emergence of extremist rent seeking: (1) an actual or perceived asymmetry in the distribution of rents; (2) political leadership to act on this; (3) conformity; and (4) the presence of a social hole or gap in trust between the centre and the potential extremist movement. Given the presence of the four elements, the leadership of the "outsiders" (those who are not allowed to bid) may act in one of two ways: it could seek to bridge the gap or social hole between the potentially extremist group and the centrist majority, or it could seek to mobilize or inflame the passions of the group in an extremist fashion. The key point is that extremism requires mobilization whereas compromise does not. So one implication is that the greater the control a leader has over his followers, the more likely an extremist action is to be chosen. Another prediction is that the more some exogenous change deepens the social hole or trust gap, the more likely the leadership is to choose the extremist course. A third prediction is that an increase in conformity at the centre is more likely to increase extremist behaviour, and a fourth is that an increase in the perception of dominance or exploitation of outsiders by the centre makes it more likely that political extremism will arise.

### REFERENCES

Alesina, Alberto. 1988. "Credibility and Policy Convergence in a Two-Party System with Rational Voters," *American Economic Review* **78**, 796–807.

Appleby, R. Scott, ed. 1997. *Spokesmen for the Despised: Fundamentalist Leaders of the Middle East*. Chicago: Chicago University Press.

Altemeyer, Robert. 1981. *Right Wing Authoritarianism*. Winnipeg, Man.: University of Manitoba Press.

Becker, Gary S. 1974. "A Theory of Social Interactions", *Journal of Political Economy* **82**, 1063–93.

Becker, Gary S. 1996. *Accounting for Tastes*. Cambridge, Mass.: Harvard University Press.

Bernheim, B. Douglas. 1994. "A Theory of Conformity," *Journal of Political Economy* **102**, 841–77.

Burt, Ronald S. 1992. *Structural Holes: The Social Structure of Competition*. Cambridge, Mass.: Harvard University Press.

Coleman, James S. 1990. *Foundations of Social Theory*. Cambridge: Harvard University Press.

Chong, Dennis. 1991. *Collective Action and the Civil Rights Movement*. Chicago: University of Chicago Press.

Downs, Anthony. 1957. *An Economic Theory of Democracy*. New York: Harper and Row.

Fukuyama, Francis. 1995. *Trust: The Social Virtues and the Creation of Prosperity*. London: Hamish Hamilton.

Gibson, James L. 1992. "The Political Consequences of Intolerance: Cultural Conformity and Political Freedom," *American Political Science Review* **86**, 338–56.

Iannaccone, Lawrence R. 1988 supplement. "A Formal Model of Church and Sect," *American Journal of Sociology* **94**, S241–S268.

_____. 1992. "Sacrifice and Stigma: Reducing Free Riding in Cults, Communes and Other Collectives," *Journal of Political Economy* **100**, 271–91.

_____. 1997. "Towards an Economic Theory of Fundamentalism," *Journal of Institutional and Theoretical Economics* **153**, 100–21.

Jones, Stephen R. G. 1984. *The Economics of Conformism*. Oxford: Basil Blackwell.

Kitschelt, Herbert. 1997. *The Radical Right in Western Europe: A Comparative Analysis*. Ann Arbor: The University of Michigan Press.

Knack, Stephen, and Phillip Keefer. 1997. "Does Social Capital Have An Economic Payoff?" *Quarterly Journal of Economics* **112**, 1251–89.

Klein, Benjamin, and Keith Leffler. 1981. "The Role of Market Forces in Contractual Performance", *Journal of Political Economy* **89**, 615–41.

Knoke, David. 1990. *Political Networks: The Structural Perspective*. New York: Cambridge University Press.

Kuran, Timur. 1995. *Private Truths, Public Lies: The Social Consequences of Preference Falsification*. Cambridge: Harvard University Press.

Morton, Rebecca. 1991. "Groups in Rational Turnout Models," *American Journal of Political Science* **35**, 758–76.

Mueller, Dennis. 1989. *Public Choice II*. New York: Cambridge University Press.

Olson, Mancur. 1965. *The Logic of Collective Action*. Cambridge, Mass.: Harvard University Press.

Opp, Karl-Dieter, and P. Hartmann. 1989. *The Rationality of Political Protest: A Comparative Analysis of Rational Choice Theory*. Boulder, Colo.: Westview Press.

Rodrik, Dani. 1997. *Has Globalization Gone Too Far?* Washington, DC: Institute for International Economics.

Shapiro, Carl. 1983. "Premiums for High-Quality Products As Returns to Reputations," *Quarterly Journal of Economics* **98**, 659–79.

Uhlaner, Carol. 1989. "Rational Turnout: the Neglected Role of Groups," *American Journal of Political Science*, **33**, 390–422.

Wilson, William Julius. 1987. *The Truly Disadvantaged: The Inner City, The Underclass, and Public Policy*. Chicago: University of Chicago Press.

Wintrobe, Ronald. 1998. *The Political Economy of Dictatorship*. New York: Cambridge University Press.

# 3

# Information Control, Loss of Autonomy, and the Emergence of Political Extremism

*Albert Breton and Silvana Dalmazzone**

## 1. INTRODUCTION

Political extremism is a multidimensional phenomenon. It can be taken to refer to, for example, the tail ends of the distribution of worldviews and beliefs held by individuals in a society, the kind of objectives sought, the means used in the pursuit of those objectives, or the preeminent position accorded to one specific issue over all others. In this chapter, we focus on a particular dimension of extremism – namely the intolerance, unwillingness to compromise, and rejection of evidence contradicting one's beliefs that are often associated with the phenomenon.

We look at the forces, within a social environment, that can contribute to the development of the above attitudes (Section 2). We then look at mechanisms that help reinforce and diffuse extreme positions (Sections 3 and 4). Much of what we say in these sections applies to all forms of extremism – whether religious, social, scientific, cultural or political. We focus on the last.[1]

Political extremism becomes a socially relevant phenomenon when it involves the mobilization of individuals and the formation of groups that pursue objectives and make use of means that impose external costs deemed to be unacceptable. We list, in Table 3.1, the 26 groups we

* We are grateful to Marilyn McKim, head of the Toronto Office of Amnesty International, for allowing us to consult AI's files on a number of extremist groups; to the International Centre for Economic Research in Turin for its financial support; in a special way to Alessandra Calosso for help in making our research leaves at the Centre productive ones, and to Stefano Valvano for competent research assistance. We are also grateful to two anonymous referees for their comments. Finally, we acknowledge our indebtedness to the Donner Canadian Foundation without whose generous financial assistance this research would not have been possible.
[1] To do so is, to a degree, artificial as often extremist political formations pursue goals which are religious and social at the same time as they seek to achieve political ends. It is, however, a useful simplification.

have examined and used as markers in formulating the model of this chapter. The evidence on these groups was culled from academic monographs,[2] book-length narratives by investigative journalists,[3] newspaper stories on the activities of extremists as these stories were breaking, articles in magazines and reviews, chronicles from the pen of erstwhile extremists,[4] and the files of Toronto branch of Amnesty International.

**Table 3.1 A sample of extremist groups**

1. Abu Nidal groups (Libya, Lebanon)
2. Action Directe (France)
3. American Militias and paramilitary groups (USA) (Among which the Militia of Montana, the Michigan Militia, the Posse Comitatus, and many others)
4. Anti-abortionists (Canada and USA)
5. Aryan Nation (USA)
6. Brigate Rosse (Italy)
7. Common Law (USA)
8. Euzkadi Ta Askatasuna (Basque Fatherland and Freedom, ETA) (Spain)
9. Groupe Islamique Armé, GIA (Algeria)
10. Gush Emunim (Block of the Faithful) (Israel)
11. Haiderism (Austria)
12. Hamas (West Bank and Gaza)
13. Heszbollah (Lebanon)
14. Irish Republic Army, IRA (Ireland)
15. Islamic Jihad
16. Khmer Rouge (Cambodia)
17. Ku Klux Klan, KKK (USA)
18. Lepenisme (France)
19. Liberation Tigers of Tamil Eelam, LTTE (Sri Lanka)
20. Palestinian Liberation Organization, PLO
21. Québec separatist groups (including the Rassemblement pour l'Indépendance Nationale, the Action Socialiste pour l'Indépendance du Québec, the Ralliement National, and others)[5]
22. Red Guards (China)
23. Rote Armee Fraktion, RAF (Germany)
24. Sendero Luminoso (Peru)
25. Silent Brotherhood (USA)
26. Taliban (Afghanistan)

---

[2] Chalmers (1951), Sargent (1995), George and Wilcox (1996), McNicol Stock (1996), Barkun (1997).
[3] Flynn and Gerhardt (1990), Karl (1995).
[4] Curcio (1993), O'Callaghan (1998).
[5] In the late 1960s and 1970s almost all separatist groups merged and dissolved in René Lévesque's Parti Québécois.

These groups are not only a small sample of a large universe, they have been and in many instances continue to be determinant elements in the evolution of political cultures and societies.

Their emergence, we argue, requires political entrepreneurs and leaders (Section 5). Like the entrepreneurs of economic analysis and those of democratic party politics, these canvass the landscape in search of opportunities that they can profitably exploit. The opportunities that will be selected will be a function of (a) the proclivities and abilities of the entrepreneurs themselves, and (b), the configuration of the map of available opportunities. The latter can originate in innate as well as historically determined demands of people, or they can derive from, or be reinforced by, controls over information that lead to more or less subtle forms of indoctrination. The last part of the chapter is concerned with the rational response of political extremists to changes in environmental parameters. Specifically, we provide a rationale for some of the activities of political extremists (Section 6). Section 7 concludes the chapter.

## 2.  A MODEL OF INFORMATION CONTROL

It is costly to ascertain objectively the different states of the world. To minimize these costs, individuals form beliefs over those states of the world that are of relevance to them. These beliefs then serve as a basis for making decisions. Once acquired – once they have become part of an individual's identity – beliefs are costly to revise. In other words, we suppose that persons have preferences over their beliefs; individuals whose beliefs are at variance with the evidence will change these beliefs only when the cost of holding onto them exceeds the benefits they generate. As a consequence, individual preferences over beliefs will act as a filter on available information. This is the same mechanism in which cognitive dissonance is anchored in the Akerlof and Dickens's (1982) model. One implication is that different individuals weigh beliefs differently.[6]

Among beliefs, some are given a large weight. Though the majority of beliefs that form a person's worldview evolve under the influence of education, experience, changing environment, interactions with others, and so on, a subset of these beliefs is more permanent. The abandonment of any of the beliefs in that subset is felt as a loss of identity – changing them is more costly than altering beliefs not in that subset.

---

[6] Purkitt and Dyson (1989, p. 329) provide experimental evidence that "choosers ignore highly relevant information in favor of evoking latent preferences" – in other words, that beliefs act as a filter on information.

In the model of extremism we propose, a process of socialization (and of resocialization) takes place through which an individual's beliefs are molded – a process which, in its most extreme expression, takes the form of brainwashing and indoctrination.[7]

The further the conditioning process is carried, the more the subset of beliefs that individuals will find costly to revise is expanded. Their critical ability is progressively dismantled. At the limit, brainwashing and indoctrination neutralize the power of mental checks and balances. Individuals, in the language of Hoffer (1951), become "true believers".[8] Their capacity or willingness to compromise contracts. They become more intolerant, more intransigent, less open-minded. True believers, as a consequence, will often refuse to question empirical evidence supportive of their beliefs, and to accept evidence contradicting these beliefs. For true believers certain issues become dominant in that they structure all or part of their *Weltanschauung*.

For us, then, individuals are not extremists as a consequence of the relative position they occupy in the distribution of beliefs. Extremism, in other words, does not necessarily refer to those whose habitats are the tails of that distribution. It refers, instead, to the inability to revise a large set of one's beliefs even in the face of contradicting evidence, to the consequent lack of independence in the formation of one's judgements, and to expressions of closed-mindedness and intolerance. Immediately below, we argue that extremism is characterized by a loss of autonomy or, equivalently, by a propensity to conform to beliefs and orientations determined within a given reference group.[9] Conforming, as we use the term, does not mean converging where the majority is located, but rather, metaphorically speaking, delegating one's critical abilities to an external agent. In other words, individuals

[7] Brainwashing is often a process in which physical coercion plays a part. According to Broom and Selznick (1968, p. 108) "brainwashing consists of an extreme, intensive, and in itself brutal application of the entire range of re-socialization measures". In the usage we make of the term, no physical coercion is implied. Indeed, our usage of the term matches quite closely Berlin's (1998, p. 57) characterization of a similar process. He writes: "I find Nazi values detestable, but I can understand how, given enough misinformation, enough false belief about reality, one could come to believe that they are the only salvation."

[8] Hoffer's hypothesis regarding the origin and evolution of mass movements has been found inconsistent with the evidence (Pinard, 1971). That notwithstanding, his book contains many shrewd observations and offers a number of felicitous expressions among which is that of the "true believer". We need not insist that one can be more or less of a true believer.

[9] Indeed, the whole of our argument could be translated into the sociological language of reference group theory (see Light and Keller, 1982).

who have lost autonomy may conform to beliefs that can be at any point in the distribution of beliefs.[10]

The process of socialization refers to the adjustment or adaptation of individuals to their social environment, defined to include individual agents such as parents, friends, and teachers as well as societal agents like churches, schools, peer groups, media, and governments. According to the use we make of the term, individuals become socialized by acquiring a "potential to conform" as well as a "potential for autonomy". The potential to conform $(c)$ leads individuals to accept and internalize a particular set of beliefs and adopt the norms and rules of conduct associated with these beliefs. The ability to accept complex situations, to tolerate ambiguity and to compromise, on the other hand, is part of the potential for autonomy $(a)$.[11]

There is a trade-off between $c$ and $a$ in the sense that a unit increase in $c$ is acquired at the cost of a decrease in $a$. Given the monotone negative character of such a trade-off and assuming it to be linear, our analysis can be conducted in terms of only one of these two variables. We focus on $a$.

We assume that the rate at which an individual acquires $a$ is higher in earlier stages of socialization and slows down as it approaches a steady state level $a^*$. Socialization can then be described by a function such as:

$$da/dt = ra(t)\frac{1 - a(t)}{a^*} \tag{1}$$

where $r$ and $a^*$ are parameters describing the individual's aptitudes and skills in handling information. The parameters account respectively for the rate at which the individual's potential for autonomy increases over time as a result of the use she makes of the information in her environment, and for the steady state level towards which she tends. An individual's talent and proficiency contribute to determine the shape of the

---

[10] Individuals who kidnap for the purpose of extortion or who, like narcoterrorists, practice terrorism for the sole purpose of protecting their business interests are not extremists. In some cases the distinction between extremists and non-extremists may not be straightforward: there can be disagreement, for example, over individuals like Abu Nidal (Sabri al-Banna) who are considered by some to be no more than contract killers (MacLeod, 1992, p. 6), and by others to be ideologically motivated extremists (Ibrahim, 1998, pp. A1 and A10).

[11] We owe to Loevinger (1976, p. 23) the idea that the ability to tolerate ambiguity is a characteristic of autonomy. There are important sociological and social work literatures on the concept of "competence" – a concept that is also closely related to that of autonomy – which examine the ability of individuals to deal with their environment and the conditions under which this is best accomplished. See, among others, White (1959), and Maluccio (1981).

function, as do factors such as cognitive dissonance that contribute to lower both the rate of acquisition and the steady state level of $a$.

In an idealized situation where the social environment can be supposed to exercise no intentional control over information, the individual attains a full potential level of autonomy. However, information control is a ubiquitous feature of the social environment. It may take innumerable forms, such as outright censorship, repression of social interaction, deception through misinformation, creation of falsehoods, as well as more subtle forms such as advertising-like repetition of messages and manipulation of the relative weight given to different issues in the diffusion of information.[12]

The controls reduce the potential for autonomy while increasing that for conformity. A consequence of a loss of autonomy is that individuals are led to perceive reality, and particularly situations of conflict, in polarized terms. Examples include the belief of American militias that most social problems in the United States derive from the fact that America is not all-white; the belief held in extreme right-wing formations in some European countries that the only solution to a host of social problems – crime and unemployment, for example – is to be found in the expulsion of immigrants; the belief of integralist Muslims that the root of moral decadence is a consequence of the emancipation of women; and the belief of some extra parliamentary left-wing groups that all social problems derive from capitalism.

The trade-off between $c$ and $a$ has some similarity to that implicit in Bernheim's (1994) model of conformity. In that model, making consumption choices that conform to a homogeneous standard of behavior is rewarding in terms of status but costly in terms of deviation from individual preferences. The difference between Bernheim's trade-off and ours is that in his model choices are completely voluntary and internal to the individual whereas in ours there is an external background component of information control which the individual cannot avoid.

---

[12] We are indebted to Nachman Ben-Yehuda for his help in clarifying the notion of information control and for bringing to our attention important documentation of its existence and weight even in modern democracies. A number of studies substantiate, for example, the systematic misrepresentation of experimental results, data, or historical information in textbooks to the benefit of a particular bias. Examples include Berkowitz's (1971) survey of research on psychology textbooks in the United States and Stille's (1998) analysis of information control by larger American textbook publishers. A wide and well-documented literature on deception and misinformation in wartime (Knightley, 1975) as well as in the areas of collective memory and commemoration (Ben-Yehuda, 1995; Schwartz, 1996, 1997) also documents the centrality of information control in the formation of beliefs.

The foregoing can be given diagrammatic representation. Equation (1), which describes the idealized process of socialization unimpeded by information controls, is portrayed in the three panels of Figure 3.1 as *FP*. It represents the full potential that an individual is capable of acquiring in terms of autonomy, the maximum level being equal to $a*$.

Information control is shown as curve *IC*. That curve describes the extent to which information control substracts from the rate at which an individual's potential for autonomy develops. In other words, it describes the susceptibility of the individual learning process to the conditioning effect of intentional manipulations of information by the social environment.[13] In effect we assume, first, that information is an input in the production of a potential for autonomy and, second, that increments in information are subject to diminishing returns. As a consequence the marginal effect of information control increases with the level of autonomy or, to put it differently, when an individual approaches her full potential level of autonomy a unit increase in $a$ requires more information.

The *IC* function has two additional core properties. First, because information control cannot affect an individual whose autonomy has been reduced to zero, the curve passes through the origin. Second, the only relevant portion of the *IC* curve is the one in the positive quadrant; in other words the marginal cost of information control in terms of an individual's autonomy (the marginal loss of autonomy) is always positive.

A range of functions can fit these properties, thus accounting for the fact that the way information control affects the potential for autonomy

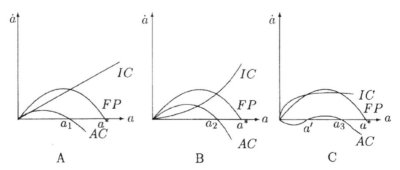

Figure 3.1 Effect of information control on the potential for autonomy

---

[13] The level of information control existent in the environment is constant along any *IC* curve. An increase in the control of information is represented by an upward shift of the curve itself.

differs across individuals. Different shapes of the *IC* curves represent different ways an individual is susceptible to information control. Figure 3.1, 3.2, and 3.3 illustrate some prototypes. In Figure 3.1 the marginal cost of information control in terms of autonomy is everywhere non-decreasing. In this case, an increase in information control always results in a decrease in the equilibrium level of *a*. For example, the linear relationship depicted in Panel A of Figure 3.1 refers to a situation in which the marginal cost of information control to the individual increases at a constant rate. In Panel B, the *IC* curve is convex: the marginal cost of information control is increasing at an increasing rate with the level of *a*. In Panel C, the marginal cost of information control increases at a decreasing rate with the level of *a*, with the effect of information control felt strongly from the very beginning of the socialization process. The substraction of the *IC* from the *FP* curve, as represented in curve *AC*, gives us a visual representation of the actual capacity for autonomy. The height of such *AC* curves is a measure of the resistance that a subject is capable of, given the amount of information control. The distance between $a^*$ and $a_i$ ($i = 1, 2, 3$), measures the steady state loss in autonomy and, given the ability of the individual as portrayed by the *FP* curve, is a measure of the effect of information control.[14]

In Panel A – as in Panel B – $a_i$ is the unique steady state because everywhere to the left of $a_i$ the rate of accumulation of *a* is positive whereas everywhere to its right it is negative. In Panel C, however, because the *FP* and the *IC* curves intersect twice, there are two steady states – one stable ($a_3$) and one unstable ($a'$). The existence of multiple equilibria opens up the possibility that exogenous events will lead to discontinuous changes in the level of *a*. In Panel C, for example, an exogenous disturbance, if large enough to push an individual across the threshold at $a'$, will have extinguished all resistance to the conditioning effect of the environment and, consequently, the individual's potential for autonomy. In the case of more than two intersections of the *FP* and *IC* curves, there will be more than one stable steady state. In Figure 3.2, where the curves intersect three times, the resulting two steady states are shown as $a_4$ and $a_5$. One implication of the above is that the potential for autonomy need not be completely choked off as a result of a discontinuous decrease in *a*.

As long as the marginal autonomy cost of information control is increasing, the *AC* curve is always flatter than the full potential (*FP*)

---

[14] Because of cognitive dissonance, the new steady state $a_i$ is a self-reinforcing equilibrium: among the available information, individuals will operate a further selection by attaching a higher relevance to that confirming their beliefs and ignoring that contradicting them.

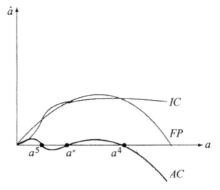

Figure 3.2 Effect of information control on the potential for autonomy: multiple equilibria

curve.[15] Therefore the resistance to displacements due to exogenous shocks – such as events that lead to social discontent – will be dampened. In other words, the more severe the information control, the weaker will be the self-correcting mechanism that brings an individual back to the steady state. If, however, the *IC* curve has a decreasing marginal cost segment, that will no longer hold. The level of the *AC* curve will anyway always be below or equal to that of the *FP* curve (Figure 3.3): in all cases, information control will impair the capacity of the socialization process, as a production mechanism, to generate autonomy.

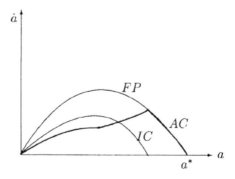

Figure 3.3 Effect of information control on the potential for autonomy: decreasing marginal cost of information control

---

[15] The slope of the *AC* curve is, in fact, the difference between the derivatives of the *FP* and *IC* functions.

## 3. REINFORCEMENT MECHANISMS

We have already introduced the social environment as the set of agents that influence individuals. We have focused on the influence that is manifested in information control. Additional mechanisms are at work. The most apparent is the pressure to conform associated with incentives such as ostracism, rejection, penalization, and rewards. These incentives tend to influence the behavior of individuals, rather than their beliefs. They do not therefore significantly contribute to the radicalization and hardening of beliefs that is at the root of extremism.

There are other mechanisms, however, through which the influence of the social environment acts upon the beliefs of individuals. These mechanisms have the power not only to weaken autonomy and foster a homogenization of behavior within groups, but also to heighten the extremity of opinions. We elaborate briefly on three of them which we label persuasion, social comparison, and social corroboration.

Social influence takes place through persuasion when individuals become more entrenched in their beliefs as social interaction brings them into contact with previously unconsidered and compelling arguments in support of their original position. In other words, by interacting with their social environment, individuals access novel information that may allow them to reinforce and consolidate their opinions and beliefs (Burnstein and Vinokur, 1977).

In addition to information sharing – the essence of persuasion – social interaction also allows individuals to compare the differences between their beliefs and those of others on a quantitative scale. Social comparison, in other words, may reveal interpersonal differences in the intensity of beliefs, differences which in principle can be measured on a numerical index based on techniques such as Guttman's (1944) "scale analysis," Lazarsfeld's (1954) "latent structure analysis," and Coombs's (1950) "unfolding scale analysis".[16] To go from such measurement techniques to the idea that individuals are capable of quantitative comparisons it is necessary to assume, somewhat as is done in rational expectations theory, that individuals can amass information on latent structures and scales like analysts do. It is not necessary, however, any more than in the analysis of expectations, to assume that the information is perfect. When individuals holding a given belief are immersed in a social environment that is more strongly wedded to that same belief, the social comparison mechanism tends to induce them to adjust their beliefs

---

[16] For a critical discussion of these various techniques, see Coleman (1964, pp. 16–21).

upwards in quantitative terms. The mechanism is akin to that which governs Duesenberry's (1949) demonstration effect which pertains to income and consumption comparisons.[17] According to the social comparison mechanism, if an individual's opinions and beliefs are less categorical than those of the group, social interaction will push the individual higher up on the scale. A fortiori, once attitudes and beliefs are shared equally by all, no further change occurs.

Social influence can take yet another form which "does not require the exchange, understanding, evaluation, and integration of persuasive material into one's value or belief system nor does it even require knowledge of other specific actions and opinions (as reflected on some continuous scale)" (Baron et al., 1996, p. 559). This third mechanism – social corroboration – is the least apparent but is, in our opinion, crucial in the development of extreme beliefs. It explains how the simple perception that others share her tendency or inclination to be for or against a given position may be sufficient for an individual to become more radically wedded to that position.

The reason why social corroboration leads to the above result is to be found in the fact that taking an extreme position is costly in terms of the risk of social sanctions that often befalls outliers. As a consequence, whenever someone in the social environment of the individual who takes an extreme position endorses that position, the costs of social interaction are reduced. This can be seen as the result of diffuse, generally non-localizable externalities among agents. The cost reduction takes place no matter the intensity with which the endorser holds to the opinions and beliefs. Moreover, social corroboration can be intentionally cultivated in the form of subtle verbal and non-verbal cues. For example, participation in parades, the wearing of insignias, the display of posters, applause, and other signs of approval may act as endorsements of particular beliefs and be sufficient to reinforce them.

The three foregoing inducements are always at work in ordinary social interactions. They may, however, become central in the genesis of extremism when the collectivity within which the interactions take place reaches a critical level of internal homogeneity. Why? Because in a homogeneous environment discordant and contrary opinions and positions are, by definition, not present to act as checks and balances to the sway of particular beliefs. In other words, the information that is shared in the persuasion mechanism is of a unique variety; the parallels that are drawn in the social comparison mechanism are between like opinions and

---

[17] See also Frank (1985).

beliefs; and the expressions of confirmation that make one more intransigent are not challenged by alternatives in the social corroboration mechanism.

The strength of the mechanisms that reinforce the rigidity with which one holds to certain opinions will therefore be positively correlated with the ratio of validating to opposing inputs from the environment. High values of such a ratio are more easily attained in groups than in society at large.[18] This is why groups are the natural habitat of extremism.[19] A corollary of the foregoing is that if an individual is a member only of groups that share like opinions and beliefs, that individual's capacity for autonomy will tend to be impaired.

## 4. AGGREGATE DYNAMICS IN THE DIFFUSION OF BELIEFS

The extent to which a collective is internally homogeneous in terms of opinions and beliefs – the ratio of opposing to validating inputs – is, we have argued, a key parameter that determines the strength of the reinforcement mechanisms. The relationship between such a parameter's value and its effect on the radicalization and entrenchment of beliefs is, however, not necessarily a linear one. It is, indeed, widely documented that optimal adjustments by microeconomic agents are not always small or continuous. Rather, a specific adjustment or decision is often triggered when some key parameter which measures the discrepancy between a desired or ideal value and the actual one reaches or exceeds some preset threshold.[20] It is when the uniformity of beliefs within a group, for example, reaches or exceeds a given threshold that the reinforcement mechanisms may trigger a bandwagon effect – a sudden diffusion of group sentiments or pressures, as happens in witch-hunts, scapegoating, and other like phenomena. Individual choices such as mobilization in extremist activities do not in fact depend only on relative costs (price signals) of different courses of action faced by each agent in isolation, but also on the fraction of agents inclined towards the same choice. Decisions, in other words, are not completely decentralized as in standard atomistic decision models because the fraction of units that make the

---

[18] Along certain dimensions, however – anti-communism in the United States following McCarthyism or anti-Semitism in Germany during the Third Reich – a large degree of homogeneity is sometimes achieved over the whole of society.

[19] This does not mean that some extremists are not "loners". However, when extremists are identified as loners, as was the case with Timothy McVeigh (see end of Section 6.1), it often transpires that they interact with other individuals via the Internet, fax messages, and other means.

[20] Examples of this kind of behavior have been reported and shown to be optimal in several classes of problems in finance, operations research, and control. See Aoki (1996).

same choices affects, through the reinforcement mechanisms described above, the desirability or effectiveness of the decision.[21]

Besides the gathering of agents around a uniform set of beliefs and a common expectational state, other factors intervene in determining aggregate dynamics conducive to the onset of social expressions of extremism. A key factor is the level of discontent and dissatisfaction with the existing order of things – due, for example, to past or present discrimination, to the inability to adapt to fast social change, or to high and protracted degrees of uncertainty about economic prospects – experienced by agents within a given society. A second key factor is a society's degree of polarization. A society is said to be polarized when its population can be classified into different clusters, with each cluster containing people with similar attributes (intra-group homogeneity), but different clusters having people with dissimilar attributes (inter-group heterogeneity). Polarization differs from standard measures of inequality. Imagine a society in which the distance between internally homogeneous income clusters is small, and contrast it with one in which the distance between clusters is large. Clusters in the second society must be fewer in number than in the first. Even if, in passing from the first to the second society, we observe a decrease in inequality, the latter is more polarized. In an empirical analysis based on a large sample of countries, Penubarti and Asea (1996) establish that there exists a positive link between polarization in terms of wealth and control over resources and the incidence of political violence.

These streams of literature are of great relevance for an understanding of the links between political extremism and some key economic variables. We do not further elaborate on them as our concern in this chapter is primarily the dynamics that lead to extremism as an individually rational choice.

## 5. POLITICAL ENTREPRENEURS, LEADERS, AND GROUPS

As is clear from the preceding discussion, individuals who become extremists do not generally do so in isolation, but in a social context of which groups are an essential component. Political entrepreneurs and leaders mobilize individuals for the pursuit of particular objectives and

---

[21] In the economics literature there are many examples of interaction between agents and their social environment affecting microeconomic decisions. Leibenstein (1950), for example, reformulated some aspects of the static theory of consumer demand while relaxing the assumption that the consumption behavior of an individual is independent of the consumption of others. Schelling (1978), Becker (1991), and Banerjee (1992), among others, also deal with the effects of interdependencies among a large number of small decision-making units.

thus play a crucial role in the formation of groups – an activity in many ways analogous to the employment of labor by the entrepreneurs of conventional microeconomic analysis.[22]

We distinguish between leaders and entrepreneurs to account for the fact that for some extremist groups it is a shared *Weltanschauung* that sets individuals in opposition and conflict with the larger society, whereas other groups arise out of individual entrepreneurial initiative. In the role they play in group formation and in group activity, leaders are endogenous, whereas entrepreneurs are initially exogenous to the groups.

Leaders shape and activate existing beliefs – in that sense, they act as catalysts. They also seek to control the centrifugal forces which threaten dissension in the groups.

Entrepreneurs, on the other hand, play two different roles in the genesis and dissemination of extremism. First, they deliberately implant and disseminate beliefs that are conducive to their objectives. Second, they are essential in engineering a transition from a state in which beliefs are held by isolated individuals to a state in which the sharing of such beliefs becomes constitutive of a community.

Entrepreneurs need groups because, being essential agents of information control and the repositories of the reinforcement mechanisms of persuasion, social comparison and social corroboration, groups are the most efficient instruments that entrepreneurs can employ to achieve their ends.

Groups will vary in size. If we assume temporarily that the only arguments of the utility functions of entrepreneurs and leaders are policy objectives, then the largest possible dissemination of the relevant beliefs and therefore the largest possible group size will be optimal.[23] However, to the extent that extremist groups engage in unlawful or in socially unacceptable activities, such as lynchings (for example, the Ku Klux Klan), political assassinations, bombings and other acts of terrorism (the Red Brigades, Euzkadi Ta Askatasuna, the Irish Republican Army, Hamas), robberies and counterfeiting (the Silent Brotherhood), the danger of infiltration and the risk of information leakage calls for groups of smaller size. Control over members and dissimulation generate diminishing returns to the diffusion of beliefs.

The influence of these forces will be larger the greater the effort of society to suppress the groups. This will depend, generally, on the extent to which the extremist beliefs are perceived as alien and threatening by

---

[22] These entrepreneurs also invest capital, borrow funds, combine factors of production, manage conflict, advertise, and so on.

[23] Some extremist groups may, however, choose to remain small in the pursuit of an elitist image and/or objective.

the rest of society. Ku Klux Klan groups in the United States, for example, tended to be largest in southern states where the variance between their beliefs and those of society at large was lower than elsewhere.

## 6.  ON THE MEANING OF EXTREMIST ACTIVITIES

In the preceding discussion, we performed an exercise which is seldom undertaken in conventional economic analysis – that of identifying mechanisms which contribute to the delineation of the map of available opportunities which entrepreneurs and leaders can exploit.[24] To put it differently, we investigated the role of information control and of a set of self-reinforcing mechanisms which can help explain both the origin and perdurance of extremism in individuals and groups and why entrepreneurs and leaders will be able to capitalize profitably on the opportunities thus created.

In what follows we limit ourselves to providing an explanation for why, in the pursuit of certain political objectives – for example territorial independence, ethnic cleansing, fundamentalist Islamic constitutionalism, redistribution of resources among classes, supremacy of white Christians, the obtention of a right, the redress of abuse, and so on – the extremist political groupings we have studied engage in terrorism, make use of violence, promote hatred and/or cultivate resentment.

These activities, we suggest, can be explained by reference to two general drives: signaling and destabilization.[25] The social and political changes that political extremists pursue are sought under some circumstances by communicating a message, a signal aimed at modifications in the behavior of those in the audience to which the message is addressed (often the general public and a fortiori the ruling establishment). In this case terrorist attacks and violence, as well as incitements to hatred and resentment, may all function as media for the transmission of a message to the general public and to the establishment, so as to generate a response congruent with the desires of the extremists.

Under other circumstances, the purpose of extremist activities is to destabilize the system in order to capture the apparatus of state and replace the existing establishment, rather than seek change from the inside.

---

[24] The techniques to alter and shape the maps of opportunities, however, have an important place in the management literature.

[25] There exist, both in the economic and the political science literatures, several analyses pointing to the signaling nature of terrorism (for example, Lapan and Sandler, 1993; Enders and Sandler, 1995 and references therein). The aim of such studies, mostly based on a game-theoretic representation of the interaction between terrorists and governments, is the evaluation of alternative anti-terrorist strategies. We focus instead on the meaning of extremist activities and behaviors from a microeconomic perspective.

Which of the two motives prevails will depend on the responsiveness of audiences.

## 6.1 Signaling

As communication, political extremist activities serve two functions. The first is to signal discontent when the extremists believe that the establishment would not, unprompted, address the problems which are seen to be at the root of their discontent, but that it could be forced to do so. Extremists try to elicit the response they desire by using terror, violence, hatred, and resentment in order to raise the costs of maintaining a status quo they wish changed. Even more importantly, by repeatedly signaling one or more problems they want to see on the agenda, the actions of extremists are aimed at influencing and altering the way the issues they care about are perceived by their own society or the international community. The media of mass communication clearly are a crucial counterpart in such signaling games. Mass media, in fact, determine the saliency of issues as well as their relative weight in the perception of audiences by deciding on the share of attention they accord to different issues. For example, it is reasonable in the light of the foregoing to understand Palestinian Liberation Organization terrorism, until recently, as attempts to keep the Palestinian problem alive in public opinion and at the top of the international political agenda.

The second mass communication function of extremist activities is to frustrate solutions of compromise to given political problems. Hamas's suicide bombings at Mahane Yehuda in July 1997, on the eve of a U.S. mission to relaunch the peace process in Israel, are an example. The activities of the Italian Red Brigades in the 1970s and 1980s have been seen as attempts to stop the development of a larger coalition of democratic forces that could eventually have led the Communist Party to participate in the government of the country.[26]

The signaling of activities of extremists are costly in that they absorb resources.[27] Given the constraint of eliciting the desired response from a target audience, we should expect a tendency on the part of extremists to minimize resource costs with respect to that constraint, leading to an optimal combination of economy of signaling costs for the extremists and detectability of signals by the targed audience. Indeed, when a signal points to real intentions and, in a situation of conflict, to real fighting

---

[26] The view that a principal objective of the Red Brigades was to drive what they saw as a collusive and monolithic political establishment into a crisis that would lead to its collapse is developed in Curcio (1993).

[27] This term must be defined broadly to cover members, popular and institutional support, finances, human capital, and so on.

potential, its detection is beneficial to both the signalers, if contestants potentially have an averse response to the signal, and to the receivers, because it reduces the receivers' uncertainty about the signalers' future behavior and it provides information useful in devising an appropriate response. An evolutionary perspective on social communication suggests that, for this reason, signals with a content of mutually beneficial com-munication tend to evolve towards cost-minimizing muted forms (Tanaka, 1996).

Both theory and empirical evidence tell us, however, that things do not always turn out that way. As an inevitable by-product of the fact that individuals are selected to respond to their environment in ways that are on average beneficial to themselves, other individuals can be selected to subvert this responsiveness for their own benefit. Can signals with a genuine information content be distinguished from manipulative signals? It is known that in nature two kinds of evolution lead to different kinds of signals: in the presence of a low information content in a message we expect to see heightened sales resistance leading, through form of arm's-race coevolution, to exaggerated, conspicuous, repetitive signaling (Krebs and Dawkins, 1984). The minimum size of a signal capable of eliciting some response increases; that is, the constraint on the minimization of signaling costs moves upwards.

This is similar to what happens in advertising. The optimal size and repetitiveness of a message about the existence or the quality of a given product – which conveys information relevant for the audience – can be expected to be smaller than the size and repetitiveness of messages devoid of informational content whose aim is to create new needs or merely to shift consumption between different brands of equivalent products. Moreover, the noisier the environment – the stron-ger the volume of existing advertising – the higher up, again, will the detectability constraint move. Escalated competition will lead to a higher repetitiveness and redundancy of messages. When the purpose of extremist activities is to signal discontent and opposition and to exacerbate conflicts, we suggest that a logic similar to that discussed above applies.

A diagram may help formalize some of the foregoing discussion. In Figure 3.4, the ordinate measures the response ($R$) of a given audience to the activities of a particular extremist group, and the abscissa the inten-sity of such activities ($A$). An increase in the intensity of extremist activ-ities may manifest itself in an increased repetitiveness of signals, and/or in a switch to more vehement terror and violence.

The relationship between $A$ and $R$ can be portrayed by a curve starting at the origin (in the absence of extremist activities the response is zero). That curve, labeled $OP$, is divided into two regions: a first in

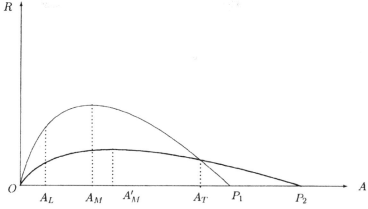

Figure 3.4 The response of audiences to extremist activities

which responsiveness is increasing but at a decreasing rate, followed by a second in which it is falling.[28] In the first region, in other words, the marginal product of the extremist activities is positive but diminishing, whereas in the second it is negative. Decreasing and negative returns are the consequence of the application of a more intensive effort to fixed "endowments." Two of these are: (i) the value that a given audience attaches to life, security, and property; and (ii) the receptivity it grants to the demands of extremists. In what follows we hold these two factors constant, although we contrast two audiences (or societies) which differ from each other in the size and quality of those endowments. The position of $OP_1$ relative to $OP_2$ is a reflection of the assumption that audience 1 attaches a higher value to life, security, and property than does audience 2 and that it is also initially more open to the demands of extremists than is the second audience.

To clarify the role of the fixed endowments in the generation of diminishing and negative returns to signaling, we begin by focusing on audience 1. At a low intensity level of activity (such as $A_L$ in Figure 3.4), that audience exhibits a given response. As extremist activities become more intense while the endowments are held constant, that audience becomes more and more reluctant – a reluctance that manifests itself in ever smaller increments in responsiveness until eventually the responsiveness declines. In the diagram, that happens once the level of intensity rises above $A_M$. Audience 2, because it attaches less value to

---

[28] The curve $OP$ could have been drawn to display an initial region in which the response increases at an increasing rate. The curve would then have had three regions.

life, security, and property and is less receptive to the demands of extremists than is audience 1, offers less responsiveness at all intensities of extremist activities less than $A_T$. The shape of the $OP_2$ curve reflects that behavior.

Given $OP_1$ and $OP_2$, Figure 3.4 tells us that for extremist activities up to intensity $A_T$, the responsiveness of audience 1 is greater than that of audience 2. When extremist activities exceed an intensity threshold such as $A_T$, the responsiveness of audience 1 falls below that of audience 2; and beyond $P_1$ society 1 withdraws all recognition to the demands of extremists, is no longer willing to search for compromises, and switches to repression alone.

There is therefore an optimal level of intensity in extremist activities which will necessarily be located to the left of $A_M$ on $OP_1$ (and of $A'_M$ on $OP_2$) and which will be determined by equating the marginal cost of resources absorbed in signaling to the marginal benefits of the responsiveness of the audience.[29] Too loud a signal may consequently be counterproductive. That was, no doubt, the case of the bombing of the Alfred P. Murrah Federal Building in Oklahoma City in April 1995 by Timothy McVeigh and Terry Nichols, of the assassination of George Besse, President of Renault, in 1986 by Action Directe, of the killing of Aldo Moro in 1978 by the Red Brigades, as well as the 1970 strangulation of Pierre Laporte, a Cabinet Minister in the Quebec Government, by the Front de Libération du Québec.

Our examination of the groups listed in Table 3.1 revealed that extremist formations that had the same orientation and pursued similar objectives often used different instruments in the pursuit of these objectives. The reason for the use of different instruments by extremists is to be found in characteristics of audiences. For example, Quebec separatist groups have made and continue to make use of low intensity signals – relying mostly on cultivating hatred and resentment – while groups such as the PLO and the LTTE relied on terrorism – a much higher intensity activity. The analysis just outlined tells us that the explanation for the differential behavior of these groups is the greater responsiveness of the audience of the Quebec separatist groups – first, the local population of the province whose support is needed if the separatists are to garner the votes necessary to win the referendum that would allow them to secede, and second, the Canadian government which the separatists can hope to blackmail. The PLO and the LTTE target mainly an international audience, whose responsiveness is much lower.

---

[29] The exact point depending on the exogenously given unit cost resources used for signaling.

## 6.2 Destabilization

Beside signaling, destabilization is the other main motive behind political extremism. It is pursued through a set of activities, which may range from subversive maneuvers to open warfare, aimed at creating the conditions for overthrowing and replacing the existing establishment.

Attempts at destabilization take place when extremists perceive that an acceptable solution to the issues at stake requires more radical change than that achievable by forcing the ruling elites to negotiate with them.

This is the case of the Algerian radical Islamists who, arbitrarily denied access to the political process, believe that only violent confrontation and destruction of the apparatus of state can lead to the establishment of an Islamic order. Such a perception is grounded in two aspects of the state of the world: (i) the prospects for peaceful change are objectively bleak – in the past half a century not a single Arab country has permitted the transfer of power to an opposition party through fair and open elections; (ii) the worldview of the contestants – in the case of Algeria, the military government and the Islamic radicals – are so incompatible as to forestall any possibility of compromise. It is also the case of the Taliban rebels who, appearing in 1994 as one more faction in the Afghan civil war, overthrew the former communist president Mohammed Najibullah in September 1996 and gained control of two-thirds of the country, where they imposed a fanatically extreme Islamic rule.

When the purpose of political extremism is to capture the apparatus of state through open confrontation, the intensity of extremist activities is no longer dictated by the rule of minimizing signaling costs. Once engaged in an escalated contest, the probability of success becomes directly correlated with the real fighting potential – the amount of resources employed and the extent of the terror, violence, and destruction caused by the activities of the extremists. If we refer to the logic surrounding Figure 3.4, we could say that extremist groups opt for destabilization when they cannot achieve the desired response from audiences. For the purpose of extremists, it is as if the *OP* curve in that diagram had collapsed to zero.

In this context, it is worth noting that the existence of extremist groups that persist in their activities when the chance of capturing the apparatus of state appears to be zero is not inconsistent with our approach. Indeed, violence can continue beyond what would be predicted on the basis of a comparison of current costs and expected beliefs, if sunk costs are assumed to exist. The prospect of penalties and of a loss of status as well as barriers to alternative career paths once one has been publicly identified as an extremist may replace the expected future rewards and act as incentives for continuing to engage in extremist activities.

## 7. CONCLUSIONS

We have been concerned with two broad problems. We have first tried to understand what forces help shape the map of extremist opportunities that political entrepreneurs and leaders can exploit. To that end, we have sought an answer to the question of who becomes an extremist and we have looked into mechanisms that are conducive to the radicalization of potential candidates. Borrowing from the sociological literature on socialization, we have suggested that persons whose individual makeup in terms of a potential for autonomy – or in terms of a competence to deal with change, confusion, difficult situations, and other like circumstances – makes them susceptible to adverse effects of information control are potential extremists as they assign higher weight to certain beliefs regarding states of the world and become unwilling to revise them even in the face of contradicting evidence. We have then examined a number of mechanisms through which beliefs become entrenched in persons and diffused or disseminated in groups.

The second problem, which has retained our attention is that of explaining why political extremists engage in activities such as terrorism, violence, hatred, and resentment. We noted that groups that appear to have the same broad orientation and to be moved by the desire to achieve similar goals often engage in different kinds of activities, and we offered an analysis of signaling and destabilization that appears capable of explaining some of the behaviors of political extremist groups.

### REFERENCES

Akerlof, George A. and William T. Dickens. 1982. "The economic consequences of cognitive dissonance," *American Economic Review* **72**(3), June, 307–19, reprinted in G. A. Akerlof, 1984, *An Economic Theorist's Book of Tales: Essays that Entertain the Consequences of New Assumptions in Economic Theory*, Cambridge University Press, Cambridge, 123–44.

Aoki, Masanao. 1996. *New Approaches to Macroeconomic Modeling. Evolutionary Stochastic Dynamics, Multiple Equilibria, and Externalities as Field Effects*, Cambridge University Press, New York.

Banerjee, Abhilit V. 1992. "A simple model of herd behavior," *Quarterly Journal of Economics* **107**(3), August, 797–817.

Barkun, Michael. 1997. *Religion and the Racist Right. The Origins of the Christian Identity Movement*, rev. edn, University of North Carolina Press, Chapel Hill.

Baron, Robert S. et al. 1996. "Social corroboration and opinion extremity," *Journal of Experimental Psychology* **32**(6), November, 537–60.

Becker, Gary S. 1991. "A note on restaurant pricing and other examples of social influences on price," *Journal of Political Economy* **99**(5), October, 1109–16.

Ben-Yehuda, Nachman. 1995. *The Masada Myth*, University of Wisconsin Press, Madison.

Berkowitz, Leonard. 1971. "Reporting an experiment. A case study in leveling, sharpening, and assimilation," *Journal of Experimental Social Psychology* **7**(2), March, 237–43.

Berlin, Isaiah. 1998. "My intellectual path," *New York Review of Books* **45**(8), May 14, 53–60.

Bernheim, Douglas B. 1994. "A theory of conformity," *Journal of Political Economy* **102**(5), October, 841–77.

Broom, Leonard and Philip Selznick. 1968. *Sociology. A Text with Adapted Readings*, 4th edn, Harper & Row, New York.

Burnstein, Eugene and Amiram Vinokur. 1977. "Persuasive argumentation and social comparison as determinants of attitude polarization," *Journal of Experimental Social Psychology* **13**(4), July, 315–32.

Chalmers, David M. 1951. *Hooded Americanism: The History of the Ku Klux Klan*, Franklin Watts, New York.

Coleman, James S. 1964. *Introduction to Mathematical Sociology*, Free Press, Glencoe.

Coombs, Clyde H. 1950. "Psychological scaling without a unit of measurement," *Psychological Review* **57**(3), May, 145–58.

Curcio, Renato. 1993. *A Viso Aperto* (Intervista di Mario Scialoja), Mondadori, Milano.

Duesenberry, James S. 1949. *Income, Saving and the Theory of Consumer Behavior*, Harvard University Press, Cambridge, MA.

Enders, Walter and Todd Sandler. 1995. "Terrorism: Theory and applications," in Keith Hartley and Todd Sandler (eds), *Handbook of Defense Economics*, Vol. 1, Elsevier Science, Amsterdam, chapter 9, 213–49.

Flynn, Kevin and Gary Gerhardt. 1990. *The Silent Brotherhood*, Penguin, New York.

Frank, Robert H. 1985. *Choosing the Right Pond: Human Behavior and the Quest for Status*, Oxford University Press, New York.

George, John and Laird Wilcox. 1996. *American Extremists. Militias, Supremacists, Klansmen, Communists, and Others*, Prometheus, Amherst, New York.

Guttman Louis. 1944. "A basis for scaling qualitative data," *American Sociological Review* **9**(2), April, 139–50.

Hoffer, Eric. 1951. *The True Believer. Thoughts on the Nature of Mass Movements*, Harper & Brothers, New York.

Ibrahim, Youssem. 1998. "Mystery shrouds capture of top terrorist," *Globe and Mail*, August 26.

Karl, Jonathan. 1995. *The Right to Bear Arms: The Rise of America's New Militias*, Harper Paperback, HarperCollins, New York.

Knightley, Phillip. 1975. *The First Casualty: From Crimea to Vietnam: The War Correspondent as Hero, Propagandist, and Myth Maker*, Harcourt Brace Jovanovich, New York.

Krebs, John R. and Richard Dawkins. 1984. "Animal signals: Mind-reading and manipulation," in John R. Krebs (ed.), *Behavioural Ecology: An Evolutionary Approach*, Blackwell, Oxford, 380–405.

Lapan, Harvey E. and Todd Sandler. 1993. "Terrorism and signalling," *European Journal of Political Economy* 9, 383–97.

Lazarsfeld, Paul F. 1954. "A conceptual introduction to latent structure analysis," in P. F. Lazarsfeld (ed.), *Mathematical Thinking in the Social Sciences*, Free Press, Glencoe, 347–87.

Leibenstein, Harvey. 1950. "Bandwagon, snob, and Veblen effects in the theory of consumers' demand," *Quarterly Journal of Economics* **64**(2), May, 183–207.

Light Jr, Donald and Suzanne Keller. 1982. *Sociology*, 3rd edn, Knopf, New York.

Loevinger, Jane. 1976. *Ego Development*, Jossey-Bass, San Francisco.

MacLeod, Scott. 1992. "The terrorist's terrorist," *New York Review of Books* **39**(10), May 28, 6–11.

Maluccio, Anthony N. 1981. "Competence-oriented social work practice: An ecological approach," in A. N. Maluccio (ed.), *Promoting Competence in Clients*, The Free Press, New York.

McNicol Stock, Catherine. 1996. *Rural Radicals: Righteous Rage in the American Grain*, Cornell University Press, Ithaca and London.

O'Callaghan, Sean. 1998. *The Informer*, Bantam Press, London.

Penubarti, Mohan and Patrick Asea. 1996. "Polarization and political violence," Paper presented at the Summer Meeting of the *APSA*, Political Methodology Section, Ann Arbor, Michigan, 1996.
   URL: http://pundit.sscnet.ucla.edu.

Pinard, Maurice. 1971. *The Rise of a Third Party. A Study in Crisis Politics*, Prentice-Hall, Englewood Cliffs, NJ.

Purkitt, Helen E. and James W. Dyson. 1989. "An experimental study of cognitive processes and information in political problem solving," in Bernd Rohrmann, Lee R. Beach, Charles Vlek, and Stephen R. Watson (eds), *Advances in Decision Research*, North-Holland, Amsterdam.

Sargent, Lyman T. (ed.) 1995. *Extremism in America: A Reader*, New York University Press, New York.

Schelling, Thomas. 1978. *Micromotives and Macrobehavior*, W.W. Norton, New York.

Schwartz, Barry. 1996. "Memory as a cultural system: Abraham Lincoln in World War II," *American Sociological Review* **61**(6), December, 908–27.

Schwartz, Barry. 1997. "Collective memory and history: How Abraham Lincoln became a symbol of racial equality," *Sociological Quarterly* **38**(3), Summer, 469–94.

Stille, Alexander. 1998. "The betrayal of history," *New York Review of Books*, **XVL**(10), June 11, 15–20.

Tanaka, Yoshinary. 1996. "Social selection and the evolution of animal signals," *Evolution* **50**(2), 512–23.

White, Robert W. 1959. "Motivation reconsidered: The concept of competence," *Psychological Review* **66**(5), September, 297–333.

# PART II

# EXTREMISM IN CONSTITUTIONAL DEMOCRACIES

# 4

# Extremism and Monomania

*Pierre Salmon**

## 1. INTRODUCTION

Although the literature on political extremism tends to be structured around monographical descriptions of national experiences, a number of interesting regularities do emerge. I will treat as established facts the following ones. First, successful extremist movements and politicians (as well, of course, as extremist governments) generally stress several issues that are only loosely connected.[1] Second, these movements or politicians often – but by no means always – adopt extremist positions on most or all of these issues. Third, when polled, supporters of extremist movements or politicians typically express *moderate views* on many issues.[2]

---

* For useful comments on earlier versions of this chapter, I am very grateful to two anonymous referees, to Isidoro Mazza and other participants in the 8th Villa Colombella Seminar, to participants in the Lisbon meeting of the European Public Choice Society – especially Johanna Jakobsson, Annick Laruelle and Ekkart Zimmermann – and to Roger Congleton and Alain Wolfelsperger.

[1] The heterogeneity of many large-scale extremist movements not in power as well as of support for extremist regimes such as Mussolini's, Hitler's or Vichy, has been observed by many authors. In the case of France, this applies to the fascist or quasi-fascist impressive Croix de Feu league in the thirties (Passmore, 1997), to the Vichy regime in 1940–44 (see the excellent commented bibliography at the end of the new, 1997, French edition of Paxton, 1972), and to Jean-Marie Le Pen's Front National more recently (see Mayer and Perrineau, 1989; Mayer, 1996, 1999). Thus, according to Alain de Benoist, one of the founders of the "Nouvelle Droite," the Front National is "a national-populist party which, on a deep level, presents itself as a true ideological patchwork" (cf. Chebel d'Appollonia, 1988, p. 392 of the 1996 edition). On the Liberal Party of Austria under Jörg Haider, see Moreau (1998, pp. 63, 67). On Nazism in Germany, see Kershaw (1992), Ayçoberry (1998). On the radical right in Israel, see Sprinzak (1993).

[2] An illustration of an extremist position adopted by a party but not by most of its members is provided by the Flemish Bloc, in respect both of the self-location at the extreme right and of the question of Flemish nationalism (De Witte and Scheepers, 1998, pp. 106–7). For a comparison of the positions of supporters of the Front National and of supporters of other parties on a number of issues, see Mayer (1996), Mayer and Perrineau (1989), Safran (1993).

Fourth, many supporters of *moderate parties* hold views or adopt positions that are extremist with regard to some issues. This is especially true in countries such as the United States or Britain, in which there is no successful extremist party, but it can also be observed in countries in which one such party exists and defends these views.[3] Fifth, it is often the case that people who support an extremist movement sincerely do not feel responsible for most of the positions adopted by this movement. This extends to the retrospective sentiments of many people with regard to their or others' past support of extremist movements, governments or regimes. Sixth, assessments of extremism vary over time. This applies in particular to retrospective assessments.[4]

This chapter is an attempt to account for these "facts" and a few others. They clearly suggest, it seems to me, that we should be careful to distinguish extremist *views*, extremist *politicians* and extremist *supporters*. Extremist views are widespread and definitely not the privilege of extremist politicians or of their supporters. Extremist politicians can be assumed here as elsewhere to express views or advocate policies for the purpose of getting support rather than because they themselves share all the views that they defend, or believe in all the policies that they recommend. To be precise, my assumption with regard to extremist politicians is that they maximize support (electoral or other) in a short-run perspective, not necessarily at the same time the long-run probability of getting into power.[5] The major assumption made in the chapter, however, concerns neither extremist views nor extremist politicians, but the extremist individuals who support (not necessarily electorally) extremist politicians. I will assume that most of these individuals are "monomaniac extremists" (no derogatory intention). In Section 2, I will elaborate on this characterization, using for that purpose concepts borrowed from the spatial theory of voting, in particular the concept of salience. The section will also include a discussion of types that cannot be characterized as monomaniac extremists but who play a role in the story that follows.

---

[3] In addition to the references given in the last sentence of footnote 2, see, for example, Messina (1989), Falter and Schumann (1988), and Zimmermann and Saafeld (1993, pp. 72–3).

[4] Points 4, 5 and 6 are discussed in Section 4.

[5] The assumption is a bit awkward. It is ill suited to conventional theoretical settings. But it fares better if some room is left for genuine uncertainty. The extremist politicians I have in mind are motivated by the hope that some unforeseen circumstances, generating a political collapse or earthquake, will offer them an occasion to get into power.

What is interesting about monomaniac extremists is the way they can be aggregated into coalitions.[6] I read the descriptive evidence as consistent with the view that, inasmuch as they have a minimum of success (the case of what is called in French "groupuscules" is another matter), extremist movements and politicians are typically supported, at least in a first phase, by coalitions of individuals who deserve to be called (non-derogatorily) monomaniac extremists. Section 3 is devoted to the study of these coalitions and others that are similar in some respects. The fact that many extremist movements, governments or regimes are based on coalitions of monomaniac extremists has noteworthy consequences, some of which I will consider in Section 4. Section 5 is a brief conclusion.

## 2. MONOMANIAC EXTREMISTS AND THEIR BRETHRENS

I do not really need a justification for the assumption that extremists are often monomaniacs (no pejorative intention in the term). First, I could point to historical examples and widespread opinion. Second, "often" is not "always," and the analysis presented in this chapter can very well be asserted to be relevant only when extremists are monomaniacs.

I will however provide an interpretation of monomaniac extremism, which is the following. Extremist *policies* are generally unreasonable because there is so much uncertainty about the indirect effects of policies that the reasonable way to act at the level of society is in the form of what Popper (1945) called piecemeal social engineering: a little step forward in one direction, based on a little conjecture, the step maintained if the conjecture is corroborated, cancelled if it (the conjecture) is refuted. But there are exceptions to the unreasonableness of extremist policies. Uncertainty about the effects of policies may be mitigated by the knowledge of what has obtained in the past or is currently obtaining in other countries. When this is so, radical or revolutionary (or counter-revolutionary) policies may become quite reasonable. Such policies may also be reasonable when the status quo is vanishing or becoming unbearable anyway, when all the alternatives, including the status quo, are equally radical and risky, or when deontological (that is, non-consequential) considerations dominate.

Even in the case of extremist policies that are unreasonable, this does not extend to the acts of advocating or supporting them. These acts can merely express protest, suggest the direction of action, or aim at putting unheeded issues on the political agenda. All of this can be quite reasonable. In the remainder of this chapter, however, I assume "sincere"

---

[6] For a previous analysis of how "single-issue" voters can be aggregated into coalitions whose positions are far from the center, see Congleton (1991). His Figure 2 is close to Figure 4.3 below. A somewhat similar diagram can be found in Tullock (1970).

extremism – "sincere" meaning here both "non-strategic" and "non-merely expressive."[7]

Under that assumption, it seems to me that the main mechanisms which may transform otherwise sensible persons into sincere extremists are those that involve a drastic narrowing of these persons' vision or concerns. Sometimes this narrowing verges on the pathological, implying a distorted and generally ominous perception of one dimension of the world's state, evolution, or future (like when everything is ascribed to a conspiracy). Often, though, and more importantly, the narrowing itself is *perfectly rational*. People are concerned with one issue only because that issue is truly essential to their life, or so they think – perhaps unwisely but not irrationally.[8] Now, the singleness of dimension or concern allows one to overcome the sobering effects of uncertainty: only the consequences of action along the dimension concerned are perceived as relevant and their prediction may be straightforward. This, then, makes extremism rational. If the other consequences of the action were equally relevant, then the fact that they are necessarily uncertain would dissuade one to favor an extremist policy, or at least would induce one to favor an extremist policy only *tentatively*. In my terminology, one would not be a monomaniac extremist, and most likely not an extremist at all.

A monomaniac extremist in a two-issue space is represented in Figure 4.1. To define extremism, I must first characterize moderation. Point R is the ideal position of a (supposedly homogeneous) moderate party, coalition or government – say, the "moderate right."[9] Assuming that the two issues are independent or separable and perceived as such, units along the two dimensions are chosen so that, first, the position of the moderate right appears close to the center of the political spectrum (represented by the origin) and, second, any departure

---

[7] Congleton (1991) discusses *strategic* single-issue voting, that is when "a single-interest voter casts his vote as *if* he were a zealot whose objective function contains only a single argument" (p. 40). Even though I agree with Congleton that such behavior plays a role in all elections, I assume it away nonetheless.

[8] Nozick (1997, p. 297) also stresses "non-compromising" as a feature of extremism but he presents it as "flowing quite naturally" from another feature – "the view of opponents as evil." This pulls the interpretation of extremism toward individually pathological behavior, which seems to me less interesting than centering it on individual behavior of a more or less rational or normal type. In any case, I do without Nozick's assumption.

[9] The figures and the reasoning apply in principle both to left-wing and right-wing extremisms. However, Gordon Tullock seems to be right when he observes (private conversation) that people who refer to political extremism almost always think of right-wing extremism. All the factual literature cited here refers to right-wing extremism and I have found some difficulty in thinking of left-wing extremist coalitions as equally plausible as right-wing ones. This certainly suggests the existence of some structural, permanent, differences between the two extremisms but I will not try to analyze them here.

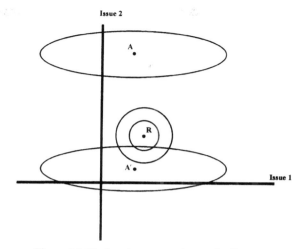

Figure 4.1 Moderation, extremism and salience

from R has the same effect on utility whatever its direction – that is, indifference or iso-preference curves are circles centered on R (the units being such that indifference or iso-preference between two points depends only on the "Euclidian distance" between these points and the ideal point R).

Now that moderation has been defined, we can see why, in Figure 4.1, both point A and the curve drawn around it reflect monomaniac extremism. First, A is an extreme position with regard to issue 2 but not to issue 1. Second, and more importantly, monomaniac extremism is reflected in the form of the indifference or iso-preference curves centered on A (only one is drawn). These curves are ellipses rather circles because the distance between any of their points and A is a "weighted Euclidian distance" rather than a Euclidian distance *tout court* (see Enelow and Hinich, 1984; Hinich and Munger, 1997). The difference in the weights assigned to issue 1 and to issue 2 reflects a difference in what is called in the literature the *salience* of the two issues. The units in which the two issues are measured have been chosen so that these issues have the same salience for the moderates, whose ideal point is R. Then, the shape of the ellipses centered on A expresses the fact that, for our individual, issue 2 is more salient than issue 1. Because the two issues are assumed to be separable, the curves' main axes are horizontal and vertical rather than inclined in one direction of the other.

Salience, or, more generally, the set of weights used in the weighted Euclidian distance formula, is often considered in the literature to be homogeneous across all individuals. For example, if at a point in time, issue 2 is more salient than issue 1, the indifference curves of all individuals are ellipses whose major axes are horizontal. In contrast to this homogeneity assumption, I assume that salience varies from one individual (or group of individuals) to the other; that is, I assume it to be heterogeneous or *idiosyncratic*.[10]

The individual whose ideal point is A in Figure 4.1 is a monomaniac extremist because the position of this ideal point is extreme in terms of one issue *and* because the individual considers that issue as the more salient and attaches relatively little importance to the other one.[11] These two characteristics – of position and of salience – are necessary conditions for one to be a monomaniac extremist. Let me consider now the case of individuals who happen to have only one of the two characteristics. In Figure 4.1 also, point A′ and the ellipse centered on it are meant to represent one such individual. In terms of position (with reference to the moderate position R), the individual concerned is certainly not an extremist. However, in terms of salience this individual, being concerned almost exclusively with issue 2, has something of a monomaniac, at least potentially. Again without pejorative intention, I will call him or her a centrist monomaniac – not so inoffensive a breed, as we shall see.

When only the other of the two characteristics is present, we have the case represented in Figure 4.2. The individual whose ideal point is A (or B) and whose indifference curves have the shape depicted in Figure 4.2 is an extremist in terms of position (being, say, a fan of Hitler, or an anarcho-syndicalist) but he or she does not attach much importance to that characteristic.[12] What counts in our individual's eyes is the other issue, with regard to which he or she is a moderate. I will call him or her an inconsequential extremist – a sometimes repulsive but generally harmless breed, again as we shall see.

## 3.   EXTREMIST COALITIONS

Extremist coalitions need not include only extremists, and coalitions of extremists are not always extremist coalitions. The most typical case,

---

[10] An assumption also made by Tullock (1970) and Congleton (1991).

[11] In the oral discussion of a previous version of the chapter, it was suggested that people could be blind to some dimensions (human rights, say) rather than "monomaniacally" concerned with others (their economic survival, for instance). In a two-issue setting such as the one explored here, there is no difference between the two possibilities but the suggestion is certainly very worth pursuing in a more general setting.

[12] In *La recherche*, Proust refers to these higher officials, like Monsieur de Norpois, who, privately, are royalists, but are legitimately trusted by the government as loyal servants of the Republic.

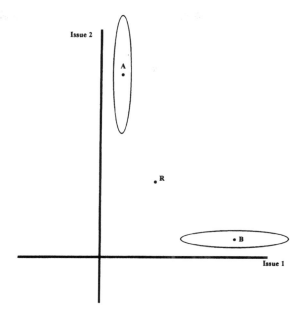

Figure 4.2 Inconsequential extremists

however, is when extremist coalitions do include exclusively extremists. I start with this first case and turn briefly to the others afterwards.

### 3.1 Extremist coalitions of extremists

In Figure 4.3, I assume two groups of monomaniac extremists, each of them perfectly homogeneous but the two groups different from one another. In one group all individuals have point A as their ideal position and the ellipse centered on A as one of their indifference curves. Members of that group are monomaniac extremists because they favor a combination of policies which is extremist in terms of issue 2 and they assign to that issue a high degree of priority, compared to the one they give to issue 1. In the other group, the situation is the same, except that the ideal point is B instead of A and the most salient issue is issue 1 rather than issue 2.

The two groups can hardly be more different. But this is exactly what makes so easy their inclusion in an extremist coalition. Suppose that a political entrepreneur, interested in maximizing his or her support, comes in and advocates a policy mix corresponding to point C. At this point an indifference curve of the first group is tangent to one of the second group. From the perspective of a coalition of the two groups, C is a Pareto optimum (that is, no other point of the issue space exists that could give more utility to one group without giving less utility to the other).

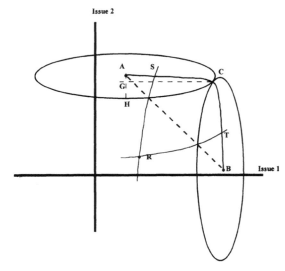

Figure 4.3 Extremist coalition of monomaniac extremists

Let us assume that the two groups can either support the extremist political entrepreneur placed in C or join a much more moderate coalition whose position is R ("R" standing, say, for "moderate right").[13] In Figure 4.3, it is clear that they prefer C to R. In other words, although each group is extremist in only one dimension (that is, with regard to one issue), both groups turn out to support an extremist movement or platform which is extremist in the two dimensions.

Now, C is not the only point corresponding to an optimum from the perspective of the two groups. Each point of tangency between an indifference curve of the first group and an indifference curve of the second group is an optimum. The locus of these points, which, following the tradition, we can call the contract curve, is the line which in Figure 4.3 goes from A to B through C. All the points on that line are Pareto optima from the perspective of a coalition between the two groups but not all of them dominate point R. If S, on the contract curve, is also on the indifference curve of group "B" (the group whose ideal point is B) that passes through R, and if similarly T is on the indifference curve of group "A"

---

[13] To explain why there is not a number of political entrepreneurs offering ideal combinations over the issue space to each homogeneous group of voters, or why only some of these entrepreneurs are considered seriously by voters, one must assume some kind of economies of scale or of scope. In fact the analysis in the text is incomplete in particular in that it does not explain why sometimes extremism is highly fragmented and why in other periods a leader manages to create a relatively encompassing coalition of extremists. I am grateful to Annick Laruelle for stressing this point.

that also passes through R, only the points of the contract curve which lie between S and T dominate R for both groups (for example, a point situated between A and S would be dominated by R, which means that if the extremist entrepreneur were to chose one such point, group B would prefer to rally the mainstream position R).

Before turning to extremist coalitions that include non-extremists, let me stress two features of the model that are apparent from the geometry itself. First, assume that the larger the portion of the contract curve which dominates R, the easier the constitution of a coalition between the two groups of monomaniac extremists. Then, if the moderates whose position is R want to make the coalition of extremists more difficult, they can just move this position R to the north-east in such a way that the distance along the contract curve between S and T gets reduced. In other words, the moderates can move a bit to a position which is less moderate. Of course, this result is fairly obvious. As shown in detail in Kitschelt (1995), the main obstacle to such strategy is its electoral cost in terms of the competition with the other side of the electorate. In all democracies, as showed by Kitschelt, the moderate left and the moderate right both oscillate between platforms that are relatively far from the center, thus leaving little space to their extremist competitors but reducing the probability of winning the election against the other side, and policies that have the inverse characteristics. As Sternhell (1978) notes, in France, except once – in 1940, under particular circumstances – the moderate right has always managed to contain, absorb or disband the waves of "revolutionary right" extremism that have followed one another since 1870.

Second, if the indifference curves were circles, that is, if the two issues were equally salient (both between one another and across individuals and groups), then the contract curve would be the straight broken line drawn, in Figure 4.3, between A and B. In that case the extremist entrepreneur would have to adopt a platform much less extreme than the one corresponding to C. In other words, a coalition of extremists who have the same positions as the monomaniacs but are not monomaniac extremists would be less extreme than the coalition of monomaniacs depicted in Figure 4.3. As things are, however, given the shape of the indifference curves as drawn in Figure 4.3, our extremist entrepreneur has no incentive to move towards R.

I must also stress again that support should not be seen as exclusively electoral. For instance, one of the two groups of Figure 4.3 could consist of a subset of activists or party members and the other group of a subset of voters. This could explain, for instance, why the leaders of the contemporary extreme right in France (Jean-Marie Le Pen in particular) indulge from time to time in coded anti-Semitic allusions that are prob-

*Pierre Salmon*

ably counterproductive in electoral terms. Rather than ascribing to the leaders particular anti-Semitic preferences (perhaps plausible but besides the point), I interpret this behavior as reflecting the need to please not only voters but also party activists coming originally from particularly extreme segments of the extreme right. Generally speaking, we can give the "groups" or "individuals" of our model whatever content we like (the army, the church, industrialists, the bureaucracy, or even foreign interests if they can provide significant support). A corollary of this versatility is that the model may be used both in democratic and non-democratic settings.

### 3.2 Non-extremist membership of extremist coalitions

As alluded to in Section 2, it is a feature of the model that people or groups whose position is moderate along all dimensions can become quite dangerous in some circumstances. What makes them dangerous is the incentive that they may have to join extremist coalitions. For this to happen, our moderates must be somewhat monomaniac in the sense that they consider one issue as much more salient than the others and are willing to defend even at a high cost their position with regard to that issue. In Figure 4.4, I assume that a homogeneous group of individuals have A as an ideal point and an infinitely large family of ellipses centered on A, similar to the one drawn, as their indifference curves. They treat issue 2 as the most salient. Another group of individuals are monomaniac extremists, treating issue 1 as the most salient. Their ideal point is B and the form of their indifference curves is as drawn. As long as the policy mix

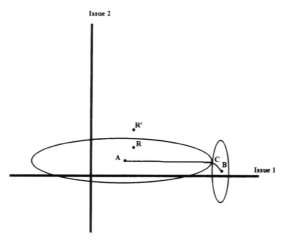

Figure 4.4 Non-extremist membership of an extremist coalition

adopted or advocated by the moderate government or coalition corresponds, say, to point R, our first group has no reason to form a coalition with the monomaniac extremists whose ideal point is B. But let me assume that, for some reason, the moderate policy mix moves to $R'$. Then a political entrepreneur can offer a platform situated in C (on the contract curve AB) and this will be preferred by our monomaniac centrists to the moderate position $R'$. As a consequence, monomaniac centrists turn out to support policies that are extremist in terms of issue 1.[14]

Many illustrations of this mechanism come to mind. One is the fact that Hitler found electoral support among voters who normally voted for parties of the center, and more generally the fact that fascism can be interpreted with some degree of plausibility as "an extremism of the center" (see, for example, Kershaw 1992, Sternhell 1978). In that case, what could motivate the middle classes is their fear of the consequences of the adoption of some economic policies reflected in the move of the mainstream position from R to $R'$.[15] Another case could be the behavior of the French settlers in Algeria and elsewhere when they felt endangered by independence movements. Lastly, if issue 2 is collectivization, socialization, and so on, the "A" group in Figure 4.4 could well be industrialists of the kind of those who were convinced by Von Papen to support Hitler (one reason why Hitler is cited here several times is that he was typically at the head of an extremist coalition in which there were many non-extremists).

### 3.3  Extremist membership of non-extremist coalitions

We already saw, in Section 2 and Figure 3.2, the case of people who have an extreme position on some issue but assign much more weight to another issue with regard to which they are moderates. Within our framework, these people cannot enter extremist coalitions. However, they may form, together with other non-monomaniac extremists, non-extremist

---

[14] Why is the platform proposed by the entrepreneur located at C rather than at another point nearer A on the contract curve AB? One reason might be that the flexibility of the monomaniac extremist group is lower than that of the monomaniac centrist group, and that this pulls the outcome of any implicit and indirect bargaining between the two groups towards the position of the monomaniac extremists (this applies also to the location of equilibrium on the contract curve in Figure 4.3). One reason for this lack of flexibility, in turn, may be that the entrepreneur deals separately with many groups, the one constraining him or her most being always the "core" group, so to say, whose ideal point is B. If there are more than two groups it is quite likely that delicate problems of equilibrium arise, however.

[15] In fact, in the case of pre-war Germany, a violent (and not completely unfounded) fear of communism was probably the most important factor, as argued by Nolte (1987) and many other historians.

*Pierre Salmon*

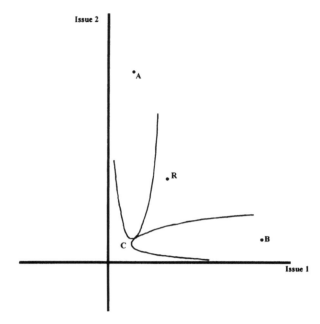

Figure 4.5 Non-extremist coalition of extremists

coalitions as shown in Figure 4.5. The result (point C in Figure 4.5) may be so moderate a combination of policies that it is more moderate than the position R, which we attribute to the moderate coalition. The case confirms that we should be careful not to confuse an individual's position and the position of the movement or coalition that he or she supports. But any elaboration of this point belongs to the consequences of the model, to which I now turn.

## 4. CONSEQUENCES

I will consider three consequences.

### 4.1 The need for additional caution in the interpretation of data

An important implication of the foregoing analysis is that one must be very careful in the interpretation of answers to surveys. When people are asked about their preferences or opinions on an issue, we can expect them to answer according to their ideal point, whereas the position of the party, movement or coalition that they support does not as a rule correspond at all to that ideal point. With regard to our usual concerns, however, what counts is support. Thus, we should not draw great comfort from the knowledge that on many issues people supporting an extremist movement may have quite moderate views, nor even that within these supporters no extremist position gets a majority. The last result, for instance, could be the observable outcome of a coalition of dangerous fanatics. Assume that there are five groups of equal size and five issues. Each of the groups has very moderate positions on four of the issues and an extreme position on the fifth, a different one for each group. The observable implication is that approval of the extreme positions is expressed only by 20 percent of respondents, and, as a consequence, the supporters of extremism may well turn out to look more moderate on average than the supporters of moderate coalitions. In addition, of course, as we saw, salience is essential. Without a high degree of salience, an extremist position is harmless, we argued. Thus one should not be unduly alarmed, perhaps, to learn that many supporters of moderate parties or coalitions are extremists on some issues.[16]

## 4.2 Feelings of non-responsibility

The positions of extremist coalitions are not the preferred position of their supporters. In fact, in Figure 4.3, the individuals whose ideal point is A and who support a program situated in C would pay to have less extremism in regard of the policy they are less concerned with. To be precise, they would give up distance GH in terms of issue 2 (the issue they are mostly concerned with) to get the coalition's position with regard to issue 1 brought down to the moderate level they prefer. As a consequence, there is some reason for them not to feel really responsible for the extreme position which is adopted by the extremist coalition with regard to issue 1. If there had been a vote within the members of the extremist coalition, individuals whose ideal point is A would have voted against issue-1 extremism. This kind of reasoning is of course even more likely on the part of the non-extremist members of the extremist coalition. They can point out that the solution that they favor is particularly moderate on all dimensions. They also would have paid something for extremism to be avoided along the dimension they are little concerned with.

---

[16] On average, voters supporting the French Front National are moderate with regard to many issues, economic as well as social ones (see footnote 3). But the fact that supporters of the FN have on average a moderate position on issue X – say, abortion – does not mean that there are not a number of monomaniac extremists on that issue among them and that the platform of the movement will not reflect their presence in the coalition. This heterogeneity within the electoral support of the extremist coalition – rather than a difference between the "mindset" of leaders and that of voters (DeClair, 1999, p. 136) – is, I submit, the proper explanation of the observed discrepancy between the priorities stressed by the leadership and those expressed on average by the voters (see also Mayer, 1999, p. 285).

An additional factor explaining feelings of non-responsibility stems from the fact that efforts to get information and attention are never equally divided among issues. In particular, the utility of information about an issue, and thus, in general, the level of attention devoted to it are related to the relative salience of that issue. People will pay little attention to most of the issues that have low relative salience for them. When told about the position of the extremist coalition with regard to one such issue, they may express surprise and this surprise may be in large part sincere.

Typically, the major moral or social objections to extremism are focused on some of the dimensions only. Suppose that extremism with regard to issue 1 ("ethnocentrism," say) is the only one which is really objected to. Extremism with regard to issue 2 ("protectionism," say) is a matter of indifference or considered as admissible. In other words, from a general social perspective, extremism is measured only along the dimension of issue 1. If this is the social attitude, people whose ideal point in Figure 4.3 is A will not feel responsible for the issue-1 extremism of the coalition that they support. Since their own form of extremism is not questioned, they may well not feel responsible at all. The same kind of sentiment can be expected from the non-extremist individuals whose ideal point in Figure 4.4 is also labeled A. Only for people whose ideal point is B in either figure will it be difficult to evade responsibility.

Of course, in general, and especially under authoritarian regimes, ideal points, relative salience, feelings, and so on are not observed. What can to a larger extent be observed is support. Thus there will always be some suspicion of those who, after the demise of an extremist regime that they supported, put forward their ideal points to elude any responsibility with regard to that support. Such suspicion is legitimate given the incentives that these persons have. Or, perhaps, responsibility imposes itself for reasons of principle. What I am only saying is that no contradiction between true feelings and revealed acts is necessarily involved in their attitude.

### 4.3    Retrospective assessments varying over time: the case of Vichy

Although it included many people who were not extremists, the regime of Vichy was typically an extremist coalition in the sense given to that expression in this chapter. It brought together a number of groups who could be extremists in some respects or centrist in all dimensions but almost always monomaniac in the sense of our model. Each group was concerned with a particular issue, or small set of issues, and more or less unconcerned with the other issues. This, to a large extent, explains a complexity that historians and more generally French opinion are currently discovering or rediscovering. It also accounts for the way responsibilities and relative guilt have been sorted out in retrospect.

What I am interested in is not exactly Vichy but the way the perception of it has changed over time (Rousso, 1987). The discovery of new facts about Vichy is not the main factor of this evolution. Most facts have always been known.[17] New facts about what happened *after* Vichy are another matter. The younger generations in France progressively discover that the values they refer to when they assess responsibilities under Vichy were not those of the generations who judged Vichy and its staff after the war.

Salience is mainly attached today to issues of human rights, the Holocaust, and so on. After the war, salience was not associated at all with that type of issues. De Gaulle hardly mentions them, for example, in his *Mémoires*. The main question at the time was that of treason, and collaboration with the enemy, versus patriotism and resistance. This change in salience explains a large part of the uneasiness that many have felt about the recent trial, in Bordeaux, of Maurice Papon. I think that the foregoing theoretical analysis can capture important aspects of the phenomenon involved.

Because a large number of Frenchmen could legitimately be charged with a lack of patriotism or some form of complicity with the breach of human rights, only the cases of a small number of individuals whose acts were particularly significant could be submitted to the scrutiny of the courts. These individuals had pushed some line "beyond the limits" of what by necessity had to be tolerated from larger numbers, and this allows us to interpret their behavior in terms of extremism. Since the recent trials and current debate in France focus on the part of the French bureaucracy which collaborated with the Nazis to arrest Jews and send them to concentration camps, it is worth examining the kind of extremism, if any, that motivated the bureaucrats concerned. What emerges, quite surprisingly, from recent scholarship is the presence in the higher tiers of the bureaucracy of a genuine and somewhat absurd concern, verging on the obsessional, with safeguarding as much as possible of the sovereignty of the French State over the whole French territory, even or especially when that territory was occupied by German troops (Baruch, 1997).[18] This led some high-level bureaucrats to insist on

---

[17] This is an exaggeration. The discoveries made in the late sixties or early seventies mostly by foreign historians such as Jäckel (1968) and Paxton (1972) should not be underestimated. Still, there was a large element of wishful thinking in the interpretations of Vichy that dominated after the war, as well as concerns and criteria quite different from those that prevailed later (Rousso, 1987).

[18] This interpretation of the concerns of bureaucrats in terms of issues is compatible with an interpretation of them in terms of interests along the line of Breton and Wintrobe (1986).

doing jobs that the Germans were offering to do themselves, and in particular to participate actively in the arrest and deportation of Jews. That, in this case as in some others, collaboration with the Germans was in part inspired by a form of (misguided) patriotism was to a surprisingly large extent accepted by the courts and public opinion after the war. This is clear, it seems to me, from the way a senior official of the French police, René Bousquet, involved at a high level in the massive arrest and deportation of Jews, was treated when his case came for the first time to trial, in 1949. In Figure 4.6, Bousquet can be placed in the box labeled "Bousquet-like Vichy bureaucrats," whose location reflects an uncertain net effect of collaboration with and resistance to the Germans and a more secure net outcome in terms of breach of human rights. Given the 1950 guilt frontier, and even though the main facts were known (Conan and Rousso, 1994, p. 28), he was found not guilty.

Almost two generations later, though – thanks to a few newly revealed facts, but mainly because in the meanwhile the criteria had changed, and despite the efforts of the then President – a second trial was started (in 1991), and Bousquet would certainly have been sentenced heavily if he

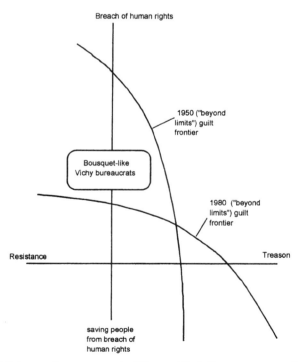

Figure 4.6 Retrospective assessment of "beyond-limits" consequences of extremism

had not been shot (in 1993). Similarly, to his undoubtedly sincere surprise, Maurice Papon – appointed "Compagnon de la Libération" and prefect by De Gaulle himself in 1945, later budget minister under Raymond Barre as prime minister – was prosecuted in 1997–98 for deeds similar to those Bousquet was charged with in his second trial.[19] In both cases, what allowed the episodes to be revisited in this way is a profound change in society's views about what is extreme, and thus intolerable, behavior. I will not attempt to explain the change itself.[20] It is depicted, in Figure 4.6, in the form of two "(beyond-limits) guilt frontiers" that refer somewhat arbitrarily to years 1950 and 1980 and conspire to explain the fate of some Vichy bureaucrats.

## 5. CONCLUSION

An army naturally eager to prepare a war of revenge, a church understandably worried by modern trends towards secularization, overly conscientious professors irritated by declining standards, policemen specialized in law and order, bureaucrats tired of being lobbied by politicians, industrialists anxious to remain in control of costs, farmers facing the perspective of leaving the farm, small shopkeepers endangered by modern forms of commerce, settlers whose horizon is darkened by nationalist claims, blue-collar workers whose jobs are threatened by relocations, even mild forms of anti-Semitism, racism and xenophobia: in itself, none of these factors may be particularly noteworthy or serious. Most of the people concerned are in many respects nice people (President Mitterrand said of his friend Bousquet that he was "charming," or had "great charm," I do not remember which of the two). The mischief that extremist coalitions of on the whole nice and transparent human beings can cause is an ominous discovery of modern times. More than in individual extremism, the danger lies in the existence of overspecialized concerns and motivations. In the vocabulary used in this chapter, the main problem is monomania. There is no seriously pejorative intention underlying recourse to that term because we all are or can become monomaniac in some circumstances.

This chapter is an attempt to address this topic with simple tools borrowed from the spatial theory of voting. An extremist is defined as an individual whose ideal point in the issue space is comparatively

---

[19] See Paxton (1999).

[20] As noted by Rousso (1998, p. 99), all of the almost 1,500 persons who were shot legally after 1944 were condemned for "intelligence avec l'ennemi", that is, treason. Nowadays, again according to Rousso (1998, p. 119), a very large majority of the French condemns Vichy without reservation and mainly for its anti-Semitic legislation and for its participation in the realization of the Final Solution.

extreme along some dimensions, and a "monomaniac" (no derogatory connotation) as an individual for whom one issue has much greater salience than all others. As a consequence of salience, monomaniacs, even though they are not necessarily also extremists, can easily be induced by extremist politicians to form or support extremist coalitions. This can account for some of the characteristics of some of the relatively successful extremist movements as they are reported in the literature. It also has implications on the questions of how the results of surveys should be interpreted, of why members or supporters of extremist coalitions can sincerely not feel responsible for some of the deeds of these coalitions, and of what may happen to social judgments of guilt and innocence when the salience of issues, as perceived in retrospect by society, changes in the course of time – as has been the case recently with regard to the nature and main aspects of the Vichy regime. I am aware that many points or assumptions need to be clarified or made explicit. This might be addressed in future work.

## REFERENCES

Ayçoberry, Pierre. 1998. *La société allemande sous le IIIe Reich, 1933–1945*. Paris: Le Seuil.

Baruch, Marc Olivier. 1997. *Servir l'Etat français: L'administration en France de 1940 à 1944*. Paris: Fayard.

Breton, Albert and Ronald Wintrobe. 1986. "The Bureaucracy of Murder Revisited," *Journal of Political Economy* **94**, no. 5 (October), pp. 905–26.

Chebel d'Appollonia, Ariane. 1988. *L'extrême-droite en France: de Maurras à Le Pen*. 2nd edn, 1996. Brussels: Editions Complexe.

Conan, Eric and Henry Rousso. 1994. *Vichy, un passé qui ne passe pas*. Paris: Fayard. New edn, 1996, Paris: Gallimard.

Congleton, Roger D. 1991. "Information, special interests, and single-issue voting," *Public Choice* **69**, no. 1, pp. 38–49.

DeClair, Edward G. 1999. *Politics on the Fringe: The People, Policies, and Organization of the French National Front*. Durham and London: Duke University Press.

De Witte, Hans, and Peer Scheepers. 1998. "En Flandre: origines, évolution et avenir du Vlaams Blok et de ses électeurs," *Pouvoirs*, no. 87 ("L'extrême droite en Europe"), pp. 95–113.

Enelow, James M. and Melvin J. Hinich. 1984. *The Spatial Theory of Voting: An Introduction*. Cambridge and New York: Cambridge University Press.

Falter, Jürgen W. and Siegfried Schumann. 1988. "Affinity towards right-wing extremism in Western Europe," *West European Politics* **11**, no. 2, pp. 96–110.

Hinich, Melvin J. and Michael C. Munger. 1997. *Analytical Politics*. Cambridge and New York: Cambridge University Press.

Jäckel, Eberhard. 1968. *La France dans l'Europe de Hitler*. Paris: Fayard.

Kershaw, Ian. (1992). *Qu'est-ce que le nazisme? Problèmes et perspectives d'inter-prétation*. French trans. of a book published in English in 1985. 2nd French edn, 1997. Paris: Gallimard.

Kitschelt, Herbert. 1995. *The Radical Right in Western Europe: A Comparative Analysis*. Ann Arbor: The University of Michigan Press.

Mayer, Nonna. 1996. "The National Front and right-wing extremism, 1988–1995," in Frederick D. Weil et al. (eds), *Extremism, Protest, Social Movements, and Democracy*, Greenwich (Connecticut) and London: JAI Press, pp. 197–222.

Mayer, Nonna. 1999. *Ces Français qui votent FN*. Paris: Flammarion.

Mayer, Nonna and Pascal Perrineau (eds). 1989. *Le Front National à découvert*. 2nd edn, 1996, Paris: Presses de Sciences Po.

Messina, Anthony. 1989. *Race and Party Competition in Britain*. Oxford: Clarendon Press.

Moreau, Patrick. 1998. "Le Freiheitliche Partei Österreich, parti national-libéral ou pulsion austro-fasciste?," *Pouvoirs*, no. 87 ("L'extrême droite en Europe"), pp. 61–82.

Nolte, Ernst. 1987. *Der europäische Bürgerkrieg 1917–1945*. French augmented edn, 2000, *La guerre civile européenne 1917–1945*. Paris: Edition des Syrtes.

Nozick, Robert. 1997. "The characteristic features of extremism," chapter 16 of *Socratic Puzzles*, Cambridge (Mass.): Harvard University Press, pp. 296–9.

Passmore, Kevin. 1997. *From Liberalism to Fascism: The Right in a French Province, 1928–1939*. Cambridge and New York: Cambridge University Press.

Paxton, Robert O. 1972. *Vichy France: Old Guard and New Order, 1940–1944*. New French edn, 1997, *La France de Vichy 1940–1944*, Paris: Le Seuil.

Paxton, Robert O. 1999. "The trial of Maurice Papon," *The New York Review of Books* **46**, no. 20 (16 December), pp. 32–8.

Popper, Karl R. 1945. *The Open Society and its Enemies, Vol. 1: Plato*. London: Routledge and Kegan Paul.

Proust, Marcel. 1913–27. *A la recherche du temps perdu*. Edition de la Pléiade, 1954, Paris: Gallimard.

Rousso, Henry. 1987. *Le syndrome de Vichy de 1944 à nos jours*. Paris: Le Seuil.

Rousso, Henry. 1998. *La hantise du passé: entretien avec Philippe Petit*. Paris: Textuel.

Safran, William. 1993. "The National Front in France: From lunatic fringe to limited respectability," in Peter H. Merkl and Leonard Weinberg (eds), *Encounters with the Contemporary Radical Right*, Boulder (Colorado): Westview Press, pp. 19–49.

Sprinzak, Ehud. 1993. "The Israeli radical right: History, culture, and politics," in Peter H. Merkl and Leonard Weinberg (eds), *Encounters with the Contemporary Radical Right*, Boulder (Colorado): Westview Press, pp. 132–61.

Sternhell, Zeev. 1978. *La droite révolutionnaire 1885–1914: Les origines françaises du fascisme*. New edn, 1997, Paris: Gallimard.

Tullock, Gordon. 1970. "A simple algebraic logrolling model," *American Economic Review* **60**, pp. 419–26.

Zimmermann, Ekkart and Thomas Saalfeld. 1993. "The three waves of West German right-wing extremism," in Peter H. Merkl and Leonard Weinberg (eds), *Encounters with the Contemporary Radical Right*, Boulder (Colorado): Westview Press, pp. 50–74.

# 5

# Some Democratic Propensities for Extreme Results

*Geoffrey Brennan*

## 1. PRELUDE

There are at least two possible approaches to the issue of political extremism. One is to study the operation of groups that are considered on some independent grounds to be extremist – perhaps in terms of the methods they use – and that see themselves and/or are seen by others to be broadly political in some meaningful sense. Thus, we might study the behaviour of the Red Guards or various of the nineteenth-century Russian anarchist groups for whom violence was an explicit tool in the pursuit of their political agenda. And we would distinguish such political terrorism from violence used by organized groups for merely criminal purposes. All such groups are extremist in *method*. Only those who have an explicit political agenda would be classified as relevant to *political* extremism. The reference in such a classification would be to the methods such groups use. Whether their political *ends* are extreme, and how indeed we would identify extremism of political ends, are separable questions. It is these latter questions with which I shall be concerned here. And I shall be concerned about them in a narrow, though not unfamiliar, context – the context of equilibrium outcomes in standard rational actor models of democratic political determination. Part of my reason for taking this approach is that this is where my expertise, such as it is, lies. But there is another reason, one perhaps more defensible. It is that the appeal to independent notions of extremism in terms of political ends begs the question of the standards by which such extremism is to be assessed. It is all too tempting to label as extreme policies or political positions which one happens to find strongly disagreeable without any reference to the distribution of prevailing views among the general population or any attempt to specify how the mean of the implicit distribution is derived or the metric of distance calculated. What *is* clear is that any claim of extremism must make reference, implicit or otherwise, to some standard position against which distance from the position under consideration is assessed. And we should be careful not to import our own private ideal as the standard in question – not least since many of us academics have ideas about what would be politically ideal that are, by popular standards, somewhat eccentric.

An example might help here. Recently, the Australian State of Queensland distinguished itself by providing the location for the electoral success of a new party, the One Nation Party. This is a party which by consensus among all middle-class commentators is an extremist party. And it is true that some of the remarks of the leaders within this party have a distinct racist overtone (though it perhaps ought to be noted that One Nation has already expelled from its ranks one notable who expressed indignation over the international Jewish capital conspiracy). Moreover, there is no suggestion that One Nation supports the use of violence – except, of course, by the duly appointed authorities. (That is, like many right-wing populist parties, One Nation is especially tough on crime.) But the alleged extremism of One Nation has to come to terms with the brute empirical fact that about one quarter of the Queensland population voted for the party. How exactly are we to square the party's putative extremism with its electoral success? What benchmark are we to use against which this extremism is to be judged? Not, it would seem, a benchmark derived from the actual voting behaviour of the relevant citizens. Or might we concede the possibility that a party that garnered a *majority* of the votes might have extremist ends in some meaningful sense? And, if so, what meaningful sense exactly do we have in mind? And, no less relevant, what kind of model of political process do we have in mind? These are the questions I intend to engage in what follows.

## 2.  RATIONALITY AND EXTREMISM

On the face of things, political extremism does not seem to be a topic that is particularly conducive to rational actor analysis. There are three reasons that strike me as to why the match of tool and task might seem poor. First, rational actor political theory has been pursued mostly in the context of specifically democratic institutional arrangements. (There are several notable exceptions to this claim, of which McGuire and Olson, 1996 and Wintrobe, 1998 are two examples.) By and large, and with a few exceptions to be pursued in greater detail below, one of the main propositions in rational actor democratic theory is that equilibria tend to be centrist. That is, if an equilibrium position exists, it will involve competing electoral candidates/parties locating towards the centre of the distribution of individual citizens' ideal points. This result seems to be a reasonably robust one – robust, at least, to assumptions about voter motivation (see Brennan and Hamlin, 1998, for example). And though standard democratic models *can* give rise to extreme outcomes (most notably in the majoritarian cycling context), the outcomes in question are inherently unstable. If we could conclude from all this that political extremism is an essentially *non*-democratic phenomenon, that would be a reassuring conclusion. One question that then arises is whether any such conclusion is really justified. That is one question that I will engage in what follows.

The second reason why rational choice political theory seems ill equipped to deal with political extremism is that extremism is not an attribute that we normally associate with interests. The (apparent) triumph in social theory of interests over passions as the prime motivator of human behaviour – of which triumph public choice theory could claim to be the latest exemplar – seems to reduce the heat in politics and make the possibility of extremism less plausible. If one wanted a model of individual behaviour most congenial to political extremism, one would probably be more inclined to look for it in Freud than in modern economics. Perhaps this is a mistake. Perhaps rational actor analysis is perfectly consistent with political passion – but that has not been the standard public choice interpretation. Again, this is an intuition that we shall want to scrutinize.

The third reason why rational choice political theory might seem to be poorly connected to political extremism is that the theory rather encourages the view that social outcomes will be broadly rational. Of course, we all (or at least most of us rational choice theorists) accept the proposition that rationality is properly an attribute only of individuals, and that it can only contingently be an attribute of collectives. This, I take it, is the central message of the prisoner's dilemma – that what is rational for each is not rational for all (if indeed the latter concept has any meaning). The same general message, though in a somewhat different guise, is delivered by Arrow's impossibility theorem: we cannot assume that, because individual agents have transitive orderings, the aggregate ordering will be transitive unless we either allow irrelevant alternatives to influence the aggregate ordering or have one of the individuals as dictator. All the same, there *is* a general impulse within the rational actor scheme towards efficient outcomes. The tale of the Chicago economist who allegedly won't pick up ten dollars lying on the pavement because it can't really be there may overstate the point; but there *is* a relevant point to be made. To the extent that individuals act in order to promote their own interests, and to the extent that those individuals choose both the political outcomes to which they are to be subject and the constitutional rules under which politics itself operates, there ought to be limits to the political disasters that can be expected.

The intellectual scheme tends to constrain social outcomes to lie within a tolerable range of the efficient, because when the distance becomes too great, someone will be motivated to act to obtain the benefits that are, by definition, on offer. Indeed, if no one is so motivated – either because there is no institutional technology that will get us closer to soaking up all conceptually available gains from exchange, or because no one can be motivated to introduce that technology – then there is a sense (a net of transactions cost sense) in which the world *is* efficient after all.

To think that efficiency, even so weakly construed, is inhospitable to political extremism is of course to make a presumption about something that ought to be interrogated. And so this proposition becomes the third of the three specific questions that I want here to raise. They are in turn:

(i) Does democracy (and electoral competition in particular) inhibit extremism in political outcomes?

(ii) Does the logic of rationality suggest that extremism in political behaviour and/or motivations is unlikely?

(iii) Is it the case that extremism in political outcomes is inefficient?

In what follows, I shall have a crack at all three questions. But I shall deal with the first and last only cursorily, and focus most of my attention on the second. I shall, somewhat perversely, discuss the questions in inverse order.

### 3.   IS EXTREMISM INEFFICIENT?

I am taking it in what follows that extremism is to be understood in terms of the normal framework of analysis used in public choice theory. That is, we can conceptualize a map of the ideal points of citizen-voters, expressed over the domain of political concerns that actually matter to them (that is, that actually enter their utility functions). This map may be uni-dimensional as in the simple *median voter* analogue of the Hotelling spatial equilibrium theorem, but that seems unlikely. It is easier to conceptualize the map in a small number of dimensions, though, and I shall suppose there to be only two. Consider the set of such ideal points. This set will have a boundary such that any point on that boundary will either be an ideal point for some citizen or a point on the contract curve between two citizens who have ideal points that lie on the boundary (given normal assumptions about preferences).

The understanding of extremism can be framed by reference to this set. First, I shall take it that a point outside the set is more extreme than any point within it. (It is not of course the case that any point inside the set Pareto-dominates any point outside it, so this is not a direct efficiency test in the sense of the Pareto criterion. All we can say is that any point outside the set is Pareto-dominated by some other point and that the latter point lies within the set.) Of course, we might ask how it could be that any point outside the set could ever arise as an equilibrium – but I want to assert here that it is possible and postpone further discussion of that aspect until later. To go beyond the distinction between points within and points outside the set (the Pareto options), we would need some metric for making more aggregated efficiency measures (a simple utilitarian metric or some social welfare function approach, for example). We would then be able to distinguish between points on the border and points that are more centrist.

Under almost any conceivable normative scheme of the consequentialist type that economists (and ultimately, most political theorists) adopt, there is a strong presumption in favour of centrism in the second sense. This presumption has two sources. First, most social welfare function metrics embody diminishing marginal value of any one individual's flourishing. The Rawlsian difference principle is an extreme form of this idea, but of course the notion is familiar in more modified form among public economics scholars of all stripes. The second source relies not on any direct egalitarian impulse, but on the convexity of individual preference. To put the point at its least controversial, perhaps, citizens behind a Buchanan/Rawls/Harsanyi veil of ignorance will have reason to choose institutions that produce more centrist outcomes than more extreme ones. This is true even if the cost to each of failing to achieve her ideal is linearly related to the degree of failure (measured by the distance between the actual outcome and her ideal). But in fact, we have persuasive reasons for thinking that the loss each sustains is a convex function of the distance between each's ideal point and the actual, and hence that the benefits of centrism are potentially quite considerable. The point is easily illustrated in terms of a simple single-dimensional three-person example, as indicated in Figure 5.1. You know behind the veil of ignorance that there are three ideal points, a, b and c in Figure 5.1 – but you do not know which will be your own. You can, however, choose an arrangement that will either deliver a centrist result (b) or an extreme result (a or c with equal probability). Which arrangement is to be preferred?

To focus on what is at stake, suppose that the preferences of all agents A, B and C have the same form: namely,

$$U(x) = U(I) - m(I - x)^2 = K - m(I - x)^2$$

where $U(I) = K$ is constant across persons. This is the simplest form of a value function that incorporates convexity (the equivalent of downward-sloping demand curves across the outcome space). On this basis, if a prevails, there is an expected return to each of:

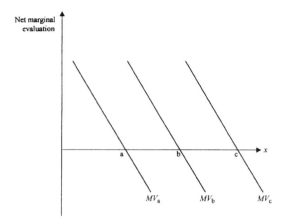

Figure 5.1 Centrism in the three-person case

$$V(a) = \tfrac{1}{3}E_A(a) + \tfrac{1}{3}E_B(a) + \tfrac{1}{3}E_C(a)$$

where $E_I$ is the value to individual $I$ of having a prevail.

$$= \tfrac{1}{3}[K + K - m(a - b)^2 + K - m(a - c)^2]$$

$$= K - m\frac{(a - b)^2 + (a - c)^2}{3}$$

If b prevails,

$$V(b) = \tfrac{1}{3}E_A(b) - \tfrac{1}{3}E_B(b) + \tfrac{1}{3}E_C(b)$$

$$= \tfrac{1}{3}[K - m(a - b)^2 + K + K - m(b - c)^2]$$

$$= K - m\frac{(a - b)^2 + (b - c)^2}{3}$$

Therefore

$$V(b) - V(a) = m[(a - c)^2 - (b - c)^2] > 0, \quad \text{because } (a - c) > (b - c)$$

In other words, the expected return to a centrist outcome is greater than the expected return to an extreme outcome. Of course, the centrism presumption could be overturned under a variety of conditions: for example, if the extremists are sufficiently more efficient utility-generating machines than centrists; or if individuals at one of the extremes happened to be more sensitive to not achieving his ideal than individuals at the other extreme. But even in the latter circumstances, the probability of achieving the correct extreme would have to be quite high to overturn the centrist presumption. In general, there seem to be no *a priori* reasons why any of the contrary conditions would apply. Accordingly, there is a reasonably strong presumption that extremism is undesirable – within the terms of the sorts of normative frameworks customary in liberal political theory (or indeed in any theory where the relation between political outcome and the interests/preferences of citizens is the predominant normative concern).

This strong presumption in favour of centrist outcomes in the sense understood here (that is, centrist in terms of the prevailing distribution of voters' ideal points) constitutes the background for the remainder of this chapter. If this normative premise is accepted, the question then arises as to what institutional arrangements promote centrism – and this in turn requires us to diagnose the sources of extremism (so understood) with which such institutional arrangements will have to deal.

## 4. EXTREMISM IN POLITICAL OUTCOME

Let us begin with the simple median voter theorem. If this theorem were taken to be applicable to actual democratic electoral competition, then no anxiety about political extremism (in democratic politics at least) would arise. We could, for example, relegate to second-order concern the question of extremism in political preferences, because we could have reasonable confidence that electoral competition – in the appropriate circumstances – would generate a centrist outcome whatever the variance of the individual ideal points. The issue of extremism in political preference as such would be irrelevant.[1]

Accordingly, one important issue is: what are the appropriate circumstances for the centrist co-location propositions to apply? Put another way, what is it about the median voter theorem that generates the co-location equilibrium? What plausible modifications can we make to that model that would break the co-location result?

One obvious initial response to this question revolves around the possibility of global cycling. The idea here is that the median voter model only applies when voter preferences are uni-dimensional. When voter preferences are two-dimensional (or higher) the centrist co-location result evaporates, except under apparently very special restrictions. Indeed, in the two-(plus) dimensional setting, there is no stable majoritarian equilibrium at all. This fact immediately suggests a puzzle. Either we ought to observe very much more political instability in democratic systems than

---

[1] In a modified median voter model in which (rational) abstention is allowed for, the midpoint of the extremes or the mean can be the equilibrium outcome. That outcome is centrist but is also sensitive to the range of ideal points. However, the central morals – that political outcome is what matters, and that political outcome can be invariant to the variance of preference – remain more or less intact.

we seem to, or the median voter theorem, implying rather implausibly simple voter preferences, is a tolerable approximation to reality. There may, however, be other possibilities. Here are several:

  (i)   Tullock's (1981) conjecture is that in a large-number log-rolling context, every representative is a participant in a majority coalition to bring about special-interest legislation at a minority's expense, but because the identity of each majority (and corresponding minority) is different, no particular coalition offers to break the arrangement: to do so would be to refrain from one's *own* special-interest programme, without any guarantee that others would do likewise in response. The outcome is that of the $n$-person prisoners' dilemma – and as such is both stable and non-optimal (that is, lies outside the uncovered set).

  (ii)  McKelvey (1976) offers a strategic agenda-setter solution, in which the process of agenda manipulation leads to an outcome that is the agenda-setter's own preferred outcome. This outcome seems likely to be an extremist one: any random dictator model admits the possibility that any voter ideal point could emerge (and in particular not just centrist ones). The McKelvey model is one in which formal democracy is a façade for effective dictatorship – with majority rule providing no long-term constraint on the exercise of political power at all.

  (iii) Suppose that voters do not reliably vote for the party/candidate/ policy that leaves them best off – that rather they vote for that party only probabilistically, where the probability of so voting is positively related to the amount at stake. Here, the idea is that the knife-edge effect of redistribution among voters (such that each votes with certainty for the policy that he believes leaves him best off) is blunted: the *size* of the pay-off difference becomes relevant to the (likely) direction of the vote, rather than merely the sign. In these circumstances, a stable centrist outcome can occur – one that has attractive normative properties. (See, for example, Coughlin, 1982).

  (iv)  A fourth possible solution to global cycling instability is the structure-induced equilibrium solution in the style of Shepsle and Weingast (1981). The natural instability of unharnessed majoritarianism is, according to this account, checked by the operation of institutional arrangements (a committee system, perhaps) which imposes uni-dimensionality on each policy area considered separately, so that something like the median voter model applies with respect to each dimension in the $n$-dimensional policy arena. Stability here depends on the suppression of any capacity to trade votes across policy areas. The resultant equilibrium is centrist, in the spirit of the median voter result, though it may lack the normatively ideal character of the probabilistic voting outcome.

These possible solutions to the 'problem' of instability vary in the extent to which they produce specifically centrist outcomes. Part of the interest in global cycling is analytic/descriptive – how can we explain the stability we observe – rather than normative. The message I draw from this literature is that we have good reason not to put too much faith in electoral competition to produce centrist equilibria; and that we may be more dependent than we know on institutional details even to give electoral stability at all.

Increased dimensionality is not the only move that might modify the centrist co-location result of the standard median voter model. Several other modifications have been introduced into the median voter construction that can have this effect. One is the threat of entry of third parties. The standard result in the Hotelling–Downs model deals with a winner-take-all race in which there are only two candidates, and in which every citizen votes. Suppose, as in that model, the two parties locate at the median voter's ideal point, M. Each voter will be indifferent between the two parties and vote between them (if at all) randomly: each party will have an expected level of voter support equal to 50 per cent of the voter population and a 50 per cent chance of victory. A new entrant could locate at some point close to, but distinct from, M and ensure a level of voter support equal to say 48 per cent of the voter population, while the original two parties share the remaining 52 per cent more or less equally. In the absence of preferential voting, the new entrant will win. In order to protect against such a contingency, parties have an incentive to locate at some distance from the median. Then voters will not be indifferent between the two parties. In any resultant equilibrium, each party will receive 50 per cent of the vote and have a 50 per cent chance of victory, but parties will not be located at the same point in policy space. In short, while maximizing the probability of victory in a *two-*candidate race encourages centrist co-location, protecting against threat of entry encourages divergence to some extent.

The degree of divergence is magnified if the race is not a winner-take-all race (say, like a contest among presidential candidates or rivals for a single seat) but rather a contest between two parties, one of which is to be the government and the other the opposition. In the two-party case, though the winner clearly takes *most*, there are *some* gains to being the opposition party; hence, parties in such races need to worry not only about winning but also about maximizing their chances of doing better than coming third! Put another way, in a winner-take-all election, third entrants can be excluded by ensuring that the entrant has no prospect of winning: in a winner-take-*most* election, third entrants (and more) might enter if they have a prospect of coming second.

This winner-take-all versus winner-take-most distinction is relevant in the context of another reason for the collapse of the co-location result. This additional reason is that there may be some uncertainty in the system – uncertainty perhaps about where the median voter's ideal lies. For, if we postulate that parties/candidates seek election for instrumental reasons, we might model each party's maximand as expected surplus from victory:

$$E(S) = p_A S_A$$
$$\text{where} \quad p_A \text{ is A's probability of victory}$$
$$\text{and} \quad S_A \text{ is the pure surplus that A accrues if A wins.}$$

In the standard median voter context, $p_A$ is either $1, \frac{1}{2}$ or 0 depending on whether A is closer, equally close or less close to (known) M than is party B. But in the presence of uncertainty about M, $p_A$ becomes a continuous function and can be traded off against $S_A$. And likewise for B. So, party surplus is *not* driven to zero by electoral competition: parties are not mere ciphers for the median voter. If parties seek to spend some of their political surplus on policies that reflect their distinctive ideological leanings, the centrist co-location result breaks down. And it will break down further, the greater the extent to which some surplus accrues to the non-winner(s) – as is characteristically the case with oppositional parties. A specific implication is that electoral contests in Westminster-type systems will tend to involve more ideological purity than U.S. presidential races.

But why does the assumption that party rents will be spent on indulging ideological preferences seem plausible? One reason is that adduced by James Coleman in an early public choice paper (1971) – namely, because candidates in party systems must satisfy a pre-selection test. If candidates benefit from a party label, then parties can constrain their candidates to some extent to follow a party line. Pre-selection imposes a double hurdle, in which candidates must first satisfy the median within the local party (or the group which determines pre-selection) and then the median within the larger constituency. In a strong party system, one would expect the former test to predominate – especially in those seats where the party has a relatively safe majority. Pre-selection affords, then, one reason why ideological differences between parties might be a stable feature of electoral equilibrium, although the moderating influence of the general contest for office will still be present.

A second reason for parties taking on an ideological identity connects to the expressive account of voting behaviour. The median voter theorem derives from a model of instrumentally based location choice, in which firms locate so as to maximize customer profits. As I have argued at doubtless tedious length elsewhere (in particular, with Lomasky in Brennan and Lomasky, 1993), this model presupposes a direct analogy between voter behaviour and consumer choice that is extremely dubious. When I make a choice as to whether or not to buy an ice-cream on the beach, I make that choice in order to get an ice-cream – not in order to influence the location of the seller. Seller's location emerges as the by-product of a large number of consumer choices. If my buying or not was meant to *influence* ice-cream seller location (rather than atomistically respond to it), then I would have to reckon with the fact that *my* behaviour, as an individual, makes negligible difference to the seller's location. In fact, I am not buying a seller's location; I am buying an ice-cream which I enjoy for its own sake.

But what then is it that electoral candidates sell to voters? Not policies that will prevail if the party is elected, because my behaviour as an individual makes negligible difference to that outcome. Voters vote (if they do) because voting is a consumption good – because voting is a way of identifying themselves, or because they like to cheer for the things they like (or something of the kind). Thus moral and/or ideological postures and symbols play a role in politics to an extent and of a kind that they do not play in markets. And parties respond to that fact about voter behaviour: electoral competition induces parties to provide those things that voters *qua* voters want – namely, strong ideological and moral identification.

Now, as Alan Hamlin and I argue elsewhere (Brennan and Hamlin, 1998), the fact that voting is expressive does not directly undermine the co-location tendency. Expressive voting does modify where the colloca-tion equilibrium occurs: that equilibrium will lie at the mode of voters' ideal points rather than the median. However, the expressive voting account does raise some doubt about how easily candidates/parties might find it to shift to such a point. If individual voters are conceived to be voting on an instrumental basis as a means to get the policy package that is best for themselves, there is no constraint on parties' choice of location imposed by the party's history or ideological tradition. If, on the other hand, voting is a means of self-identification, then parties become the signs by which such identification is possible: it is not, one would have thought, particularly attractive to any voter to identify with a party that is slavishly following public opinion or whoring after votes. Just as words have to mean something, parties have to stand for something – and a vote for a particular party has to signify something – if anyone is to find identification with the party valuable. The party's objective in electoral competition, on this (expressive) reading, is to stake a position in whatever affective domains are at hand that will induce voters to seek to associate themselves with that position. There is an element of capital intrinsic in a party's choice of location. And this capital element is an important constraint on party conduct and on policy choice specifically because it means that parties cannot respond to every whim of a sometimes febrile popular opinion. The question I shall want to take up in somewhat greater detail in the following section is whether there is anything in this expressive argument that specifically encourages extremism in a different sense. For even if the expressive model generates a co-location equilibrium or invokes co-location tendencies, there is a separate and more basic question as to whether the resultant equilibrium bears the kind of relationship to individual interests that the standard median voter/instrumental voting account presupposes. If, as I believe, the expressive account of voting is right, then reference to the prevailing distribution of political preferences is normatively questionable: there is no case for co-location in a domain that bears no relation to the interests or indeed the real preferences of the participant citizens.

## 5. EXPRESSIVE VOTING AND EXTREMISM: THE DYNAMICS OF THE RHETORICAL CONSTRAINT

It seems self-evident that there is considerable scope within the expressive account of voting for political extremism, in the sense of a radical departure from political outcomes that seem in any way connected with aggregate citizen interests. Even if electoral competition encourages co-location (within the expressive domain), and even if parties are unencumbered by their own ideological histories in pursuing electoral support, the resultant political equilibrium may lie a long way from the ideal point of the median voter model, and may well be located in an utterly different domain. The voter's dilemma, outlined at length in *Democracy and Decision*, is an articulation of a kind of rational irrationality in electoral politics, a kind of irrationality that becomes embedded in voters' motivations (rather than mere behaviour) and runs sufficiently deep that most voters (and many commentators) cannot see the problem as one of irrationality at all. In my view, however, a proper view of democratic electoral politics takes very seriously the dark side of the (popular electoral) force. This darker side is what underlies traditional anxieties about mob rule and figures extensively in Schumpeter and more mutedly in Downs (via his rational ignorance arguments), but it plays virtually no role in most modern public choice scholarship. As I understand it, traditional political thought drew a sharp distinction between the *demos*, as the constitutional expression of the people, and the *ochlos*, understood as the people unmediated by any constitutional restraint. In effect, the distinction is one between what the citizenry may vote for and what is in the citizens' interests (or accords with the citizens' true preferences). The expressive voting model provides a decision-theoretic ground for that distinction. It also implies that an assessment of extremism independent of actual voting behaviour cannot be avoided: it is simply an open question whether the expressed will of the people is in the people's interests or not. (This observation is not, as it may seem, an invitation to authoritarian politics. It is simply a rejection of the idea that direct determination of policy outcomes by electoral means is what democracy properly understood either requires or admits.)

So far so good. In what follows, I shall take the expressive account of voting and its constitutional implications as given. I will term the problem to which expressive voting gives rise the motivation problem – though this is a rather loose description, since the problem is really a behavioural one in the sense that it involves a rational response to incentives embedded in the collective-decision-making setting.

Here, I wish to illustrate how the interaction between the motivation problem and the behaviour of political agents in a representative democracy might serve to produce political outcomes that are even more extreme than the nature of expressive preferences might lead one to think. What I have in mind goes something like this.

A critical piece of electoral competition within the expressive account is essentially rhetorical. Rivals are engaged in a battle in which those who can put the best spin on themselves and the positions with which they are associated are the most likely to win. Political candidates will (rationally) appeal to *any* affective symbols that are to hand: that is why so much of political speech is of the motherhood genre. But political candidates will seek to go beyond motherhood. The true political entrepreneur on this reading is not one who can broker strategic redistributions among various interests (as in the conventional public choice picture) but rather one who can invent new and arresting symbols and develop a rhetoric that is both distinctive and compelling. Call the attribute of the successful political entrepreneur, so understood, charisma. Then, two questions. What are the dynamics of charisma creation? and in particular do those dynamics have extremist implications? To the extent that charisma remains contained in such innocent arenas as good looks, an excellent dress sense, a certain facility on the saxophone, having an attractive spouse and charming children, nothing much of policy significance follows. But when charisma extends to the development of persuasive rhetorical defences of particular policies, and indeed to choice of policies themselves with an eye to their charisma-generating potential, then the possibility of a kind of extremism clearly looms.

The recent film *Primary Colors* provides a morality tale that bears on these issues. In the film, the U.S. president, in trouble for some sexual peccadilloes and confronting a re-election hurdle, orchestrates through his spin doctor a phoney war against Albania. The inspiration for this story-line might well be Maggie Thatcher's assault on the Falklands; or the fact that George Bush at the height of the post Iraqi-war euphoria was the most popular president in U.S. history (he was the most *un*popular a mere 12 months later when he fronted up to the election).

Whatever the inspiration, the tale captures a disturbing feature of populist democracy – namely that a good war, with clever rhetorical support and quickly won, can be extremely rewarding electorally. Democraphiles often take some comfort from the (apparently statistically supported) claim that democracies do not make war on other democracies – but this may primarily be a reflection of the availability of plenty of tin-pot dictatorships around. If the United States was to declare war tomorrow, the most plausible list of traditional enemies lying on the shelf would be mainly composed of non-democratic regimes – but this fact does not necessarily allow us to conclude that democracy has deeply pacific tendencies. Nor necessarily bellicose ones. My point is simply that policies that are particularly congenial to extravagant rhetoric and provide a hospitable platform for exploiting charismatic gifts in leaders are often not in the public interest (as I think, for example, Sam Brittan effectively demonstrates in relation to the Falklands War).

Let me take a different example. In the early 1970s, I spent a sabbatical in Nova Scotia. This was a depressed area of Canada, and accordingly a plausible claimant on support from Ottawa. It was difficult not to be impressed with the way in which the national government would periodically embark on some megalomaniacal scheme to save the Atlantic provinces. First, it was a huge heavy-water plant, that was planned to supply a significant fraction of the entire world's needs. Then there was a project to harness the power of the tides in the Bay of Fundy to supply hydroelectric power to the U.S. north-east. What impressed me with these schemes at the time was their grandiose quality: it was as if salience was the chief political object of Atlantic province policy – as if what was most important to voters was not so much to redistribute income to the Atlantic provinces as to persuade the Atlantic citizens that they were *loved*. For that purpose, one large gesture was much better than many less visible ones. This, as I see it, is a form of political extremism.

The connection between salience and extremism has in addition a dynamic element. What is at stake here is nicely captured in that wonderful soliloquy sung by Bunthorne in Gilbert and Sullivan's *Patience*. Having confessed to the audience that his every action is "born of a morbid love of admiration", Bunthorne proceeds to offer a recipe for how he might go about increasing the admiration in which he basks. His second recommendation runs:

Be extravagant in praise of the very dull old days which have long since passed away,
And convince 'em if you can that the reign of Good Queen Anne was culture's palmiest day,
Of course you will pooh-pooh whatever's bright and new as simply vulgar and obscene
For art stopped short in the cultivated court of the empress Josephine.
And everyone will say as you walk your mystic way
If that's not good enough for him which is good enough for me,
Why, what a most discriminating kind of youth this kind of youth must be.

I have often enough seen something of the kind go on in gatherings where there is a presumed ideological commonality. Participants seem to strive to outdo one another in terms of ideological purity: they seek to make themselves salient by staking out more extreme positions than everyone else. Each serves to egg the others on. The same thing often happens in religious revival meetings.

It is notable that the antipathy to political parties and to factions that one finds in David Hume and the American Founding Fathers more reflects this kind of anxiety than it does the majority interest line more familiar in contemporary public choice theory. Public choice theorists are fond of quoting (I have done so many times myself) from Hume's essay on the independency of parliament to the effect that "in designing the various checks and balances of the constitution, every man ought to be supposed a knave and have no other purpose in all his actions than private interest". But Hume's actual argument in this essay involves an appeal to the natural tendency for representatives to seek out and associate those with like views, and for these views to become both more extreme and more confidently held by virtue of the support and enthusiasm found for them within the biased audience that each gathers to himself.

Moreover, as Hume notes in another essay (on political parties), factions can often form around the most arbitrary and apparently trivial distinctions. It is as if the securing of salience in public life requires one to distinguish oneself from one's rivals: so distinguishing oneself lends a distinctiveness; and the quest for distinctiveness naturally leads in the political arena to a kind of perverse oppositionality. Hence the antics of political parties in those systems where political parties are strong are often vigorously reactive, with each party seeking to distinguish itself from the other(s) rather than establishing a position that reflects its best judgment of the public interest.

I do not mean here to deny that there is much to be said for party politics and in particular for the two-party systems of the kind that exist in Britain and Australia. But I do claim that public choice theory has brought to the study of democratic politics an excessively rationalist mode of analysis, or better put, public choice theorists have interpreted the requirements of rationality in the political arena too simple-mindedly. One aspect of this excessive rationalism is that the theory paints a picture of democracy that is much less accommodating to extremism and eccentricity in political outcomes than democracy actually is, and than the logic of rational actor analysis, faithfully applied, admits.

## REFERENCES

Arrow, Kenneth J. 1951/1963. *Social Choice and Individual Values*. John Wiley & Sons, New York.

Brennan, Geoffrey and Hamlin, Alan. 1998. "Expressive Voting and Electoral Equilibrium", *Public Choice* **95**: 149–75.

Brennan, Geoffrey and Lomasky, Loren. 1993. *Democracy and Decision: The Pure Theory of Electoral Preference*. Cambridge University Press, New York.

Coleman, James. 1971. "Internal Processes Governing Party Positions in Elections", *Public Choice* **11**: 35–60.

Coughlin, Peter. 1982. "Pareto Optimality of Policy Proposals with Probalistic Voting", *Public Choice* **39**: 427–33.

Downs, Anthony. 1957. *An Economic Theory of Democracy*. Harper & Row, New York.

Hume, David. 1994. *Political Essays* (edited by Knut Haakonssen). Cambridge University Press, Cambridge.

McGuire, Martin and Olson, Mancur. 1996. "The Economics of Autocracy and Majority Rule", *Journal of Economic Literature*, **XXXIV**, March, 72–96.

McKelvey, Richard D. 1976. "Intransitivities in Multidimensional Voting Models and Some Implications for Agenda Control", *Journal of Economic Theory* **12**: 472–82.

Schumpeter, Joseph A. 1950. *Capitalism, Socialism and Democracy*. 3rd ed., Harper & Row, New York.

Shepsle, Ken A. and Barry Weingast. 1981. "Structure Induced Equilibrium and Legislative Choice", *Public Choice* **37**: 503–19.

Tullock, Gordon. 1981. "Why So Much Stability?", *Public Choice* **37**: 189–202.

Wintrobe, Ronald. 1998. *The Political Economy of Dictatorship*. Cambridge University Press, New York.

# 6

# Strategic Positioning and Campaigning

*Amihai Glazer**

## 1. INTRODUCTION

To give a sense of the politics of extreme parties, the Appendix lists all candidates in U.S. presidential elections who won at least half a percent of the popular vote. For each election year, the table lists candidates by my reading of their ideology, with the most conservative candidate listed at the top, and the most liberal candidate listed at the bottom. Candidates not belonging to one of the two major parties are shown with an asterisk after the party affiliation. Also shown is the percentage of the popular vote each won. The data begin with the election of 1832, the first election in which virtually all states chose presidential electors by popular vote.

Ordering parties by ideology entails some subjective judgment. A principal difficulty is that for much of the nineteenth century slavery and the consequences of the Civil War were the main issues, whereas in the twentieth century economic issues can distinguish parties. I classify Republicans as more liberal than Democrats through the election of 1872. From 1876 (when Reconstruction ended) and thereafter I classify Republicans as more conservative than Democrats.

Two features are of note:

- Third parties, even popular ones, rarely become major parties. Indeed, only one minor party, the Republican Party, ever became a major party.
- Most small parties have extreme ideologies, in the sense of not lying between the ideologies of the two major parties. Of the 41 elections, 28 had small parties which won at least 0.5 percent of the vote. Of these 28 elections, only four had a moderate party.

* I am grateful for comments by Isidoro Mazza and by an anonymous referee.

Two of these four elections occurred in elections just before the Civil War. Summing the number of small parties running in these elections, shows that 44 were extreme, and only 4 moderate. It is thus fair to say that moderate third parties rarely appear in the United States.

Why the pattern of extremism among third parties? One approach to understanding lies in looking at the appeal of parties to voters.[1] But here I pursue a different approach: to understand the electoral strength of an extreme party we must understand the conditions under which major parties will and will not campaign among persons attracted to the extreme party.

## 2.  LITERATURE

This chapter builds on the work of Skaperdas and Grofman (1995), who consider negative campaigning with three candidates. They show that were the two weaker candidates to engage in negative campaigning, they would both attack the front-runner. A front-runner who engaged in negative campaigning would attack the stronger opponent. As Skaperdas and Grofman note, a similar result appears in game-theoretic models of a three-way duel: the most accurate duelist has a lower probability of survival than the second-best (or even the third-best) shooter. The reason is that the optimal strategy of either of the other duelists is to shoot at the duelist who has the best shot. By analogy, small extreme parties will not be attacked by large parties. But the same model would also predict that an extreme party could grow almost to the size of a major party without being attacked. That conclusion appears unrealistic, motivating my analysis that predicts immunity for an extreme party only for some small size. My reasoning for the conclusions presented below also differ from earlier analysis: Skaperdas and Grofman ask where the most votes are, whereas I ask about the comparative opportunities for attracting voters. That is, even if the extreme party were large, the mainstream parties may choose not to campaign against it.

One of my results is that an extreme party may do worse when it moves towards the center. The result appears because it would thereby

---

[1] Another approach may also be important in studying parliamentary democracies with coalition governments. A large moderate party may avoid dealing with an extreme party, and even more so if it campaigned against it. A small party may then choose its position with coalition bargaining in mind (cf. Baron, 1991). That may explain the prevalence in Europe of small parties with moderate platforms.

increase campaigning against it. The explanation thus differs from recent literature which asks how a party in power in the current period can increase its electoral chances by adopting extreme positions.[2]

## 2.1 Expressive voting

I shall consider below instrumental voters – they vote for a party to give it the power of implementing the policies it announces. But other motives for voting can explain some features of extremism in politics – why a voter may support a party whose positions he opposes, and why he may be more willing to support an extremist party he expects will lose.

Voting is a peculiar activity since any one vote is highly unlikely to change the outcome of the election. Several authors (see Brennan and Lomasky, 1993, Kuran, 1995, Glazer, 1987, and Brennan and Hamlin, 1998) argue that people may therefore vote not to affect outcomes, but for expressive reasons, showing their anger or emotions. They may therefore vote for an extremist party even though they hope it will not win office. A voter, however, who thinks that his vote can significantly affect policy will not support the extreme party. The appeal of an extremist party may thus be self-limiting.

A related idea sees voting as an act of communication. Consider a voter who expects party $X$ to win office, and who prefers its position over the position of an extreme party. Suppose, however, that he prefers a policy that lies somewhere between the positions of party $X$ and the extreme party. Suppose further that party $X$ is uncertain about the preferences of the voters. Then a person who votes for the extreme party signals his preferences to the winning party, inducing the party to adopt a different position once in government or in anticipation of the next election.

Although undoubtedly some persons vote for such expressive reasons, to explain why an extreme party's appeal to moderate voters often declines as the number of its supporters grow, models of expressive voting must also consider instrumental voting. It is therefore worthwhile to see how well a model of instrumental voting can explain elections with extreme parties. Moreover, since my interest lies largely in understanding political campaigns, it appears useful to extend the standard Downsian model in one way, rather than in several.

---

[2] For instance, the incumbent may commit to a policy because he wants to remove an issue from the electoral agenda. See Aghion and Bolton (1990), Milesi-Ferretti and Spolaore (1994), and Glazer and Lohmann (1999). The incumbent may also adopt an extreme policy to reduce the benefits from electing an opposing party that would want to incur a costly reversal of that policy; see Glazer, Gradstein, and Konrad (1998).

### 3   CAMPAIGN STRATEGIES

## 3.1   Assumptions

*3.1.1 Parties*

I start with the standard Downsian model. Each party aims to maximize the number of votes it wins. But unlike the Downsian model, I let the positions of some parties be fixed.[3] I also let parties make non-policy choices to attract voters. In particular, a party can campaign (either to its right or to its left) by offering bribes, promising jobs to supporters, emphasizing its competence and honesty, and so on.[4] The assumption that a party campaigns in only one direction simplifies the analysis. And it is a plausible assumption under some conditions. A politician who is reported to be campaigning both to his left and to his right may be viewed as speaking from both sides of his mouth, confuse voters about his message, and lose credibility among them. Or the media through which voters learn about candidates may simplify and dramatize the contest by reporting it as a simple left–right contest. Lastly, in the years before mass communication and air travel, a candidate might have to decide in which region of the country to campaign, thereby limiting his ability to campaign among any set of voters he wishes.

The election is contested by two Big parties and one Small party. The Big party on the left, party $L$, has position $p_L$. The Big party on the right, party $R$, has position $p_R$. The Small party's position is at $p_S$.

Each party aims to maximize the number of its votes. Under a plurality system, where the candidate with the largest number of votes wins office, such maximization is equivalent to maximizing the chance of winning. Of course, under some conditions a party may care not only about its vote, but also about the distribution of votes among the other parties. For example, in a parliamentary democracy a liberal party may prefer to form a coalition with a left-wing party; it may then avoid campaigning against its likely coalition partner, even if such campaigning could win it more votes. But even in parliamentary systems, vote maximization is a reasonable goal. For example, it is common in parliamentary democracies for the largest party to be called on first to form a coalition, or to be viewed as the party with the greatest legitimacy to head a government. A party would therefore aim to maximize its share of the vote.

---

[3] Perhaps because parties selected platforms as the result of their interaction with the groups which offered position-induced contributions in a previous period.

[4] More generally, a campaign may reduce support by some voters – a liberal voter may object to a putatively liberal candidate who campaigns among conservatives. For simplicity, I ignore here such effects.

### 3.1.2 Voters

A voter's utility from voting for party $i$ varies with the voter's ideal point, with the position of the party, and with the party's campaigning.[5] The first two effects are captured by the function $U(v, p)$ with the voter having ideal point at $v$ and considering a party with position at $p$. At times I use a quadratic utility function, $U = -(v - p)^2$. The distribution of voters' ideal points is given by $F(x)$. That is, the fraction of voters with ideal points to the left of $x$ is $F(x)$.

The effect of campaigning is captured as follows. If the party campaigns to the left, and the voter's ideal point lies to the left of the party's position, then he is targeted. If his ideal point lies to the right when the party campaigns to the left, he is not targeted by that party. Similar statements hold for other possible combinations. A targeted voter gets additional utility from voting for the targeting party of $B(p - v)$, with $B > 0$ and $B' < 0$. I shall at times more specifically assume that the function is $\alpha/p - v$, with $\alpha$ a positive constant. This captures the idea that campaigning is ineffective when directed at voters with preferences very different from the party's. The difference between a Big and a Small party is that a Big party has the resources to campaign; the Small party does not.

Combining a voter's policy preferences and the effects of campaigning gives the utility of a targeted voter in voting for a party with position $p$:

$$U(v, p) + B(v, p), \tag{1}$$

or more specifically

$$U = -(v - p)^2 + \frac{\alpha}{|p - v|}. \tag{2}$$

The utility of a non-targeted voter does not include the last term.

## 3.2 Campaign strategies

### 3.2.1 Two Big parties

With only two Big parties, the Nash equilibrium strategies are simple. The conservative party campaigns to its left; the liberal party campaigns to its right. Campaigning may have no net effect: when the median voter's ideal point lies midway between the two parties' positions, his utility from each party increases by the same amount, and so he is still indifferent between them.

---

[5] For evidence that campaign expenditures increase support for a candidate, see Banaian and Luksetich (1991). For theoretical analyses of campaigning see Mueller and Stratmann (1994), and Myerson and Weber (1993).

### 3.2.2 One Big party and one Small party

Let the Big party's position be at $p_B$, and let the Small party's position lie to the left of $p_B$, at $p_S$. Critical to determining the votes each party wins is determining the position of the voter who is indifferent between them. Describe this voter by the distance, $d$, of his ideal point from the Small party's position. Then with the utility function (2) $d$ satisfies

$$-(p_s - d)^2 + \frac{\alpha}{p_S - d} = -d^2, \tag{3}$$

with the solution

$$d = \frac{3p_S^2 - \sqrt{(p_S^4 + 8p_S\alpha)}}{4p_S}. \tag{4}$$

More generally, what matters to the determination of $d$ is the distance between the positions of the two parties. Let this distance be $p_B - p_S$. Then the voter who is indifferent has a position at

$$p_S + \frac{3(p_B - p_S)^2 - \sqrt{(p_B - p_S)^4 + 8\alpha(p_B - p_S)}}{4(p_B - p_S)}. \tag{5}$$

To find the Small party's vote-maximizing position, assume that voters' ideal points are uniformly distributed on $(0, 1)$, and solve the first-order condition to obtain

$$p_S = p_B - \sqrt[3]{\alpha}. \tag{6}$$

The first result, then, is that the Small party will not position itself next to the Big party, but instead some distance from it, with the Small party's position more extreme the greater is $\alpha$, or the greater the effectiveness of campaigning.

To determine which voter is indifferent between the two parties at this solution substitute (6) in (5) to obtain

$$p_S + \frac{3(p_B - p_B + \sqrt[3]{\alpha})^2 - \sqrt{(p_B - p_B + \sqrt[3]{\alpha})^4 + 8\alpha(p_B - p_B + \sqrt[3]{\alpha})}}{4(p_B - p_B + \sqrt[3]{\alpha})} = p_S. \tag{7}$$

This yields a second result, that the most successful extreme party will attract the support only of voters with preferences more extreme than the party's position; it will attract no voters with ideal points that lie between the positions of the extreme party and the moderate one. Put differently, a successful party that cannot campaign will attract only extreme voters. That also implies that if the extreme party moved in the direction of its supporters, it would lose votes.

### 3.2.3 Two Big parties and a moderate Small party

Consider a Small party with a position between $p_L$ and $p_R$. Clearly, party $L$ will campaign to the right of $p_L$, and party $R$ will campaign to the left of $p_R$. Both Big parties may therefore attract voters who in the absence of campaigning would support the Small party. An instructive case occurs with $p_L$ and $p_R$ arbitrarily close, bracketing the ideal point of the median voter. Clearly, if $\alpha$ is sufficiently large, the Small party in the middle wins no votes. It therefore wins more votes with a position to the left of $p_L$ or to the right of $p_R$. Assuming again that ideal points are uniformly distributed and using equation (6), this means that the Small party may choose an extreme position.

### 3.2.4 Two Big parties and an extreme Small party

Accordingly, consider an extreme Small party, with a position $p_S$ to the left of $p_L$. Party $R$ will campaign to its left. Party $L$ must choose whether to campaign to its right or to its left.

Suppose first that $L$ campaigns to its right (so that it does not campaign among the Small party's backers). With the utility function the voter with ideal point at $(p_S + p_L)/2$ is indifferent between parties $S$ and $L$.

Some voter to the left of $p_L$ may prefer $R$ over $L$. Again using (2), the ideal point of this voter is determined by the value of $d$ satisfying

$$-d^2 = -(p_R - p_L + d)^2 + \alpha/(p_R - p_L + d), \tag{8}$$

with the solution

$$d = \frac{-3p_R^2 - 3p_L^2 + 6p_R p_L - \sqrt{p_R^4 + 6p_R^2 p_L^2 - 4p_R^3 p_L + p_L^4 - 4p_L^3 p_R + 8\alpha(p_R - p_L)}}{4(p_R - p_L)}. \tag{9}$$

For simplicity, I ignore such jumping over; I instead assume that campaigning by party $R$ is ineffective among voters to the left of $p_L$. And if $\alpha$ is not too large, or if $p_R - p_L$ is sufficiently large, even without such a constraint each voter with an ideal point to the left of $p_L$ will prefer $L$ over $R$.

What is the best the extreme party can do? That depends on how $L$ campaigns. We saw in (6) that if $L$ campaigns to its left, then $S$'s share of the vote is greatest when its position is at $p_S = p_L - \sqrt[3]{\alpha}$, and that the voter indifferent between $L$ and $S$ has his ideal point there.

If party $L$ campaigns to its right while $S$ is at $p_L$, then $L$'s vote is $F((p_L + p_R)/2) - F(p_L)$. If party $L$ campaigns to its left while $S$ is at $p_L$, then $L$'s vote is

$$F\left(p_L + \frac{3(p_R - p_L)^2 - \sqrt{(p_R - p_L)^4 + 8\alpha(p_R - p_L)}}{4(p_R - p_L)}\right)$$

$$- F\left(p_S + \frac{3(p_L - p_S)^2 - \sqrt{(p_L - p_S)^4 + 8\alpha(p_L - p_S)}}{4(p_L - p_S)}\right). \tag{10}$$

Thus if

$$F((p_L + p_R)/2) - F(p_L)$$

$$> F\left(p_L + \frac{3(p_R - p_L)^2 - \sqrt{(p_R - p_L)^4 + 8\alpha(p_R - p_L)}}{4(p_R - p_L)}\right)$$

$$- F\left(p_S + \frac{3(p_L - p_S)^2 - \sqrt{(p_L - p_S)^4 + 8\alpha(p_L - p_S)}}{4(p_L - p_S)}\right), \tag{11}$$

then $S$ does best when its position is $p_L$.

What if the inequality is reversed? Then with $L$ campaigning to its left, $S$ does best at $p_L - \sqrt[3]{\alpha}$, and the number of votes it wins is $F(p_L - \sqrt[3]{\alpha})$. But $S$ may do even better with a position to the left of $p_L$, if it can thereby induce $L$ to campaign to its right. Let $S$ be at $p_L - \sqrt[3]{\alpha} - \delta$, with $\delta > 0$. If $L$ campaigns to its left its vote is

$$F\left(p_L + \frac{3(p_R - p_L)^2 - \sqrt{(p_R - p_L)^4 + 8\alpha(p_R - p_L)}}{4(p_R - p_L)}\right) - F(p_L - \sqrt[3]{\alpha} - \delta).$$

If, given $S$'s position at $p_L - \sqrt[3]{\alpha} - \delta$, party $L$ instead campaigns to its right, then $L$'s vote is $F((p_L + p_R)/2) - F((p_L - \sqrt[3]{\alpha} - \delta + p_L)/2)$. That is, suppose

$$F\left(p_L + \frac{3(p_R - p_L)^2 - \sqrt{(p_R - p_L)^4 + 8\alpha(p_R - p_L)}}{4(p_R - p_L)}\right) - F(p_L - \sqrt[3]{\alpha} - \delta)$$

$$< F((p_L + p_R)/2) - F((p_L - \sqrt[3]{\alpha} - \delta + p_L)/2)$$

holds for sufficiently small $\delta$ but does not hold when $\delta = 0$. The reversal can happen if $F'(p_L - \sqrt[3]{\alpha} - \delta) > F'((p_L - \sqrt[3]{\alpha} - \delta + p_L)/2)$. Then the Small party may maximize its vote when its position is to the left of $p_L - \sqrt[3]{\alpha}$.

The next task is to compare support for $S$ when it is to the left of $L$ to support for $S$ when its position lies between $L$ and $R$. I cannot obtain an analytic solution. But clearly as $p_R - p_L$ approaches zero, the share of the vote won by a moderate Small party also approaches zero, but the share of the vote won by an extreme party does not. Thus, a Small party may do better when its position is extreme.

To review, when the Small party positions itself to the left of $L$, a movement to the left has three opposing effects. First, in the absence of campaigning by party $L$, party $S$ attracts fewer votes. Second, if $L$ does campaign against $S$, the campaigning may switch fewer votes. Third, by moving to the left, party $S$ makes it less attractive for party $L$ to campaign to $L$'s left, and so may induce $L$ to campaign to $L$'s right.

Note that I do not merely say that a Small party is more likely to be targeted the more popular it becomes. What is critical for my results is that a Big party's campaigning is more effective when the Small party's position is close. Thus, my results would continue to hold if a Small party which moved to the right lost voters on its left.

If the Big party on the right is far to the right, then campaigning by $L$ to its right will switch few votes. The indifferent voter under no campaigning, with ideal point $(p_L + p_R)/2$, is far from either party, so that campaigning by either of the Big parties will little affect voters near him, and will thus switch few votes. Thus, if the Big parties are far apart, the Big party on the Left has incentive to campaign to its left. That drives the Small extreme party to an even more extreme position, but also reduces the share of the vote won by the Small party.

## 3.3 Extensions

I assumed that a Big party must choose between campaigning to its right or to its left. This can be generalized in several ways. If campaigning in either direction entails a fixed cost, then a party may find it optimal to campaign to its right, to its left, or to allocate its resources between campaigning in both directions. Such a generalization will not affect the qualitative results obtained here – a Small party still does better when its position reduces a Big party's incentive to campaign in its direction, and when its position reduces the effects of any such campaigning.

To determine some comparative statics, let the effectiveness of campaigning by party $L$ differ when it campaigns to its right (against the Big party) from when it campaigns to its left (against the Small party). Call the parameters $\alpha_R$ and $\alpha_L$. What happens when $\alpha_L$ increases? Party $L$ benefits more from campaigning to its left. The Small party, if it can choose its position or if selection effects cause a change in the position of such a party, will therefore move further to the left. Thus, increased effectiveness of political campaigns against an extreme party will reduce support for the extreme party, but will also cause the extreme party to become even more extreme.

The extremist-moving effect of campaigning also means that data on how an extreme party fares as it moves to the right or to the left may give little evidence of voters' preferences, but may instead reflect the effects of campaign decisions by a Big party. For example, as the Small party moves to the right, the effectiveness of $L$'s campaign against it will increase, and $L$ will find it more attractive to campaign against $S$. The Small party's support will therefore decline. And it will decline even if no voter finds $S$'s new position less attractive than before.

## 4.  HIDE INFORMATION ON POPULARITY OF SMALL PARTY

We saw that a major party may choose not to campaign against a small one. That is one reason for the success of some small parties. To check for robustness, we can ask what happens when voters are imperfectly rather than perfectly informed about the Small party. The immediate intuition is that support for a Small party will decline, since with the quadratic utility function I have been assuming voters are essentially risk averse, and therefore will find a party with unknown positions less attractive. But as shown above, more than voters' preferences must be considered. We must also look into the campaign decisions of a Big party. Here I will outline how uncertainty can reduce campaigning, and thus increase support for an extreme party.

Since I examine the informational content of an action, my approach necessarily relates to the classic signaling model (see Spence, 1973). Several works, which do not refer to signaling, consider how a candidate may gain from imperfect information about himself. Shepsle (1972) shows that ambiguity pays when voters are risk loving. Glazer (1990) shows that if each candidate is uncertain about the median voter's preferred policy (and therefore faces the risk of stating an unpopular position), then in equilibrium both candidates may adopt ambiguous positions. The benefits of ambiguity are even larger if the position announced by one candidate allows the other candidate to estimate more accurately the preferences of the voters. Similarly, Alesina and Cukierman (1990) show that a party can increase its popularity by hiding from voters its preferences.

We saw above that a Big party may campaign against the other Big party rather than against the Small party, thereby increasing the success of the Small party. The above analysis was made under the assumption of complete information. But an important characteristic of small parties is that voters are unsure about their positions. A Big party that campaigns against the Small party thereby signals that it believes the Small party is a threat, with a position that may appeal to many voters. Campaigning against that party may therefore backfire.

To see how backfiring can arise, suppose voters are of two types. A fraction $f$ are perfectly informed about the position of the Small party. A fraction $1 - f$ are imperfectly informed: they believe that with probability $\pi_1$ the Small party's position is $p_1$, and that with probability $\pi_2$ its position is $p_2$. Let $p_2 > p_1$, so that $p_2$ represents a more moderate position.

Suppose for the moment the Small party is at $p_1$, that party $L$ knows it, and that the informed voters know it. As shown above, party $L$ may gain little from campaigning against $S$ – few voters would support the extreme party anyway. Suppose next the Small party is at $p_2$. In terms of gaining votes from informed voters, party $L$ has greater incentive to campaign against $S$ than were $S$ at $p_1$.

If party $L$ adopted such a campaign strategy, then it would signal uninformed voters about party $S$'s position – uninformed voters would infer that if $L$ campaigns against $S$ then $S$'s position must be at $p_2$ rather than at $p_1$, or that party $S$'s position is relatively moderate. That signal would then increase support for party $S$ among initially uninformed voters. This signaling effect thus reduces the benefits to $L$ of campaigning against $S$, and can thus increase the electoral support of an extreme party. Moreover, since knowledge about a party's position will most hurt the most extreme party, the absence of campaigning by the Big party differentially helps an especially extreme party.

## 5. CONCLUSION

The results obtained here can be summarized by thinking of how a party that cannot campaign should position itself to maximize votes. Surely it must consider the preferences of voters, and these considerations are extensively studied in the literature. The novel effect discussed here is that a party can reduce the effectiveness of a major party's campaign against it by adopting a position that strongly appeals to extremist voters. Indeed, the Small party may want to appeal only to voters more extreme than itself.

In addition, the Small party must consider how its position affects the campaign strategy of a large party. The Small Party has an interest in inducing large parties to campaign against each other rather than against itself. This consideration may drive the Small party even further to the extreme. We reached the paradoxical result that effective campaigning by a major party against a small one may drive the Small party to extreme positions. The existence of very extreme rather than moderately extreme parties may point to the difficulty the extreme may have in increasing its vote, and to the success or potential for success of campaigns against it.

## 6.  APPENDIX: CANDIDATES IN U.S. PRESIDENTIAL ELECTIONS

| Election | Candidate | Party | Percentage vote |
|---|---|---|---|
| 1832 | Henry Clay | National Republican | 37.63 |
|  | Andrew Jackson | Democratic | 54.54 |
|  | William Wirt | Anti-Masonic* | 7.83 |
| 1836 | Daniel Webster | Whig | 2.74 |
|  | Martin Van Buren | Democratic | 50.87 |
|  | William H. Harrison | Whig | 36.66 |
|  | Hugh L. White | Whig | 9.73 |
| 1840 | William H. Harrison | Whig | 53.05 |
|  | Martin Van Buren | Democratic | 46.95 |
| 1844 | James K. Polk | Democratic | 49.58 |
|  | Henry Clay | Whig | 48.12 |
|  | James G. Birney | Liberty* | 2.30 |
| 1848 | Lewis Cass | Democratic | 42.54 |
|  | Zachary Taylor | Whig | 47.33 |
|  | Martin Van Buren | Free Soil* | 10.13 |
| 1852 | Franklin Pierce | Democratic | 51.04 |
|  | Winfield Scott | Whig | 44.03 |
|  | John P. Hale | Free Soil* | 4.93 |
| 1854 | James Buchanan | Democratic | 45.32 |
|  | Millard Fillmore | American* | 21.55 |
|  | John C. Fremont | Republican | 33.13 |
| 1860 | John C. Breckinridge | Southern Democratic* | 18.10 |
|  | Stephen A. Douglas | Democratic | 29.46 |
|  | John Bell | Constitutional Union* | 12.61 |
|  | Abraham Lincoln | Republican | 39.83 |
| 1864 | George B. McClellan | Democratic | 44.97 |
|  | Abraham Lincoln | Unionist | 55.03 |
| 1868 | Horatio Seymour | Democratic | 47.34 |
|  | Ulysses S. Grant | Republican | 52.66 |

| Election | Candidate | Party | Percentage vote |
|----------|-----------|-------|-----------------|
| 1872 | Ulysses S. Grant | Republican | 55.77 |
| | Horace Greeley | Democratic–Liberal Republican | 43.94 |
| 1876 | Samuel J. Tilden | Democratic | 51.06 |
| | Rutherford B. Hayes | Republican | 48.03 |
| | Peter Cooper | Greenback* | 0.90 |
| 1880 | James A. Garfield | Republican | 48.30 |
| | Winfield S. Hancock | Democratic | 48.28 |
| | James B. Weaver | Greenback–Labor* | 3.32 |
| 1884 | John P. St. John | Prohibition* | 1.47 |
| | James G. Blaine | Republican | 48.27 |
| | Grover Cleveland | Democratic | 48.52 |
| | Benjamin F. Butler | Greenback–Labor/ Anti-Monopoly* | 1.74 |
| 1888 | Clinton B. Fisk | Prohibition* | 2.20 |
| | Benjamin Harrison | Republican | 47.86 |
| | Grover Cleveland | Democratic | 48.66 |
| | Anson J. Streeter | Union Labor* | 1.29 |
| 1892 | John Bidwell | Prohibition* | 2.25 |
| | Benjamin Harrison | Republican | 42.99 |
| | Grover Cleveland | Democratic | 46.08 |
| | James B. Weaver | People's* | 8.50 |
| 1896 | Joshua Levering | Prohibition* | 0.90 |
| | William McKinley | Republican | 51.01 |
| | John M. Palmer | National Democratic* | 0.96 |
| | William J. Bryan | Democratic | 46.73 |
| 1900 | John G. Woolley | Prohibition* | 1.50 |
| | William McKinley | Republican | 51.69 |
| | William J. Bryan | Democratic | 45.54 |
| | Eugene V. Debs | Socialist* | 0.62 |
| 1904 | Silas C. Swallow | Prohibition* | 1.91 |
| | Theodore Roosevelt | Republican | 56.42 |
| | Alton B. Parker | Democratic | 37.60 |
| | Thomas E. Watson | People's* | 0.84 |
| | Eugene V. Debs | Socialist* | 2.98 |

(*continued*)

**Appendix** (*continued*)

| Election | Candidate | Party | Percentage vote |
|---|---|---|---|
| 1908 | Eugene W. Chafin | Prohibition* | 1.70 |
|  | William H. Taft | Republican | 51.58 |
|  | William J. Bryan | Democratic | 43.05 |
|  | Thomas L. Hisgen | Independence* | 0.55 |
|  | Eugene V. Debs | Socialist* | 2.82 |
| 1912 | Eugene W. Chafin | Prohibition* | 1.38 |
|  | William H. Taft | Republican | 23.19 |
|  | Woodrow Wilson | Democratic | 41.85 |
|  | Theodore Roosevelt | Progressive* | 27.39 |
|  | Eugene V. Debs | Socialist* | 5.99 |
| 1916 | J. Frank Hanly | Prohibition* | 1.19 |
|  | Charles E. Hughes | Republican | 46.20 |
|  | Woodrow Wilson | Democratic | 49.33 |
|  | A. L. Benson | Socialist* | 3.19 |
| 1920 | Aaron S. Watkins | Prohibition* | 0.71 |
|  | Warren G. Harding | Republican | 60.42 |
|  | James M. Cox | Democratic | 34.16 |
|  | P. P. Christensen | Farmer-Labor* | 0.99 |
|  | Eugene V. Debs | Socialist* | 3.42 |
| 1924 | Herman P. Faris | Prohibition* | 0.19 |
|  | Calvin Coolidge | Republican | 54.04 |
|  | John W. Davis | Democratic | 28.83 |
|  | Robert M. La Follette | Progressive* | 16.61 |
| 1928 | Herbert C. Hoover | Republican | 58.25 |
|  | Alfred E. Smith | Democratic | 40.78 |
| 1932 | Herbert C. Hoover | Republican | 39.65 |
|  | Franklin D. Roosevelt | Democratic | 57.44 |
|  | Norman Thomas | Socialist* | 2.23 |
| 1936 | Alfred M. Landon | Republican | 36.55 |
|  | Franklin D. Roosevelt | Democratic | 60.80 |
|  | William Lemke | Union* | 1.95 |
| 1940 | Wendell L. Willke | Republican | 44.79 |
|  | Franklin D. Roosevelt | Democratic | 54.74 |

| Election | Candidate | Party | Percentage vote |
|---|---|---|---|
| 1944 | Thomas E. Dewey | Republican | 46.03 |
| | Franklin D. Roosevelt | Democratic | 53.55 |
| 1948 | Strom Thurmond | States' Rights Democratic* | 2.41 |
| | Thomas E. Dewey | Republican | 45.07 |
| | Harry S. Truman | Democratic | 49.56 |
| | Henry Wallace | Progressive* | 2.37 |
| 1952 | Dwight D. Eisenhower | Republican | 55.14 |
| | Adlai E. Stevenson | Democratic | 44.38 |
| 1956 | Dwight D. Eisenhower | Republican | 57.58 |
| | Adlai E. Stevenson | Democratic | 42.10 |
| 1960 | Richard M. Nixon | Republican | 49.77 |
| | John F. Kennedy | Democratic | 49.94 |
| 1964 | Barry M. Goldwater | Republican | 38.60 |
| | Lyndon B. Johnson | Democratic | 61.26 |
| 1968 | George C. Wallace | American Independent* | 13.54 |
| | Richard M. Nixon | Republican | 43.43 |
| | Hubert H. Humphrey | Democratic | 42.73 |
| 1972 | John G. Schmitz | American* | 1.42 |
| | Richard M. Nixon | Republican | 60.72 |
| | George S. McGovern | Democratic | 37.55 |
| 1976 | Gerald R. Ford | Republican | 48.04 |
| | Jimmy Carter | Democratic | 50.10 |
| | Eugene J. McCarthy | Independent | 0.93 |
| 1980 | Ronald Reagan | Republican | 50.78 |
| | John B. Anderson | Independent | 6.62 |
| | Jimmy Carter | Democratic | 41.04 |
| 1984 | Ronald Reagan | Republican | 58.79 |
| | Walter F. Mondale | Democratic | 40.57 |
| 1988 | George Bush | Republican | 53.40 |
| | Michael S. Dukakis | Democratic | 45.67 |

(*continued*)

**Appendix** (*continued*)

| Election | Candidate | Party | Percentage vote |
|----------|-----------|-------|-----------------|
| 1992 | Ross Perot | Independent | 18.91 |
|      | George Bush | Republican | 37.46 |
|      | Bill Clinton | Democratic | 43.02 |
| 1996 | Ross Perot | Independent* | 8.48 |
|      | Harry Browne | Libertarian* | 0.50 |
|      | Bob Dole | Republican | 40.86 |
|      | Bill Clinton | Democratic | 49.15 |
|      | Ralph Nader | Green* | 0.63 |

Note: *, indicates Small party.
Sources: *New York Times* (various issues), *Encyclopedia Brittanica* 1998 CDRom edition, *Running for President, The Candidates and Their Images*, Vols. I & II, Arthur M.

### REFERENCES

Aghion, P. and P. Bolton. 1990. "Government domestic debt and the risk of default in a political economic model of the strategic role of debt" in: Dornbusch R. and Draghi, M. eds., *Public Debt Management: Theory and History*. Cambridge: Cambridge University Press.

Alesina, Alberto, and Alex Cukierman. 1990. "The politics of ambiguity." *Quarterly Journal of Economics*, **105**(4): 829–50.

Banaian, King and William A. Luksetich. 1991. "Campaign spending in congressional elections." *Economic Inquiry* **29**: 92–100

Baron, David P. 1991. "A spatial bargaining theory of government formation in parliamentary systems." *American Political Science Review* **85**(1): 137–64.

Brennan, Geoffrey and Loren Lomasky. 1993. *Democracy and Decision: The Pure Theory of Electoral Preference*. Cambridge: Cambridge University Press.

Brennan, Geoffrey and Alan Hamlin. 1998. "Expressive voting and electoral equilibrium." *Public Choice* **95**(1–2): 149–75.

Glazer, Amihai. 1987. "A new theory of voting: Why vote when millions of others do?" *Theory and Decision*, **22**(3): 257–70.

Glazer, Amihai. 1990. "The strategy of candidate ambiguity." *American Political Science Review* **84**(1): 237–41.

Glazer, Amihai and Kai Konrad. 1995. "Strategic lobbying by potential industry entrants." *Economics and Politics* **7**(2): 167–79.

Glazer, Amihai and Susanne Lohmann. 1999. "Setting the agenda: Electoral competition, commitment of policy, and issue salience." *Public Choice* **99**(3–4): 377–94.

Glazer, Amihai, Mark Gradstein, and Kai Konrad. 1998. "The electoral politics of extreme policies." *Economic Journal*, **108**(451): 1677–85.

Kuran, Timur. 1995. *Private Truths, Public Lies: The Social Consequences of Preference Falsification*. Cambridge, MA: Harvard University Press.

Milesi-Ferretti, Gian Maria and Enrico Spolaore. 1994. "How cynical can an incumbent be? Strategic policy in a model of government spending." *Journal of Public Economics* **55**(1): 121–40.

Mueller, Dennis C. and Thomas Stratmann. 1994. "Informative and persuasive campaigning." *Public Choice* **81**: 55–77.

Myerson, Roger and Robert J. Weber. 1993. "A theory of voting equilibria." *American Political Science Review* **87**(1): 102–14.

Shepsle, Kenneth A. 1972. "The strategy of ambiguity." *American Political Science Review* **66**(1): 555–68.

Skaperdas, Stergios and Bernard Grofman. 1995. "Modeling negative campaigning." *American Political Science Review* **89**(1): 49–61.

Spence, A. Michael. 1973. *Market Signaling: Information Transfer in Hiring and Related Processes.* Cambridge, MA: Harvard University Press.

# 7

# At the Outskirts of the Constitution

*Gianluigi Galeotti**

## 1. INTRODUCTION

Extremism is a label covering a variety of behaviors characterized by goals and methods not shared by the majority of the people. Extremism is a matter of freedom in terms of personal choices and it becomes a social issue when it generates externalities. Progress in many areas, from science to politics, is due to people challenging the common values of their times (think of the abolition of slavery and of the extension of political and social rights). That raises the question as to whether the long-run interests of a community are better served by conformist or by critical individual attitudes. Too much conformity makes the lemmings' trap inescapable,[1] but systematic criticism generates uncertainty and can undermine the cohesion of the community. In the political case, democratic societies are supposed to reduce both risks while fostering open confrontations of ideas and modulating conflicts through adaptable rules. Yet, the relationship between domestic political violence and political and economic freedom is not univocal (Muller and Weede, 1990) and Hardin (1997) calls into question the ability of democracy in dealing with major conflicts.

Extremism, interpreted as a challenge to the existing rules and values of politics, is a phenomenon that features in any constitutional order, democratic or non-democratic alike, and its evolution. We circumscribe our analysis, however, and submit that in a more or less democratic setting the presence of extremist leaders posits a problem in so far as they show apparently steadfast attitudes and an unwillingness to compromise. Does that steadfastness result from choice or from constraints?

* The author is grateful to Vani Borooah, Louis Lévy-Garboua and two anonymous referees for their comments on preliminary versions of this chapter.
[1] It seems that at times the lemmings (vole-like rodents of the Arctic) rush over the edge of cliffs and, swarm after swarm, drown themselves by swimming out to sea.

In the former case attention should be paid to the process of preference formation; in the latter to the nature of the constraints they face. In order to reduce the risk of ad hoc explanations (and the standard charge of conformist majorities against dissenters' mental health), our emphasis is not on the pathology of individual preferences, but on the presence of extremist stances relevant in terms of popular appeal. We assume well-behaved utility functions, with extremists provided with normal preferences, which in the case of their leaders include the appreciation of power and its amenity. Our working assumption is that the apparent low rate of substitution among different political goals relates to the poor trade-off they come to face, and we discuss a number of circumstances affecting that trade-off: (a) the early stages of democratic evolution, where people can be rallied only in terms of relatively simple signals, and compromises and settlements still work poorly; (b) the occurrence of decision stalemates; (c) settings in which the preferences of only a subset of citizens reach the political agenda, either because of the strong homogeneity of the passionate majority or because of hidden rules which de-franchise a significant subset of the population. In this way, our reflection on political extremism comes to be a reflection on the broader issue of the working of constitutional rules that translate pressure into political influence. In modeling competition among pressure groups, Becker (1983) considers extremist actions (disobedience, riots and the violent seizure of power) alongside the more conventional political activities. He is right in pointing out the constitutional underpinning of political influence, but the very notion of political constitution becomes void if the factors affecting the choices among those different activities are not clarified.

In what follows, Section 2 suggests a classification of the markets for political influence based on the constitutional distinction between established versus non-established interests *vis-à-vis* moderate versus extremist political activities. Section 3 shows how the accomplishments of any historical constitution – the promotion of legitimacy and consent – encourage conformity, constrain the evolution of political competition and account for the existence of an asymmetric appreciation of political violence. Following on from those underpinnings, Section 4 discusses the radicalism of the early stages of representative democracy; Section 5 the occurrence of political deadlocks which can prompt more radical conflicts; and Section 6 the instances in which groups pursuing "extremist" interests are compelled to adopt extremist methods of pressure. The concluding section reflects on the relationships between rules and substantive interests, an issue at the core of constitutional evolution.

## 2. EXTREMIST STANCES VERSUS EXTREMIST ACTIONS: THE CONSTITUTIONAL BOUNDARIES

The gladiators who revolted against Rome, the Peasants' war of sixteenth century Germany, the Irish nationalists of the nineteenth century, the organization of Guatemalan Indians in the 1980s, the recent aberrations of ethnic nationalism in Yugoslavia or of the Islamic Groups in Algeria, the excesses on the abortion issue in the United States or of the world-wide anti-capitalism globalization protests: this is a short list of the many examples of people resorting to violent political actions in the pursuit of socially unaccepted or otherwise controversial aims. Violence is a threat in itself, but can a political proposal as such be equally threatening? Do political extremists pose a problem because of what they stand for or because of what they do? The distinction is blurred in conformist settings where any dissent amounts to a challenge to the existing order, but it is not easy in more tolerant societies either. In any society the accommodation of different attitudes works within the boundaries of what is considered acceptable by the constitutional order. It is the *de facto* constitution that defines the admissible aims/interests and the instruments of legitimate influence on public decisions. Today, democratic societies respect dissent within broader limits than before and provide a wide array of political and legal instruments to settle grievances and redress wrongs. But in expanding the spheres of private freedom and public liberties, they face conflicts that traditional societies kept down by restricting both spheres. Before discussing this point in the following section, let us formulate the problem and classify the aims and methods of political influence in terms of the social consent to their legitimacy.

In Figure 7.1 the horizontal axis ranks the various aims (interests) in terms of their decreasing constitutional acknowledgment. Basic and accepted property rights are close to the origin (most of them going back to the Roman law), whilst dubious interests and positively excluded ones are located far to the right. As for the instruments of political influence, let us state that the formal or informal ways of arranging political pressure can go from normal signaling activities (requests, hearings, open debates), from the cultivation of bureaucrats and politicians, from conventional democratic instruments, to strikes, civil disobedience, corruption, riots, terrorism and the violent seizure of power. The dotted lines indicate the boundaries that at any time identify *de facto* what is legitimate and what is illegitimate in terms of interests and methods, in democratic and pre-democratic settings alike.

The purpose of the exercise is to discuss the main combinations of organized political actions that can be identified. The first (case A)

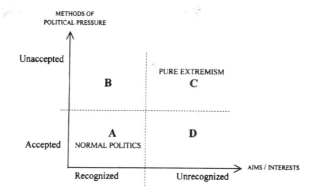

Figure 7.1 Constitutional boundaries to political action

expresses the normal political life, made of recognized interests and admissible pressures, and the remaining three the variety of combinations occurring on the outskirts of the constitutional order. The strict extremist case C, made of unrecognized interests and inadmissible methods of struggle, accounts for the subject matter of our inquiry and presents the basic issue whether that case is the cradle of constitutional evolution, in terms of the gradual empowerment of new interests and of the enlargement of the instruments of demand revelation, or simply the more or less intended failure of conventional politics.

While leaving that question open, clues can be looked for by reflecting on the occurrence of combinations B and D. Why are "extremist" interests rarely pursued through moderate methods and why are recognized interests at times pursued through extremist activities? At first sight, the occurrence of D should present no problem: interests are what they are and however extremist they can appear, they should seek recognition through normal political action. As discussed in Section 6, that is the case of any politically voiceless group trying to be heard, and we would think that in a democratic setting the German peasants would have received a better hearing than they did four centuries ago when the mere request for rights was perceived as a threat to the social order. Yet, the situation was not that much better for the Irish nationalists at the beginning of the twentieth century or for the Guatemala Indians in the 1980s, as they both found themselves engaged in extremist activities.[2] Why should a political movement move from D to C and face stronger reactions? Rational political entrepreneurs would not adopt violent meth-

---

[2] In Guatemala the 1981 electoral success of two moderate leftist parties caused a right-wing reaction that led to the formation of the Indian Revolutionary Organization of Armed People.

ods of political pressure if they could count on decent popular support
and on a receptive environment. If we exclude the case of deviant preferences, they must be compelled to make that move: it will be shown that
a perverse convergence of interests makes situation D degenerate in the
strictly extremist case C in the attempt to eliminate awkward issues from
the political agenda.

The occurrence of case B raises a different problem. Indeed, moderate
interests can occasionally find it convenient to show their muscles, and a
kind of militant median citizen is often behind authoritarian upsets. What
is puzzling, however, is the fact that extremist actions seem to be more
easily accepted when adopted in the pursuit of accepted interests than of
unaccepted ones. Consider an extremist action along the vertical axis and
move horizontally, confronting the case of a violent rally undertaken by
sanitary engineers for a pay increase with the case of the same rally
organized by illegal immigrants. Is the reaction of public opinion (and
of the authorities) going to be the same in the two instances? Why is the
interruption of a public service by school teachers felt less threatening
than a fiery gathering arranged by poor peasants or homeless people
trying to better their position? Since it cannot be a matter of costs of
repression – which would imply the opposite reaction – we have to inves-
tigate why violence is weighted in terms of goals. The following section
submits that the selective attitudes towards violence ensue from a historical pillar of constitutional stability, the fostering of legitimacy and social
consent. That result will help us to understand the extremism of the early
stages of representative democracy and the strategic use of those attitudes
in manufacturing radical extremism.

### 3.  CONSENT AND COMPETITION

In any historical polity we know of, political constitutions broadly
intended record the organization of power: they identify political leadership, establish the rules of the exercise of power, and determine the
domain of public action. Finer (1997, 28ff.) underlines how their stability
requires a certain congruence between social stratification and political
institutions, held together by belief-systems legitimizing the authority of
rulers. Along the same line, Douglass North has repeatedly stressed the
role of ideologies – shared views of the world – in controlling behaviors,
thus reducing both citizens' shirking and what Breton (1996, 64) calls
leaders' reverse-shirking. More generally, it has been shown that in coor-
dinating the activities of the leadership (power-holders and political
entrepreneurs in general) the working of the constitution is made stable
and self-enforcing because the costs of rearranging different rules induce
leaders' acceptance and people's acquiescence. In ordinary times that

acceptance and that acquiescence stick together thanks to the glue supplied by ideologies and legitimacy. By supplying *ex ante* ranking of interests and *ex post* benchmarks on the outcomes – a kind of syntax – those ideologies nurture a feeling of moral obligation in people to obey because of the legitimacy of those (an individual, a group, a bureaucracy) who apply the syntax and select the interests worthy of protection. In that sense, those shared values are experienced as pledges and the social expectations embodied in the legitimacy represent – implicitly at least – a constraint on the exercise of political power. The discretion of that exercise of power is further curtailed by political competition, as any leadership is constrained by the presence of potential rivals, of the claims of the rulers' agents and of the fact that political 'entrepreneurs spring up whenever there develop contrasting views of the world around us as a result of differential experiences' (North, 1981). Constitutional legitimacy is therefore the carrying structure within which both the maintenance of acquiescence and the evolution of competition have developed (Galeotti, 2000).

### 3.1 Culture of consent and selective violence

Political societies, born out of common experiences, have always encouraged consent and looked suspiciously at those holding views at the fringe of accepted values. In an uncertain political environment – because of external threats, social distress and limited information – the costs of mistakes are expected to be high and unanimous consent represents a value inspiring confidence, especially in the political arena where the lag between direct experience and accepted values is much greater than in other spheres of social life (Boyd and Richerson, 1985). The influence of a political culture is deep just because of its essentiality. If unanimous consent expresses a kind of reciprocal commitment, dissent is considered with suspicion (why should somebody, if reasonable, reach conclusions different from those of the overall majority?) and perceived as a threat because it creates doubts and hesitation when action is required. Those considerations are consistent with the strong social pressure exerted to restrain disagreement and dissent. What Roman and medieval historians tell us about the political life of their contemporaries in Northern Europe, whose influence shaped the European Middle Ages and our political history thenceforth, is revealing. If we combine what the Roman historian Tacitus (around the year 100) writes on the Germans and what the German bishop Thietmar (around the year 1000) writes on the Slavs, we get the following picture. When a proposal (previously arranged among the influential leaders, as underlined by Tacitus) was submitted to an assembly of warriors, the consent was manifested by banging together swords and shields. Voicing dissent was technically difficult indeed, but if a dissenting warrior was spotted he was duly beaten and, if stubborn, could be drowned in a close-by river (Ruffini, 1927, 38).

What we would consider violence today was then accepted as a device to foster cohesion and reciprocal links within the community. If culture is defined as 'the information affecting phenotype acquired by individuals by imitation and teaching' (Boyd and Richerson, 1985), we can speak of a culture of political consent. That culture sanctions the distinction between the 'right' violence in the pursuing of shared values and the 'wrong' violence jeopardizing those values. After all, it was the moderate Cicero who said that *salus populi suprema lex esto*. The historical enforcement of cohesion has left a durable trace in terms of social conformity, and conformity has always accompanied the respect of legitimate authorities. Its traces are still present today. Apart from popular sayings ('right or wrong, it is my country') and the political relevance of what is called the "raising the flag effect," it is the persistence of that culture that can explain the asymmetric consequence of the 1971 abrogation of compulsory voting in the Netherlands. If we compare the average turnout of 1946–67 to that of 1971–82 general elections, there was a fall of 9 percentage points, a not unexpected result. However, 87 percent of that drop affected the two major political parties (whose cumulated average fell from 54 percent to 46 percent), and the remaining 13 percent the many smaller parties, whose total average fell from 38 percent to 37 percent.

Social conformity is pursued through different devices, since what has changed is more the means than the substance. Today we can have externally imposed conformity or conformity enforced in a decentralized way. At the "macro" level, the imposed conformity of modern totalitarian states leads to attitudes that can be rather precarious in the presence of opposing pressures, as shown by Kuran (1989). Social pressure is stronger when enforced in a decentralized way through the binary interactions described by Wintrobe (1983). Here we have the roots of that democratic despotism feared by Alexis de Tocqueville. For our purposes, it has to be stressed how that asymmetric appreciation of violence is vulnerable to abuse (today as yesterday) by power-holders, especially in the presence of partial or distorted information (remember the famous experiments by Milgram, 1974).

### 3.2   Accepting competing views

The culture of consent explains the historical difficulty of accepting the democratic method of collecting consent in reaching a collective decision or in appointing power-holders. It took centuries of trial and error to find viable compromises between the procedural accommodation of dissent and the uniqueness of the outcome. At some point, in old Iceland the dissenting members of a jury were allowed, *after having voted with the majority,* to state in a formal way that their vote would have been different if the majority had consented to their view. And in the year 1340, the members of the City Council of Vienna were fined when their vote was different from that of the majority (Ruffini, 1927).

Pre-democratic politics recognized sectional interests, and the constitution of the time defined the subjects entitled to representation collectively, so that liberty was not an individual matter but that of the community (identified along territorial, functional, ethnic or religious lines) against outside influence. Inside each community, as well as among different communities with respect to higher political aggregations, the distribution of political power followed 'natural' hierarchies of kinship, clan, wealth or tradition. In the eighteenth century the chief function of the New England town meetings was still not to debate issues, but to confirm the harmony and the consensus reigning in the community by following the agenda and the decisions of the most influential figures (Schudson, 1998).

All that does not exclude the presence of competitive strains within the leadership: it implies only that struggles and bargains had to be internal to avoid any break in the social cohesion. In other words, the quest and maintenance of legitimacy constrained the manifestations of competition among the leaders. Contested elections and counting votes to reach a decision did not represent a spontaneous evolution, and neither did the discovery of rational devices to settle conflicts. On the contrary, they had to overcome attitudes deeply rooted in what was felt as a natural hierarchy of power. The detailed account of the electoral evolution of the British Parliament in the period 1620–80 presented by Kishlansky (1986) shows how the transition was not a smooth one and how the new leaders had to try their best to overcome the respect for the traditional hierarchy of power. Before the Glorious Revolution, the selection of representatives was firmly rooted in the social hierarchy and based on rotas among prominent families, pre-designation of borough officers and the grant of nominations to patrons. Contested elections were not only rare but indicative of a political failure:

"when contests threatened it was the obligation of country magistrates, borough officials, and officers of the state to attempt to compose them. If the communities were divided into factions or disturbed by religious dispute, then their leaders worked even harder to prevent eruptions at parliamentary selection," to bind the participants to each other and to recreate their collective identity. (p. 226)

What occurred during the Civil War

broke apart the identity of interest within the ruling classes . . . [and divisions] arose from the competition within the elite for control of boroughs or the voices

of country freeholders . . . Majoritarianism was not based upon notions of universal suffrage or the rights of man. It was as yet but a tactical development
deployed to cope with the irreconcilable division [since] ... a society which until
recently had defined disagreement as dissidence was now awash in dissident
groups.

It was only after the Restoration that

attention came to be fixed upon parliamentary constituencies, their composition,
their patrons, and their electorate . . . Competition for places in Parliament led to
new sophistication in the process of selection . . . Frequent legal battles helped to
determine franchises. Rules for polling and counting voters were gradually stan-
dardized. (p. 227–8)[3]

Those quotations support the suggested interpretation, and help to
underscore how difficult it is to graft representative democracy on to
the traditional culture of consent.

## 4.  THE RADICALISM OF THE EARLY DEMOCRATIC STAGES

The early British experience helps explain why political extremism is a
feature of many new democracies. If the subtitle of Kishlansky's book
refers to the passage from 'social' to 'political' methods of leaders' selection, an analogous contrast can be read behind the contemporary political vicissitudes of many Third World countries. Thus Hutchful (1993)
speaks of the conflict between 'society politics' and 'state politics' in
Africa, and Coomaraswamy (1993) describes the contrast in South Asia
between the traditional legitimacy of dynastic, religious or tribal nature
and the legitimacy of Western-inspired constitutions. Coomaraswamy
attributes the responsibility of the political conflicts afflicting those
societies to the tension between those two sources of legitimacy. If the
democratic 'taming' of European politics has taken centuries (and with
still yet uncertain success), we can understand why the sanction of
unknown democratic practices comes to de-legitimize time-honored political mechanisms and to drive a wedge between the formal and the much
more extensive 'informal' political sphere (Hutchful, 1993, 218).

If Western democracy has been the historical by-product of the competition for leadership (Galeotti, 2000), the radicalization that is a feature
of many new democracies today can be simply reinterpreted in terms of a
move from A to B in our initial graph. It is indeed a conflict within the
elite, that is, between those legitimized by their relationships with the ex-
colonial powers and the legitimacy of the traditional leaders. When faced

---

[3] However, when the equity based upon majority decisions had replaced the old equity
based upon social standing or magisterial solidarity, contested elections were still viewed
by the Court's party as a challenge to authority.

with such a conflict, people become confused and the presence of different credentials precludes the easy way out of taking sides with the 'legitimate' authorities. When people face a genuine uncertainty because of the gap in their competence and the ensuing difficulty in selecting the best alternative, they tend to follow simple signals and to show inflexible attitudes (Heiner, 1983). Politicians are ready to oblige: in order to capture people's attention and to ignite contrasts, they focus on straight messages inspired from old values and traditional symbols. That explains what can be called the extremism of 'headscarf politics', that is, the apparently naïve battles fought in terms of radical and easy messages (the Turkish controversy on the use in public of the headscarf) or the importance of family names for India's and Sri Lanka's voters (an effect supported by modern media in many other countries). When that occurs after repeated democratic practice, it is not necessarily a negative sign, as it can reveal that people are taking hold of the process and reinterpreting the new methods in terms of their traditional political language. In other words, radical attitudes can be a proof of vitality as democracy is taking popular roots. In this vein, Coomaraswamy (1993) finds that in South Asia Western liberal values undergo a transformation and 'a new genuine legitimacy for liberal values of indigenous constitutionalism' is engendered. If radicalism is a temporary sour fruit of democracy, in due time politics should move back from B to an enlarged A.

But there is always the risk of failure, and of degenerative shifts from B to C. Once people are rallied in terms of simple and radical signals, politicians can become entrapped in their own game and find compromises and political settlements more difficult. If the new legitimacy fails and does not provide reliability and confidence, people can only turn back to the old legitimacy. The alternative scenario, therefore, is the restoration of primordial links. Hutchful (1993) seems to fear that outcome when he observes that traditional institutions arise again and again out of the ashes to which modernization politicians try to consign them. That could include the reversal to more primitive aggregation of an ethnic nature, as happened after the dissolution of Yugoslavia with the appeal to the Serbian identity.

## 5. THE DEMOCRATIC STALEMATE

What we have been describing so far is an early democratic radicalism that can lead either to the bolstering of democracy or to its undermining. We have now to consider two sources of extremism related to the inability of more mature democratic politics to handle controversial issues. We consider in this section the occurrence of decisional deadlocks paving the way to extremist methods of pressure, that is, a move again from A to B

in terms of Figure 7.1. In the following section we deal with the move
from D to C, occurring when politicians manufacture extremism in order
to eliminate 'unpleasant' issues from the political agenda.

John Stuart Mill's notion of representative government and Joseph
Schumpeter's emphasis on responsible government express the two
horns of the democratic dilemma: the representation of different points
of view (citizens' effectiveness) and the capacity of the public action to
respond accordingly (system capacity). Constitutional features affect that
trade-off in different ways. Consider only the impact of decentralization
(discussed at length by Robert Dahl and Edward Tufte a quarter of a
century ago in their 'Size and democracy') and of electoral rules and
party organization. In comparing different voting rules, it has been
noticed that the UK politicians are more willing to take up issues and
fight political battles because they rely on the backing of well-organized
political parties, whilst the U.S. representatives prefer to avoid and to
sidestep divisive issues which may jeopardize their political future
(Newton, 1974). The contrast between representation and responsiveness
has been reinterpreted by Howitt and Wintrobe (1995) when discussing
the conditions that can lead political parties to a rational political inaction. The authors show that in a two-party system a low level of trust in
the political parties can combine with the risk aversion of their leaders to
engender a decisional paralysis where both parties prefer an unsatisfac-
tory and inefficient status quo to the risk of raising a divisive issue that
could favor the other party's policy. Howitt and Wintrobe's analysis
indeed captures a number of real-world situations, but we can ask
whether a political system can at times face a non-convex set of choices.
When the marginal rate of transformation among different solutions
exhibits increasing returns (the marginal loss of position $y$ is greater
than the gain of position $x$), compromises would be technically unavailable and only corner solutions are left. That could be the case not only
with choices of a yes/no nature (the Vietnam War, legislation on abortion) but whenever compromises are politically unfeasible: UK sovereignty in Northern Ireland, the ethnic democracy of Burundi and the
independence of Kosovo are the first examples that come to mind.
Whatever the case – rational political inaction or non-convex sets of
choice – when representative democracy reveals itself unable to cope
with highly divisive issues, direct democracy can make the conflict deeper
since both sides are pushed to adopt stronger and more extremist actions
and reactions.

One merit of democracy is its capacity for devising solutions of compromise and of accommodating different positions by granting each the
features that they consider most important. Yet people learn, and an
environment of systematic mediation can encourage extremist attitudes.

Passionate minorities can take more extremist initial positions and adopt stronger actions for the strategic purpose of getting a more favorable outcome. In such a case, not only will the mediation become more difficult, but those extremist stances and initiatives can acquire their own momentum and slip out of control, thus making compromises unavailable. In the light of that, we can wonder if the decline of political ideologies can encourage the extremism of conflicting interests: after all, the traditional malleable ideologies have always been used tc supply useful *ex post* rationalization of political compromises.

## 6. THE MANUFACTURING OF EXTREMISM

The last case of extremism we consider is that involving subsets of citizens fighting for their political recognition. In the contemporary world, this is the case of many cultural, ethnic or social minorities living in countries on all continents. However, if we view democracy as the institution through which people become empowered, 'that is come to have a degree of control over the apparatus of state and therefore over matters that affect their lives' (Breton and Breton, 1997, 179), what follows should have a more general bearing on interpreting the evolution of the constitutions themselves.

People are never equal in the political field because the relative influence of the various groups is sensitive to the characteristics of the political system (Becker, 1983). In assessing which characteristics bring advantage or disadvantage and to whom, many factors are relevant, directly and indirectly. First, the system of property rights and the social division of labor themselves provide different opportunities to affect other groups' opportunity sets, with significant political impact. Moreover, historical factors (geographical isolation, nomadic traditions, the pride of cultural autonomy, the lack of civic culture and self-organization, and so on) combine with explicit or implicit rules in making some groups politically irrelevant. Among those hidden factors let us only mention the electoral rules and their arrangements in terms of voters' registration, gerrymandering, and the like. Because of those implications, Vanhanen (1987) and Werz (1987) find that the proportional rule would be less discriminating than the first-past-the-post rule in pluralistic societies.

Along the continuum from the 'politically powerful' to the systematic 'losers' (Becker, 1983), we are concerned here with a variety of the latter, the politically irrelevant or *de facto* de-franchised citizen. When those who feel oppressed, deprived or unfairly treated do not 'passively accept their fate' (Midlarsky, 1992), they have first of all to be organized. Since their requests lie outside the constitutionally recognized tract of our abscissa – they are 'extremist' in terms of aims – their requests will interfere with the vested interests of the existing institutions. That observation is obvious, but it is important to understand the political reaction it can lead to and why their leaders resort to extremist instruments of pressure, instead of seeking recognition though ordinary politics. Is the choice of political violence a matter of perverse preferences, steadfast attitudes, or something else? We submit that it is not a matter of preferences, but an outcome obtruded upon them by the 'politically powerful' in the attempt to rouse against them the strong arm of the law thanks to the selective appreciation of violence.

That attempt is carried out exploiting a delicate moment of the process leading to the activation of those new political subjects. We do not discuss the dynamics of group organization as such,[4] but make use of Breton and Breton's (1997) analysis of what they call the 'mechanism of empowerment', reinterpreted in broader terms of political mobilization. Out of the three stylized steps described by the Bretons – acquire group awareness; organize themselves and take action; provoke a political response – we are interested in the passage from the second to the third. This is the phase of radicalization, when the group engages in provocative tactics designed to elicit public attention. Although those tactics fulfill various tasks (they help to solidify supporters and to consolidate leaders' internal power), the signals and information they supply to the external world represent the susceptible point of external exploitation. The standard panoply of political rhetoric (inflammatory speeches, simple and net propositions, strong attitudes) combines with adequate initiatives (pamphlets, demonstrations, rallies, and so on) to attract the attention of the media and to make clear the size and prospects of the challenge to the existing order (McCormik and Owen, 1996). It is the substantial value of their challenge to set the value of the counter-move. When it is a true (and somehow system-organic) minority asking for minor goals, the accommodation is easier, as in the monopoly case of judo-economics (Gelman and Salop, 1983). When the minority is relevant or invests sensitive interests, its mere presence represents a threat, and requests delivered in moderate ways can put the prevailing paradigm at stake. In order to reduce extremist leaders' trade-off, those provided with more opportunities take advantage of the internal dynamic of group organization. By reducing the space for compromises – thanks again to the oversimplification of the terms of the political issue – and by encouraging the radical phase of the group, the latter is compelled either to give up its requests or to resort to extremist methods of pressure: the aims-extremists are

---

[4] With its costs of controlling internal free-riding, use of money- or labor-intensive methods of pressure, role of education and social links, and so on. On the role of leaders within the group, see Salmon (1987).

cornered and can only become means-extremists. It is easy then to build a strong moderate consensus and to exploit the asymmetric appraisal of violence in arranging a more than adequate reaction, and when the methods come to discredit the aims, we have a fabricated extremism. The traditional trick of disqualifying opponents finds here a radical application: to make criminals out of them. In that sense, the resulting manufactured extremism we are dealing with is always a bilateral phenomenon.

There are many contemporary instances where the phase of radicalization came to coincide with a strong reaction of the authorities, and paradoxically the leaders of all colors can at times converge in the attempt to hang their respective supporters together. When by-passing the property rights of indigenous people, that can be the case of the Latin American governments (Brazil, Guatemala, and so on), or of the Algerian military establishment banning the moderate Islamic party who won the 1991 elections. In the case of Sri Lanka, Coomaraswamy (1993, 165) observes that when (in 1978) the Sixth Amendment of the Constitution banned separatist movements, the real effect was to remove the representatives of the troubled Tamil-speaking areas from democratic opposition. Once expelled from the democratic process, their leaders lost democratic accountability and turned to political terrorism.

We have to recognize, however, that the issue of preemptive repression in terms of aims is a delicate point indeed. Perplexity is unavoidable when we see the Turkish Constitutional Court banning the Welfare Party not on the grounds of violence, but on those of aims. But we have to remember how the Nazis' conquest of power was facilitated by allowing them to run in the elections once their undemocratic aims were obvious. After the failure of the Beer Hall Putsch (1924), Hitler decided to make use of the democratic rules, following the plan roughly expressed by Goebbels: 'We become Reichstag deputies in order to paralyze the spirit of Weimar with its own aid. If democracy is so stupid as to pay us our transportation and daily expenses for these 'services' of ours, that is its own affair' (Finn, 1991, 163).

## 7. CONCLUDING REMARKS

This chapter has not considered the extremism of bizarre minorities, but the circumstances in which popularly supported leaders behave in a radical or uncompromising way. Can our distinction between extremism of interests and extremism of methods shake the conventional wisdom maintaining that within democratic settings political wrongs should be righted by vote or by courts, and not by violence? Is political violence always a matter of perverse preferences?

'The possibility of passing from a state of disempowerment to one of empowerment without resorting to violence is a virtue of democratic regimes whose supply side is competitive and responsive' (Breton and Breton, 1997, 190). The lack of competition and of responsiveness, therefore, could explain why the 'bids' from the outsiders of the market of influence (to use the language of Ronald Wintrobe, Chapter 2 in this volume) are not accepted. However, the possibility of preempting awkward interests – by compelling them to adopt extremist methods – leads us to question the relationships between constitutional rules and substantive interests. Those rules are never neutral, not only because they entrench the interests of those writing them, but because they do not work in a vacuum, and are strongly influenced by traditional values and expectations. It is ironic that democratic constitutional rules conceived as rules of inclusion can be used to exclude subsets of citizens from political empowerment. Transforming rules of inclusion into rules of exclusion fulfills the dream of all those benefiting from the status quo when they try to establish a strong correlation in terms of legitimacy between interests and methods. The democratization of political constitutions was achieved by widening the instruments of participation and by the peaceful empowerment of new groups. In that sense, the combination D of Figure 7.1 could be read as the cradle of the democratic evolution.

In terms of democratic politics, we can ask whether political extremism strains the working of democracy or whether it is democracy itself that encourages extremist behaviors. Of the three manifestations of extremism we have examined, the case of decisional deadlocks expresses those limits, but the other two (the transition to new rules and the fabrication of extremism) accompany any constitutional change where leaders' competition involves the people. In that sense, extremist conflicts are more open than other political feuds. Along those lines, it could be further observed that democracy reduces the costs of political participation, thus encouraging the expectations of disempowered minorities and engendering further constitutional evolution. Voting is the canonical way of expressing political opinions and many political actions are concentrated on it (canvassing, parades, political contributions, and so on). The array of political means to voice the intensity of preferences is, however, wider and includes more extreme forms of pressure. Within the prevailing equilibrium of interests, old and new interests need at times more effective avenues to channel their voice. In that sense extremist methods are somehow within the logic of democracy, although straining its working.

A constitutional order reveals its limits when it allows vested interests – opposing any change – to compel any innovation to the combination C. Our analysis would predict that the more conformist a society is, the more uncompromising are the political attitudes and the higher the risk of bilateral extremism. That applies both to authoritarian rulers and to conformist majorities, and in that sense the occurrence of pure extremism is not a democratic oddity but a latent risk present in any polity. The eventual difference between a democratic and undemocratic setting is in the effective ability of the former to learn from its own mistakes, as stressed by Karl Popper.

### REFERENCES

Becker, Gary. 1983. "A theory of competition among pressure groups for political influence," *Quarterly Journal of Economics* **98**, 371–400.
Boyd, Robert and Peter Richerson. 1985. *Culture and the evolutionary process*, The University of Chicago Press.
Breton, Albert. 1996. *Competitive governments: an economic theory of politics and public finance*, Cambridge University Press.
Breton, Albert and Margot Breton. 1997. 'Democracy and empowerment', in A. Breton, G. Galeotti, P. Salmon, and R. Wintrobe, *Understanding democracy: economic and political perspectives*, Cambridge University Press, 176–95.
Coomaraswamy, Radhica. 1993. "Uses and usurpation of constitutional ideology," in Douglas Greenberg, Stanley N. Katz, Melanie Beth Oliviero and Steven C. Wheatley, eds., *Constitutionalism and Democracy: Transitions in the contemporary world*, Oxford University Press, 159–71.
Dahl, Robert and Edward Tufte. 1973. *Size and Democracy*, Stanford University Press.
Finer, Sammy. 1997. *The history of government*, Oxford University Press.
Finn, John E. 1991. *Constitution in crisis: political violence and the rule of law*, Oxford University Press.
Galeotti, Gianluigi. 2000. "Founding fathers vs. rotten kids: a positive approach to constitutional politics," in G. Galeotti, P. Salmon and R. Wintrobe, eds., *Competition and structure: The political economy of collective decisions. Essays in Honor of Albert Breton*, Cambridge University Press, 104–25.
Gelman, Judith and Steven Salop. 1983. "Judo economics: capacity limitations and coupon competition," *Bell Journal of Economics* **14**, 315–25.
Hardin, Russell. 1997. "Democracy on the margin," in A. Breton, G. Galeotti, P. Salmon and R. Wintrobe, eds., *Understanding democracy: economic and political perspectives*, Cambridge University Press, 249–66.
Heiner, Ronald. 1983. "The origins of predictable behavior," *American Economic Review* **73**, 560–95.
Howitt, Peter and Ronald Wintrobe. 1995. "The political economy of inaction," *Journal of Public Economics* **56**, 329–53.
Hutchful, Eboe. 1993. "Reconstructing political space: Militarism and Constitutionalism in Africa," in Douglas Greenberg, Stanley N. Katz, Melanie Beth Oliviero and Steven C. Wheatley, eds., *Constitutionalism and democracy: transitions in the contemporary world*, Oxford University Press, 215–34.

Kishlansky, Mark A. 1986. *Parliamentary selection: social and political choices in early modern England*, Cambridge University Press.

Kuran, Timur. 1989. "Sparks and prairie fires: a theory of unanticipated political revolution," *Public Choice* **61**, 41–74.

McCormick, Gordon and Guillelmo Owen. 1996. "Revolutionary origins and conditional mobilization," *European Journal of Political Economy* **12**, 377–402.

Midlarsky, Manus. 1992. "The origins of democracy in agrarian society," *Journal of Conflict Resolution* **36**, 454–77.

Milgram, S. 1974. *Obedience to authority: an experimental view*, Harper and Row.

Muller, Edward and Erich Weede. 1990. "Cross-national variations in political violence," *Journal of Conflict Resolution* **34**, 624–51.

Newton, K. 1974. "Community decision-makers and community decision-making in England and the United States," in T. N. Clarke, ed., *Comparative Community Politics*, Sage Publications, 55–86.

North, Douglass. 1981. *Structure and change in economic history,* Norton.

Ruffini, Edoardo. 1927. *Il principio maggioritario*, Milano: Adelphi edizioni.

Salmon, Pierre. 1987. "The logic of pressure groups and the structure of the public sector," *European Journal of Political Economy* **3**, 55–86.

Schudson, Michael. 1998. *The good citizen: a history of American civic life*, The Free Press.

Vanhanen, Tatu. 1987. "What kind of electoral system for plural societies? India as an example," in Manfred Holler, ed., *The logic of multiparty systems*, Kluwer Academic Publishers, 303–15.

Werz, Nikolaus. 1987. "Parties and party system in Latin America," in Manfred Holler, ed., *The logic of multiparty systems*, Kluwer Academic Publishers, 223–43.

Wintrobe, Ronald. 1983. "Taxing altruism," *Economic Inquiry* **21**, 255–70.

# 8

# Is Democracy an Antidote to Extremism?

*Harold M. Hochman\**

## 1. INTRODUCTION

While much has been written on political extremes, little is theoretical, in economics or politics. Moreover, notwithstanding appearances, the term "extremism" is far from unambiguous. A conceptual chapter on this subject, *sui generis*, entails brainstorming, and delineation. As "necessity is the mother of invention," so it will be here. Specifically, my charge is to determine what an economist, neoclassically trained, but with a more than passing understanding of the public choice canon, can contribute, *qua* economist, to our understanding of political extremes and political extremism.[1] The discussion focuses, in the main, on the relevance of political extremes to modern democracies, in which they exist on the margins of politics; but the argument extends, as appropriate, to autocratic systems.

The place to begin is by searching out, conceptually, the meanings of these terms, often used loosely as synonyms for many things, sharing but the distaste of the observer. If nothing else, the concepts in question are decidedly relativistic. Neither moderation nor extremism can be assessed, much less judged, as simple rhetoric, absent a suitably defined reference point. To be meaningful they require contextual bounds.[2] After all, what

\* This essay was prepared for a conference of the Villa Colombella Group in Vichy, France, June 27–29, 1998 and a session of the Western Economic Association honoring William A. Niskanen in Lake Tahoe, Nevada the following week. Thanks are due to two of my students at Lafayette College: Ilene Gitelson for an insight that helped me formulate the theory, and Mark Sandford, and to an anonymous referee.
[1] One useful source we unearthed, and a very helpful one at that, was a book by Seymour Martin Lipset and Earl Raab, prepared for the Anti-Defamation League of B'nai Brith, and entitled *The Politics of Unreason: Right-Wing Extremism in America, 1790–1977* (Second Edition, 1978). Unfortunately, this book contains no public choice theorizing as we know it.
[2] For example, in terms of palatability (for me) the "political extremes" discussed in this chapter range from the American third parties that Glazer (Chapter 6 in this volume) writes about to the fringe groups examined in the chapter by Breton and Dalmazzone (Chapter 3 in this volume).

is reason to me may be irresponsibility to you. But this does not take us very far. Fortunately, moral absolutes lurk in the background.

I have chosen, accordingly, to limit my efforts to the clarification of conceptual issues. Happily, this frees me of the obligation to do empirical work. In any case, hard data are scarce here; most of the allusions have an anecdotal quality. While the rhetorical answers, if any, that I produce to my rhetorical questions may seem vague, they do supply some methodological perspective, logical structure as it were, in a context of minimalist theory; and such structure is in any sense prior to positive analysis. The drill is familiar; semantics, at least to begin, embellished by hubris, and nothing fancy or openly judgmental.

Such disclaimers notwithstanding, there is actually quite a bit we can say, from a public choice perspective, about the topic of political extremes. To do so, I plan to divide the discussion, roughly, between statics and dynamics, and begin in the accustomed fashion, with the interpretation of democratic politics, within a bounded polity, in terms of a simple location-theoretic Hotelling continuum. This is the standard representation of Downsian or spatial voting. It arrays policies or platforms from left to right in two-dimensional issue space, ignoring the complex internal reconciliation of differences that goes on within political parties. The median voter calculus or theorem, a direct corollary, holds that the positioning of economic institutions, private or political, will coalesce on the center.

In democracies, collective decisions are made (more or less) by a freely elected government, responding to a voter mandate. The assumption is free political competition, within parties and at the ballot box. (Of course, this may cease to be the case if, in some election, an autocratic extreme prevails.) One effect of competition is to preserve responsiveness. When a government is separate from the population it rules and need not compete in a political marketplace to acquire or conserve power, it is convenient for those in control to define anything that disagrees with the dominant view as extreme. Whether to tolerate or suppress dissent then becomes, as in Wintrobe's dictatorship model (1998), a straightforward matter of perceived benefits and costs, inasmuch as costs of control or repression tend to be lower, generally, the less vital the political competition.[3]

To label a political platform as extreme forces the question: "compared to what?" Platforms of other parties in the same polity? Major parties, or all parties? Small differences, irrelevant in the ebb and flow of American or British politics, may be perceived very

---

[3] Thus, in some sense, the issue is to identify the conditions that blur the distinctions between democracy and dictatorship, making the former more vulnerable.

differently in a monistic state. Moreover, sovereignty is never absolute and nation-states are always constrained, somewhat, by expectations of international repercussions. Whether the extreme is to the left or right of center is indifferent. Theory's virtue is that it is generic and applies all the same, for the Michigan militia, radical vegetarians, or Iranian mullahs.[4]

So it is with these basics that I shall start my minimalist discussion of political extremism. I now turn to what my literary studies colleagues refer to as deconstruction.

## 2. DEMOCRACY'S INTERNAL DEFENSES

I concern myself, primarily but not exclusively, with participatory democracy, and the place of political extremes in democratic polities, impelled by voting, in which political agents, both legislative (representative) and bureaucratic (administrative), owe their status to a process (at some level majoritarian) in which those who are eligible to vote are the ultimate principals. In other words, I deal with governments that are, rather more than less, freely elected. The qualifier "rather more than less" leaves open whether the operative democracy is *thin* – elections conform, formally, with constitutional process; or *thick* – officials are bound as well by a bill of rights, or some universalistic expression of human rights, transcending the time or space in which the results of particular elections control political affairs. Monitoring of performance by political principals can be loose or tight. Voter participation is important, but it can be misleading, at least so far as political competition is concerned; it is readily maximized, through repression, by authoritarian regimes masquerading as democracies.[5]

Even for democracies one must distinguish up front between political extremes, or politically relevant extremes, and the extreme positions of politicians, acting individually or in a group, on particular issues. While the latter can lead to unusual coalitions, as Pierre Salmon's chapter (Chapter 4) points out, they normally have little actual or potential

---

[4] Survey research, vintage 1984, by H. McClosky and D. Chong (University of California at Berkeley), based on public opinion sampling, found that "far-right conservatives and left-wing radicals hold similar views." Unfortunately, I have been unable to track down the study itself, but a precis in Society conveys the gist of its results quite well: [American] extremists, according to McClosky and Chong, "share both authoritarian tendencies and deep feelings of distrust for American government," as well as "intolerance of ambiguity, stark enmity toward political opponents, disdain for human frailty, and paranoid tendencies . . ."

[5] Non-voters, I should note, are never irrelevant. They are simply indifferent, given their priors about the electoral outcome. I suspect that most non-voters in well-functioning democracies, confronting an objectionable extreme with a non-trivial chance (whatever this means) of prevailing, would go to the polls to prevent it.

political import. Thus, personally, a voter (or an elected representative) may think the legislature should require everyone, for nutritional reasons, to consume daily rations of seaweed, or ginseng. Surely this is extreme, not just eccentric; and, as a policy recommendation, albeit a mildly crazy one, it is not without political content, like the simplistic rantings of a latter-day Luddite in the Montana woods. (Beware, I am becoming normative!) But it involves no collective agenda or platform; thus, it is not political extremism; it is devoid of political import. Without co-religionists, in politically meaningful numbers, so that he has votes to bargain – or can, in a less palatable setting, make threats – an individual extremist can lead a cult, even wreak local havoc; but he cannot be a political force.

Political extremism is an artifact of collective choice; it articulates a collective preference, shared by an enfranchised subset of a bounded society. Extreme interests are well described, like all organizations, by enterprise theory. At least nominally, leaders, acting as agents, represent (sometimes hierarchically, sometimes laterally) a rank-and-file, from which they derive their support. The structure is essentially independent of the nominal philosophy of the political cause or the political context in which it is embedded. Moreover, principals and agents – the leaders and the rank-and-file – as in profit-seeking firms, may respond to different imperatives.[6]

Return now to the deceptively simple world of the Downsian model, in which political preferences, whether they relate to single issues or bundled sets of complementary issues, are arrayed, low to high or left to right, along a uni-dimensional Hotelling continuum. Preferentially, extremism corresponds to a platform or policy agenda, enunciated by a cohesive minority of voters or otherwise politically active individuals, that has little foreseeable likelihood of overlap – absent a major institutional shock, like a revolution – with the posture of the median voter. Thus, in straightforward, basically majoritarian democracies, political extremes seem destined to be unsuccessful, absent a crisis capable of transforming voter expectations and preferences. With respect to outcomes they are, in some ultimate sense, irrelevant, and more so the more direct the democracy.[7] Thus, to explain the influence of political extremes in democracy, at least with static analysis, a more complicated theory is required –

---

[6] Obviously, the principal–agent relationship differs along a continuum (not in binary fashion) between democracy and dictatorship. In dictatorship the distinction between principal–agent tends, in the limit, to collapse.

[7] A conversation with Roger Congleton, who has written on the related, but different topic of single-issue politics, has helped me to think through this point. For those who may be interested, see Congleton (1991).

unless, of course, even transitorily, the extremists control the guns. (But this would vitiate the premise of democracy.)

What if, at either limit of the continuum, there are competing extremes? Then, the issue space resembles a family of continua – visually analogous to a handful of spaghetti loosely held together in the middle by a strip of ribbon and fanning out at the ends – that intersect at the center of gravity, represented by the median voter. The effect is to make extremism even harder to accommodate, because it is divided. Competing extremes conjure up the image of non-majoritarian forces, sectarian or "tribal," all in vehement opposition to the parties in power and fighting with each other, often tenaciously, when they are not attacking the centrists. Only when they have a common enemy can such extreme political interests agree on anything; otherwise, they are neutralized by internecine squabbles.[8]

While the median voter model does a poor job of accommodating extreme positions, relative to the norm, when the world is described by a single-issue continuum, and perhaps when there are competing extremes, this is less so under more complicated democratic systems. There are a number of reasons – all familiar.

Of these the crucial consideration is salience. Voter attitudes are typically continuous, not binary, and elementary statistics tells us that the discontinuities fade, even if they are there, as politics aggregates preferences. Particularly in representative democracy, this broadens and deepens the range of possible outcomes, all the more when vote trading is practicable, whatever the rules of aggregation. The result is similar when a large number of parties compete under plurality rule in first-past-the-post elections.

Parliamentary democracy, in which representation is proportional and the distribution of seats corresponds to the distribution of votes in a general election[9], renders extreme positions more viable, the more evenly the centrist parties are split. A familiar case is the continuing domination of domestic politics, at the political margin, by Israel's religious parties. The religious parties (there are competing religious extremes, though the subtle distinctions tend to be lost on most of us) have managed to control the class of outcomes with which they are concerned through an unbroken succession of Labor and Likud governments because they are rela-

---

[8] In non-democratic settings, well described by Wintrobe (1998), the power to repress replaces voting as the equilibration mechanism. A recent paper by Bernholz (1998) contains an excellent discussion of the conditions, both specific and restrictive, which must be met if an extreme ideology is to gain and consolidate secular power. Predominant among these is the perception of a major crisis by a significant part of the population, in particular, by those who control the use of force, the army and/or the police.

[9] General election refers here to the jurisdiction in question, not to the nation in its entirety.

tively indifferent to the secular issues that preoccupy the rest of the Israeli population. Complex voting and weighting procedures – examples are Borda rule and point voting – may have similar effects, diminishing the dominance of median preference.

Pressure to conform, internal or imposed, plays the same role in democracy as in autocratic regimes. For example, the median voter result may break down because party discipline is imperfect. This is analogous, in the limit, to the degradation of majoritarian interests. In the United States it is common at all levels of government because legislative agents (like bureaucratic interests) are at least partially distinct from parent parties; but it is less of a factor, *ceteris paribus*, in parliamentary democracies like the UK, thanks to tradition and tighter pre-screening of candidates by the major parties.

Pluralism is the universal hallmark of Western democracy. Inclusiveness, reflecting the ubiquity of compromise in political markets, within and between parties, functions as the guarantor of political efficiency, both before the expression of voter preferences and after. I interpret efficiency, for any candidate or party, as survival (weakly) or as continuing success (strongly) in primaries and elections. At each step and level of collective decision making, specific or general, logrolling (vote trading) is an essential part of the process.

In contrast, political extremes, whatever their other characteristics and whatever the coalitions on which they are built, tend to simplism. Some extremes, as Lipset and Raab point out, reflect a preservatist backlash against institutional or social change, responding to its threat to established interests. Others, with more romantic appeal for most Western intellectuals, seem preoccupied with injustice, procedural or distributive, or with a belief that existing institutions have thwarted economic and social progress.[10] Whichever, their substantive agendas tend to be narrowly focused and characterized by views that are oversimplified, passionate, inflexible, and readily amplified by rhetoric. They are, then, well-suited to demagoguery.

The effect of all this is that extreme interests are usually unreceptive to compromise and concession, at worst blocking and at best increasing the cost of the political transactions that enable functional democracies to satisfy diverse constituencies. This assures their cohesion, because even minor (as the rest of us see things) deviations from the party line are readily construed as tantamount[11] to defec-

---

[10] I follow, in my interpretations of these concepts and definitions, the usage in Lipset and Raab (1978, Chapter 1).

[11] In this sense political extremes are analogous to cults, as discussed, among others, by Akerlof in "Procrastination and Obedience," his Richard T. Ely Lecture (1991).

tion. However, unless circumstances are conducive to paramilitary action or to controlled terror (more on this later) as a political instrument, it assures that the extreme positions will remain at the fringe – even if, as in Northern Ireland, the *cause* is one that has charismatic appeal and enjoys non-trivial external support in some other Western democracies.[12]

Consequently, when the democratic commitment to pluralism is strong, as it is in countries with heterogeneous electorates and established, competitive two-party political systems that are subordinate to a meaningful constitution, a simplist extreme has a very limited chance of capturing the political hearts of enough constituents to dominate, even transitorily – unless there is something about the dynamics (like the major crises that Bernholz invokes) that tips the scales. In effect, well-functioning democracy is itself the antidote to extremism.

Latent animosities endanger democracy because they deny pluralism, as with the internecine warfare in the independent ethnic states that comprise what we called, to a decade ago, Yugoslavia. Theory counsels that such problems are less likely to be virulent, as opposed to irritating, under two-party than proportional representation, the lower the correlation between ethnic identity and party membership, and the more educated and prosperous the electorate – because, within any polity, such attributes foster attitudinal convergence.[13] Diversity, as in the United States, and a thick form of democracy add to the resistance.

Conceptually, the problem is simple enough. With an educated, politically sophisticated, and diverse community, one which understands and accepts both the benefits of tradeoffs and the costs of failing to make them, pluralism flourishes, making simplistic, uni-dimensional political messages less credible. (Perhaps economic literacy does, after all, yield positive returns.) On the surface, at least, the probability that an extremist position, with very limited (by definition) breadth, can capture the median is invariably low, and pluralism makes it even lower.

Yet, in politics as in biology, randomness is eternal; low probability does not mean zero probability, though our reasoning is often enough guilty of this false step. Politics is decidedly not deterministic. We are all aware of many instances, during our lifetimes, in which extreme political interests have prevailed, reshaping history irreversibly. Democracy may be the best protection against this, but it is not infallible.

---

[12] Take "external" to mean, in this context, "outside the operative political boundaries," what economic statisticians call the "rest of the world."

[13] Historically, however, this reasoning is a bit circular, because pre-existing political institutions are themselves not independent of internal conflicts.

## 3. DYNAMICS

Complexity guarantees that the median voter theorem, read literally, will never prove right; on the other hand, median voter reasoning does ordinarily define the political center of gravity in democracies, at least directionally, so it is never entirely wrong. With stable institutions the likelihood that a political extreme will become dominant is always low, but never nil. Disequilibrium is the norm: attitudes and agendas are in constant flux, and cycling a real possibility. But if the most intractable and inflexible of viable political alternatives is one that demonstrates little respect for constitutional process, a chance exists, however small, of an irreversible mistake.[14]

The corollaries are evident. When the salience of a political extreme exceeds some modest threshold, there is a tendency for most people (loosely, the centrist or median interests) to hope it will be diluted by the logroll, as secular Israelis do for the platforms of the religious parties. There are, of course, cases in which the extreme represents values so abhorrent that majoritarian interests become hell bent on eliminating it. However, Western societies, respecting pluralism, tend to give dissent the benefit of the doubt and display a reluctance, constitutionally mandated, to counter extreme with extreme.

Shifts toward the political center will be greater, the more universal the commitment of the electorate to democratic institutions, and less, the greater the devotion of the extreme interests and their leaders to their nominal cause, or to retaining power within their parochial spheres of influence.[15] Menachem Begin's transformation into a statesman contrasts with the truculence of most communist leaders in the mid-twentieth century, or with Fidel Castro's long-lasting hegemony in Cuba and the failures of transformative leaders in many non-Western nations to commit their nations to pluralism and open political competition.[16]

Now consider, in a stylized way, the behavioral dynamics. One possibility is that the extreme interest, acting (at least from an econ-

---

[14] Absent political extremes, the periodic cycling of control across centrist parties can be seen as a strength, not a weakness, of representative democracy, which acts as a guarantor of compromise and cooperation. Strong democracy is generally characterized by frequent transfers of control. The longest continuous tenure of any party in the United States in the twentieth century was the twenty-year period in which the Democrats, led by Presidents Roosevelt and Truman, controlled the White House, and even this was tempered by Republican control of Congress during part of Truman's presidency.

[15] On the behavior of dictators I defer to Wintrobe (1998).

[16] Remember that it is the local, not global, center of political gravity that is germane to discussion of extremism in a particular polity. Depending on venue, for example, student riots may be interpreted as outright revolution or adolescent dissent, perhaps not the routine rites of spring but only superficially inconsistent with civil propriety.

omist's perspective) rationally, tries to gain control of the polity – more realistically, tries to significantly influence the policy agenda. Whether it is recognized at the time, by leaders or rank-and-file, such influence is accompanied by responsibilities, some of which may conflict with declared ideology. Alternatively, the extreme may withdraw, behaving more like a cult. Embracing narrower horizons, it tries to participate in and win enough skirmishes at the borders of the political system to preserve its identity and sustain the status of its leaders. It is instructive to speculate, sketchily, on how these two scenarios might play out.

The first case is consistent with the belief that in the larger, long-term scheme of things, the relevance of political extremes, despite the sound and fury, is limited. When an extreme is assimilated into a majoritarian position, the consequences are predictable.[17] In general, the extreme will gradually fade away as an independent political force, like third parties in American presidential elections – the States' Rights parties of Strom Thurmond (1948) and George Wallace (1968) and the candidacies of Eugene McCarthy (1968) and Ross Perot (1992 and 1996) – typically in the course of one or two campaigns (see the paper by Amihai Glazer, Chapter 6). Risk of random error notwithstanding, no third party, save Lincoln's Republicans, has ever won a presidential election in the United States, though there have been occasional, but not enduring, successes at the gubernatorial level.

Why, then, given the existence of alternatives, would a rational political leader affiliate with or form a new party rather than working within one of the centrist parties? The reasons vary with electoral institutions and, perhaps more importantly, personality. The romantic explanation is idealism or intense commitment, the prosaic a belief that affiliation with an extreme will lead, in the end, to better political bargains. A less cynical alternative is visceral opposition to something in the majoritarian position (abortion, desegregation, or the Vietnam War, for example). A third explanation, which reflects the distinction, in politics, between principals and agents – whose interests may be quite different – is that affiliation with an extreme provides maverick political leaders with superior opportunities for entrepreneurial gain, monetary or political.

The dynamics of the second case are complex. Presumably, political accommodation is too costly, for either the extreme (leaders? followers?) or the centrist groups, possibly because agendas are rigid and shifts of position, especially if abrupt, will impact on internal credibility. (Of

---

[17] In a state committed to democracy the effects are much like the accommodation of defeated but reputable candidates for a party's presidential nomination in primary elections through minor cabinet appointments.

course, a failure to accommodate in the short run may be part of a strategic ploy, related to optimal timing.) Costs of accommodation to leaders of a political extreme include the potential loss of followers, who are typically less sophisticated in politics, and diminution of ego; neither failed movements nor their leaders can retain serious influence or bargaining power. Maintenance of the status quo, even if desired, may not be an option; in any case, political extremists are likely to be less risk-averse than other politicians. To persevere, it may be incumbent on them to break down the majority's resistance to their agenda, even by extra-legal means.

In these circumstances, terror, always an option, may become tactically active. Terrorist acts, which are extra-political, incorporate violence, often with some randomness to their effects. Their purpose is to attract attention, induce fear, and increase the likelihood of capitulation. What does happen depends, of course, on many things, including the values, personal and communal, of leaders; shortsightedness; frustration levels among followers; and sheer numbers. The next section turns to a brief discussion of this topic.

## 4.  TERRORISM

Political extremes tend to monism. They ignore or suppress complexity and recognize or tolerate little if any ambiguity, reducing the evaluation of social institutions, according to "uniform and fixed standards" (Lipset and Raab, 1978, p. 6), to black and white, or right and wrong. Their romantic appeal to outsiders or fringe participants typically resides in their apparent devotion to a cause – in the minds of its proponents, one that is just, and eliminates the distinction between the private and communal interests of its adherents. In their own minds this sets their supporters apart, morally, from run-of-the-mill moderates, though the romance is less when the motivation is backlash, as opposed to a perception that the established status quo is unjust. Whichever, if the goal is to have an impact on median interests, as opposed to simple self-indulgence, rationality is dubious, and at best tightly bounded.

Among those of us who live our lives with reasonable satisfaction in majoritarian democracies, it is tempting to see individuals who affiliate with political extremes, despite a similar institutional background,[18] as aberrant or different, with preferences that lead to one-sided choices, like hard-core addicts who display a lexicographic preference for an addictive

---

[18] By "similar institutional background" I mean, in a Beckerian sense, essentially the same prices, implicit as well as explicit, and thus the same opportunity costs.

good.[19] Thus, they behave as extreme-seekers, rejecting balanced consumption bundles (interior solutions) and choosing extremes (corner solutions) instead. One way of interpreting this is to attribute it to a pathology, related, for example, to personality, that renders extreme-seekers relatively unresponsive to ordinary changes in relative prices.

But while this is surely the case, at times, for some people who affiliate with political extremes – perhaps to the members of Taliban – it is a mistake to overstate its relevance to political behavior (or, for that matter, to addiction). For example, it is quite plausible to interpret political extremes, at least for leaders, as dominant employment or entrepreneurial opportunities. Here, at least in fairly stable democracies, subsequent credibility requires that the agenda not be too inflexible and that political memories be limited. If leaders are indeed extreme-seekers, with preferences that lead them to prefer corner outcomes, they are virtually certain to be unsuccessful, with regard to their substantive agendas, in normal politics, because such singlemindedness would obviate any real chance of accommodation in a majority coalition. This may make them susceptible to the sponsorship or use of terror as a political instrument.

Committed functionaries typically do not operate under the same constraints, or inhibitions, as leaders; nor are they as sophisticated. To influence political outcomes, it makes sense for leaders to adapt to the median; but this troubles functionaries, who would probably have no real role in a broader coalition and would lose out in the aftermath of accommodation. Their salience is bound up with the continuing visibility of the monistic cause. This renders the most extreme, read naïve, followers vulnerable to serving the cause through terrorism.[20]

In this scenario leaders stand to gain from terrorism in at least two ways. First, not only terrorist acts, but threats, induce fear, making the general population and its agents more susceptible to acquiescence. Second, by offering to rein in and control the terrorists, leaders gain opportunities to act like statesmen. But sooner or later, to have any hope of majority acceptance, they must cut their ties with zealots, or convey a firm impression they have done so, if they seek credibility in international relations. For this among other reasons the history of poli-

---

[19] This can be depicted, as I have argued elsewhere, in terms of ordinary indifference curves – relating preferences for the goals of the political extreme and ordinary economic goods – with concave segments. See Barthold and Hochman (1988) for further discussion of this line of thought.

[20] No movement straps semtex to its rocket scientists, and no genius drives a truck laden with explosives into the garage of New York's World Trade Center.

tical extremism is replete with stories of purges; and it is also characterized by division, at least nominal, between the political and paramilitary
arms of extreme movements.

To conclude this section, recall that electoral endorsement of a
political extreme is not a zero-, but a low-probability event. Thanks
to cycling it is not, other things equal, likely to repeat; more often,
the random error will be reversed in subsequent elections, and it will
find it difficult, perhaps impossible, to anticipate a return to power –
more difficult than a defeated mainstream party. Once elected, a political extreme must, far more than a centrist party, consolidate its position. Thus, quite aside from difficulties of compromise when there are
wide differences in political views, extremes have strong incentives to
engage in repression (as the Nazis did in the aftermath of the Weimar
Republic). An obvious way of doing this is to deny legitimacy to differences of opinion that are a routine part of well-functioning democracy
and to characterize political opponents (or some other scapegoat) as
enemies of the state, or unworthy of representation (the course of action
adopted by the Nazis, the Iranian clerics, and many other extreme
groups that have gained power).

## 5. CONCLUSION

This essay has made but not substantiated many broad claims about
political extremes and their viability. These relate almost entirely to the
standing of extreme political interests in a democracy, to the likely behavior of their leaders and rank-and-file, and to their internal conflicts.
Whether it is correct to argue, as I have, that extremes tend to fade
away as a result of political accommodation remains open to proof;
but the fact is that, in the United States at least, only one third party,
the Republicans, has survived through more than two presidential elections (see Glazer's, Chapter 6 in this volume) and in the twentieth century
no third party has succeeded in national politics.

### REFERENCES

Akerlof, G. 1991. Procrastination and Obedience. *American Economic Review*, **81**,
    May, pp. 1–19.
Barthold, T. A. and Hochman, H. M. 1988. Addiction as Extreme-Seeking.
    *Economic Inquiry*, January, 89–106.
Bernholz, P. Ideology, Sects, State and Totalitarianism: A General Theory. ICER
    Working Paper No. 3/98.
Congleton, R. D. 1991. Information, Special Interests, and Single-Issue Voting.
    *Public Choice*, pp. 39–49.

Lipset, S. E. and Raab, Earl. 1978. *The Politics of Unreason: Right-Wing Extremism in America, 1790–1977* (Second edition). Chicago: The University of Chicago Press.

McClosky, H. and Chong, D. 1984. Study cited in "Social Science and the Citizen: Political Extremists." *Society*, Nov./Dec, p. 2.

Wintrobe, R. 1998. *The Political Economy of Dictatorship*. New York: Cambridge University Press.

# PART III

# EXTREMISM IN NON-DEMOCRATIC SETTINGS

# 9

# The Political Life Cycle of Extremist Organizations

*Mario Ferrero*

## 1. INTRODUCTION

Political extremism is a multi-faceted, perplexing phenomenon. To gain some understanding, a useful first approach is to look at it dispassionately from a positive, as opposed to normative, standpoint: before asking whether extremism is good or bad for society, a preliminary question is whether and why it is good or bad for the extremists themselves. In this vein, this chapter views political extremism as a policy choice that a political organization, given appropriate circumstances, may find rational to make in the pursuit of its self-interested aims. This working definition carries a number of implications that are worth stressing. First, the focus of analysis is not on individuals but on a particular kind of organization which, within the existing institutional framework, pursues political goals, and which will be called a political enterprise. Secondly, extremism is viewed as an observable form of behavior that is instrumental to some ends, not as a personality trait or a description of special individual preferences. Thirdly, no attempt is made at identifying a substantive content of extremism, or classifying policies (or platforms, or goals) into extreme and moderate categories. Rather, a turn to extremism may be thought of as redefining the (vector of) characteristic(s) of political activity in the direction of increasing its disutility to those engaged in it – by making its ends more difficult to achieve, or more distant in time, or by making the effort required more risky or more disagreeable. To put it differently, extremism comes in degrees that can be arranged monotonically on a utility scale: a given policy can only be said to be more, or less, extreme relative to the one the organization endorsed before, not relative to the policy endorsed by some other organization in some other time or place. Thus extremism in this chapter is basically synonymous with radicalization. An important advantage of this "marginalist" approach (which is perhaps the appropriate one for an economist) is that the student of extremism does not have to become entangled in the participants' self-serving definitions and evaluations. Taken together, it is hoped, these three features make it meaningful to speak of political extremism as a rational choice and thus make it possible to bring it fully into the domain of economic analysis.

The history of political thought has a canonical place for extremism in the childhood of socialist movements. In the words of Lenin's (1920) once-famous essay, extremism or, as he called it, "left-wing communism" is an infantile disorder of communism. When revolutionaries are a tiny, lonely group lost in a sea of indifference or collaboration between working-class leadership and the bourgeoisie, they cry out in the wilderness, as it were, and can indulge in extreme, provocative behavior aimed at waking up the sleeping consciousness of the workers. This is an understandable and, up to a point, healthy reaction: extremism, and more specifically anarchism, "was not infrequently a kind of penalty for the opportunist sins of the working-class movement" (Lenin 1920, p. 560). But as the movement grows to maturity and the prospect of conquering and retaining state power draws nearer, then communism has to become responsible and well behaved and, under a correct (read, Leninist) leadership, will in its own best interest steer clear of the symmetric mistakes of opportunism (right-wing deviation) and extremism (left-wing deviation). Infantile behavior no longer serves any useful purpose and naturally dies out. Thus extremism in this view is a child of failure and isolation.

There is no denying that Lenin's view of extremism – however self-serving – captures an important phenomenon that calls for explanation. Had Lenin lived longer, however, he would have had problems in reconciling his theory with observation. To him, as to Marx and Engels before him, the prototype of political extremism was anarchism and anarcho-syndicalism, but its subsequent evolution did not quite fit Lenin's characterization and predictions.[1] Even more importantly,

---

[1] While anarchism was indeed displaced by mainstream socialism and communism in most countries, this did not happen everywhere. Spain was one country where anarchism remained strong and influential, overshadowing well-behaved socialism, and finally had its day during the civil war. But when the anarchists seized their unique opportunity and conquered power in Catalonia in 1936, they turned out to be not all that extreme in their behavior and policies. Sympathetic but dispassionate first-hand observers such as Orwell (1952) and Hobsbawm (1973) report that due to their uncompromising rejection of all authority, coercion, and political centralization, the anarchists found it difficult to get anything done in Barcelona, but for precisely the same reason, they did not force any decisions on anybody who would not voluntarily cooperate. Their policies were so ineffective as to become self-defeating, and in this sense they contributed to the military defeat of the republic at the hands of the fascists; still, extreme ineffectiveness is not the same as extreme policies.

well-behaved mainstream communism itself turned to unprecedented extremes once it got firmly hold of power. The pattern was set in Russia by Lenin himself immediately following the 1917 revolution and then repeated, and greatly magnified, by Stalin since the end of the 1920s, and it was re-enacted time and again, with variations, in China, Cambodia, Cuba, and elsewhere in the communist world (though not in Nicaragua); and, in the opposing camp, it had a counterpart in Nazi Germany (though not in fascist Italy). Well before communism, however, the modern prototype of a victorious revolution that turns against its own men and women in increasingly radical steps was established by the French revolution under Robespierre – the Terror regime. A yet different, dramatic example of a successful revolution turning radical is provided more recently by Iran's Islamic republic. Here extremism is a disorder of adult age: the radicalization of revolutionary regimes shows that extremism may well be a child of success, not of failure – something that Lenin's theory clearly cannot account for. The radicalization of successful revolutions is, then, another major phenomenon that calls for explanation.

How are we to explain the puzzle of a successful political organization that alienates itself from an increasingly large fraction of its allies, its constituents, and even its own senior membership? The suggestion one can gather from conventional wisdom in the West during the Cold War era is that you can never gauge how bad communists (or totalitarians in general) are until and unless they are in full control of things: however reasonable, cooperative, and moderate they may pretend to be all along the road to state power, once power is firmly in their hands they can finally throw the mask and show what they had always been up to, that is, enforcing utopian policies through continuing revolution from above at appalling human costs[2] – the "hidden face" of communism. I find this line of argument unpromising. How can rational people such as moderate allies, "fellow travelers", veteran revolutionaries, and the supportive intelligentsia be fooled over and over again into believing that they will finally be rewarded for their labors when they end up being suppressed, expropriated, and as often as not exterminated each time? The "hidden face" theory of totalitarian regimes implies that participants are not fully rational. If political actors, like economic actors, do form rational expectations, then it must be that the extreme, terrorist outcome of revolutionary regimes is a possibility to be anticipated, not a certainty, so that it may be worthwhile for actors to run

---

[2] A sophisticated, influential version of this view is Lowenthal's (1970) contrast between a utopian urge that shapes communist policies and a development imperative that alone can make them bow to reason. See Ferrero (1994) for an alternative interpretation of revolutionary communist regimes, broadly in line with the approach taken here.

the risk and participate in the revolution. Therefore a basic requirement of a rational theory of extremism is that it should make room for its failure to occur.

To further complicate matters, sometimes a resurgence of extremism is observed as a reaction to decay and failure by aged organizations outpaced by events: for example, some embattled, dying totalitarian regimes or some long-established political organizations that are losing members to more promising ventures. Here extremism is a disorder of old age, a counterintuitive reaction to terminal failure when circumstances would seem to dictate moderation: we shall call it senile extremism. This brand of extremism is clearly inconsistent with either the Leninist or the hidden-face theories.

I will try to bring all three brands of extremism under a unified theory that revolves around a political organization faced with the choice of a platform in a policy options space. To make this choice the organization considers that a more extreme option has two effects. The first is a *productivity effect*: it may broaden or narrow the support it commands among the population at large, or it may increase or decrease the resources at its disposal. The second is a *utility effect*: a more extreme option invariably makes the task, or effort, harder for its members. By balancing out the two effects the organization finds its optimal policy mix, and reacts to exogenous changes by optimally adjusting it – where "optimally" is with respect to the organization's objective as clarified below. It will be shown that infantile extremism is to be expected as we observe an organization groping towards its equilibrium policy mix – that is, it is a growth phenomenon. Mature extremism, on the other hand, turns out to be a rational response to *favorable* environmental changes; that is, it is a comparative statics response when the organization finds it difficult otherwise to adjust optimally to success. Finally, senile extremism may likewise be a rational response to unfavorable changes under some circumstances.

Having cast the issue in terms of organizational choices and reactions, my starting point has to be a theory of the behavior of a political organization, which is sketched out in the next section. Section 3 builds a simple model to determine the degree of extremism as an optimal choice by a political organization and studies its reaction to changes in the politico-economic environment. Finally, Section 4 tries to bridge the gap between the model and the real world of extremist movements and regimes. As the introductory discussion above suggests, a privileged testing ground will be the world of totalitarian politics and revolutions, but the potential for application is very broad, including nationalist and ethnic movements, religious fundamentalism, and environmental groups.

## 2. THE POLITICAL ENTERPRISE AND THE CHOICE OF EXTREMISM

For the purposes of this chapter we will focus on a political organization, or firm, which specializes in the business of selling promises of a more or less extensive and radical reorganization of society, whatever its specific nature. It will often be convenient to refer to such an organization as a revolutionary party, although its "revolution" may well be carried out through democratic means given the appropriate institutions. Whatever the institutional environment, "selling" promises involves exchanging current support from the target population for future, expected benefits, and the time horizon over which the promises will be delivered on is typically a very long one. If and when the goal is achieved, perhaps in a piecemeal fashion, then its benefits accrue to the organization's followers and perhaps to everybody (a public good from the organization's viewpoint), and the organization's members or workers get the reward for their effort in terms of power and the rents and privileges associated with it (a private good). Before that day comes, however, there is no monetary revenue from sales that the organization can use to pay its workers. Selling promises to customers thus entails selling promises to workers as well. Therefore, a first basic feature of this political enterprise is that it is a *volunteer enterprise*. Its members are "volunteers" not because they are unselfish or altruistic; on the contrary they are ordinary, self-interested people who make an investment in labor time, that is, who engage in unpaid effort today in exchange for probabilistic reward tomorrow (Menchik and Weisbrod 1987): their compensation is the present value of the reward the firm promises to pay them in the event of success weighted by the probability of success.

Given the firm's platform or program, increased effort by workers increases popular support and/or command on resources and thereby the expected payoff, that is, the value of the rent from power and/or the probability of success, though presumably at a diminishing rate. There are thus decreasing returns to labor in political production. Also, there is a fixed factor that sets a limit to economies of scale, and this is the unique capabilities of management, or political leadership; thus the size of the firm is in principle well defined. On the other hand, the firm's "product" – its platform, goal, or program – is defined within an ideology or worldview, broadly understood, which structures political discourse and makes this firm's activities intelligible to both customers and fellow producers. But, much as with religions founded on a Book, the "true" interpretation of a given ideology is always debatable: since the ideology is there for everybody to use, that is, it is a common-property asset for political production, someone can always come up and challenge an established firm's interpretation of ideological tenets, that is, set up a competing firm. Since doing this requires only generic, unskilled labor and managerial talent (leadership), and since an unreliable leader's inability to deliver on his promises will show up only *ex post*, it follows that potential entry will be easy, that is, the market for political promises will be very competitive, even if as often as not it will be a competition from quacks.

The cornerstone of the model is the proposition that our volunteer political enterprise will typically take on a specific organizational form: it will be in fact, if not in name, a *producer cooperative*, whose workers, including the manager or leader, share among themselves the whole expected net revenue including the shadow profit, although shares may be very unequal. The argument required to establish this proposition is developed in depth in a companion paper (Ferrero 1999) and will not be repeated here. In a nutshell, full income sharing and direct exertion by the would-be owners/leaders, which together comprise the definition of a producer cooperative or labor-managed firm, appear to be the only available, if imperfect, mechanisms to control opportunism and make efficient exchange possible in an environment, such as a one-time transaction in promises, that seems to be the ideal ground for mutual cheating both between the firm and its workers and between the firm and its customers. Income sharing provides incentives to workers since, due to easy firm entry in the market for this specific kind of political product, dismissal for misconduct is not a penalty, and direct exertion by the leaders gives customers some assurance that they are not being fooled in a "fly-by-night" fashion.[3]

If we accept the proposition that a political firm engaged in long-term operations of the kind described will function like a producer cooperative, then the standard model of the labor-managed firm (LMF) can be readily put to use.[4] As a cooperative, the natural objective of the political firm is to maximize expected net income per capita (a convenient, harmless simplification) under the usual technology and demand constraints. Unlike in a profit-maximizing firm, expected labor income here is not a market parameter (a wage) but an endogenous variable that is deter-

---

[3] Additional devices further to build customer trust and improve worker monitoring and incentives, such as the development of side activities of a short-run nature which yield pecuniary revenue here and now, are usually put in place, but these only supplement the basic cooperative form of organization and will be ignored here for simplicity (for a fuller treatment see Ferrero 1999).

[4] For a good introduction to the labor management model see the survey by Bonin and Putterman (1987) and the literature cited therein. A full analytical treatment is in Ireland and Law (1982).

mined by the firm simultaneously with the employment level. Per capita worker income is maximized at an employment (and therefore output) level at which this income equals the marginal revenue product of labor. This equilibrium condition has several well-known implications, two of which are worth stressing here. First, given different levels of the fixed factor across firms (differences in leadership and organizational skill), worker income will be different across firms. Second, and consequently, marginal revenue product of labor (MRPL) will be different across firms, which implies that the overall allocation of labor among firms will be inefficient. These two features persist in equilibrium because there is no way that low-paid workers can bid entry into higher-paying cooperatives and thereby equalize marginal products. It follows that a competitive political market made up of cooperative firms will be very inefficient. The chief decentralized mechanism available to improve allocative efficiency in a system of LMFs is merger.[5] Since this source of efficiency gains from merger is not exhausted as long as there remain productivity differences across firms, the merger process may be expected to go on until a single firm, or an all-embracing cartel, is reached.[6]

For the remainder of this chapter, it will be assumed that the benefits from complete merger outweigh any transaction costs arising from committee decision making and conflicts within the cartelized leadership so that the monopsony solution obtains. As the political labor market must clear under our assumptions, however, the monopsony will not be allowed to restrict entry and maximize per capita income of its members but will be forced into a free-access equilibrium with a lower level of per capita income. Figure 9.1 plots several per capita income (denoted $y$) and labor supply price[7] (denoted $w$) curves as a function of the labor input

---

[5] If two cooperatives merge at an unchanged level of total employment, their MRPLs are equalized by relocating workers from one firm to the other and total output, and therefore per capita income, increases (though this will normally imply side payments, or inegalitarian income shares, to make the merger profitable to all concerned).

[6] This monopsony outcome – a single dominant party – corresponds closely to observation of political markets specialized in a particular product of the long-term kind considered here; on our interpretation, it arises out of the specific kind of inefficiency in labor allocation that is unique to cooperative market equilibrium.

[7] The political labor supply curve is assumed upward-sloping throughout. A downward-sloping labor supply curve would imply a kind of "old-boys' effect" which triggers participation only when the organization is hard pressed, making it less prone to mature extremism when it succeeds and less in need of a moderate shift when it fails (see Section 3 below). Its programs and policies would thus tend to become fixed and insensitive to outcomes, and the firm would never entirely run out of volunteers and collapse even under the most adverse circumstances. These predictions are at odds with the common observation that political organizations and regimes do change their degree of extremism, sometimes dramatically so, and do die out when especially hard hit.

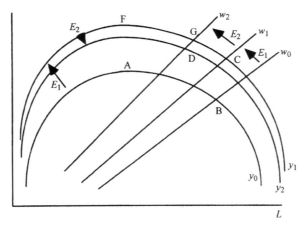

Figure 9.1 Groping toward the optimal degree of extremism ("infantile extremism")

$L$. With a given policy package or program, the monopsony's income-maximizing solution would be at A but the free-access outcome is dictated by labor supply at B.

However, unlike the textbook cooperative whose sole choice variable in the short run is the number of members, our political monopsony can do better than just sitting back at point B: it can manipulate its program or policy mix so as to achieve a superior outcome. As argued above, the empirical specification of the ideology, or of the ultimate goal it involves, is always subject to interpretation; that is, the firm can always redefine its product, or change the package of promises it offers to members and customers alike. Put otherwise, we assume that in this environment the political firm cannot credibly precommit not to change its policy package over time. Let the range of possible policy mixes, or platforms, be ordered by a scalar index $E$ (like "extremism") on the real line: a higher $E$ means a turn to "more" extreme policies. Changing $E$ then implies at once changing the product's characteristics *and* the nature of work or effort. Therefore, changing $E$ has both a utility effect and a productivity effect. The first effect is unambiguous in sign: increasing extremism invariably increases the disutility of effort and therefore reduces labor supply; the labor supply curve shifts upward and to the left. The productivity effect is more complex. If we start from a very moderate platform (a very low $E$), we are in effect telling people that very little can be accomplished by way of political action and therefore we are getting scant support because our potential customers think the outlook is so bleak. Then some degree of radicalization (an increase in $E$ over some range) may prove to people that political action pays and that something can indeed be achieved. If it is so, then over some range increasing extremism broadens the organization's popularity and increases the productivity of political action: the revenue curve shifts upward. Then, beyond some point, further increases in $E$ turn counter-productive and start alienating customers or depleting potential resources, shifting the revenue curve downward. As labor supply always shifts upward as extremism is increased, this insures that, holding all other parameters constant, there will be a unique interior optimum, that is, an equilibrium degree of extremism that defines an optimal size of the political enterprise. That is, as long as there is a finite limit to the extremism customers are willing to accept, there will be an upper bound to the policy choice before the organization's membership shrinks to zero.[8]

In Figure 9.1, suppose that curves $(y_0, w_0)$ correspond to a policy package in which extremism is still productive. Then political radicalization shifts up both curves to $(y_1, w_1)$, crossing at point C. Suppose curve $y_1$ measures the maximum per capita income attainable; that is, the productivity of extremism turns negative beyond the level implied by curve $y_1$. Hence an additional dose of extremism shifts revenue down to $y_2$ and labor supply up to $w_2$, bringing about a new equilibrium at D where per capita income is higher, and membership is lower, than at either the initial free-access position B or the maximum-productivity level of extremism C.[9]

This, then, is Lenin's infantile extremism: it is not really a pathology but a physiological phase in the development of a "young" political enterprise which is groping toward an equilibrium policy mix. Lenin's harsh judgment was thus wrong. Within limits, political radicalization does pay: it scares volunteers away and makes the job harder for those who remain, but their expected reward will be higher because it draws more followers to support the organization's actions. The performance of anarchism in the early stages of European and American working-class movements has already been cited as a case in point. As another instance,

---

[8] For ease of exposition, the argument in the text is structured around a logical sequence by which market competition and collusion occur prior to the policy choice. However, a more realistic description that viewed different platforms (in terms of extremism) as a weapon in the competition and the struggle for cartel leadership would be unlikely materially to affect our results.

[9] Notice that in this example the optimal market-clearing equilibrium D is in the region where the marginal per capita productivities of both labor and extremism are negative. At D, unlike at B, the cooperative fully exploits its monopsony potential by setting both labor and extremism at their income-maximizing levels under the constraint that labor supply must equal demand. If full employment enforced by free access, that is, by merger with all potential entrants, were not a constraint, the monopsony would choose the unconstrained maximum income solution F, where the productive potential of both labor and extremism is just exhausted.

the European student movements of 1968 provide spectacular evidence in support of this hypothesis.[10] Related examples are the idea (popularized by the French writer Debray 1967) of starting guerrilla warfare in Latin American countries from a small "fire" that propagates to an ever-broader "prairie" of peasantry hitherto acquiescent to the status quo, and the idea (forcefully argued out by Fanon 1963) that acts of violent revolt instill self-confidence and self-esteem in humiliated colonized people and so broaden popular participation in the struggle against an hitherto unchallenged colonial power. More generally, nearly a century's history of nation building and national liberation struggles throughout the colonial and dependent world can be interpreted as a case of dramatically successful radicalization of the nationalist struggle, or the takeover of the national cause from the weak, unreliable hands of the national bourgeoisie by a revolutionary, socialist-nationalist leadership, as I have examined in depth elsewhere (Ferrero 1995). Most recently, the chain of events leading up to the Kosovo war of 1999 bears witness to the success so rapidly achieved by the Kosovo Liberation Army in wresting the leadership of the ethnic Albanians' resistance to Serbian domination from the hands of traditional moderate politicians and thrusting the problem sharply into the focus of international attention and great-power interests.

Consider now an established enterprise that has already gone through the pains of growth and found its optimal degree of extremism. How will this enterprise react to changes in market conditions? In general it will not only adjust its level of employment but also reconsider its policy package and adjust its degree of extremism. An improvement in market prospects may be captured in our model by an exogenous income increase, that is, an outward shift of the y curve. In Figure 9.1, starting from equilibrium D, suppose an exogenous shock shifts up the per capita income curve back to $y_1$, with extremism unchanged. Labor supply and employment slide up along curve $w_2$ to point G, the new free-access equilibrium, where the previously set degree of extremism will no longer be optimal. Thus whereas income maximization would call for membership reduction, free access forces increased employment upon the success-

---

[10] Militant groups in the forefront of the demonstrations in Germany, France, and Italy managed to draw huge crowds to the streets and the clashes with the police showed that keeping aside or outside was no longer a viable option for the people concerned. This was made into a theory, among others, by the German student leader Rudi Dutschke (Bergmann et al. 1968): challenging the status quo elicits the state's repression which hits also those who would otherwise be apathetic and draws them into action, which in turn elicits more repression and thereby a broader mobilization, and so on in a spiralling cycle which builds up a political capital for the vanguard to exploit for its own ends.

ful enterprise, thereby diluting away the old boys' dividend from success. However, given the unique nature of political production, the political enterprise can do the trick by changing at once the characteristics of the promises it sells and the effort it asks for, that is, often by turning more radical. Increasing the degree of extremism turns volunteers away from political activity and so labor supply "voluntarily" shrinks: the supply curve shifts leftward from $w_2$ and the income curve downward from $y_1$, bringing about a new equilibrium (not shown in the figure) to the left of G with a higher per capita income and a lower membership than at G.

When such is the optimal choice, then, we have mature extremism, a child of the success that befalls to middle-aged, well-behaved political enterprises. To be concrete, the first and foremost of such successes, in the examples to be examined in Section 4, is the conquest of state power by a revolutionary organization, and mature extremism is then the radicalization of a successful revolution. It is a way of preventing newcomers and latter-hour converts ("opportunists") from sharing in the pie of rewards that success delivers to long-time fighters at last; at the same time, it is a device that solves a cooperative's classic, intractable problem of adjusting a redundant membership downward. Remarkably, the root cause of mature extremism lies in the monopsonistically cooperative nature of the political enterprise and is magnified by free-access market equilibrium, whereas it would have no *raison d'être* if political organizations were classic profit-maximizing firms. However, as the next section will show, mature extremism is a very real possibility but not an unavoidable outcome. The optimal reaction to success could be a turn away from extremism and toward moderation.[11]

To prove these claims, graphical illustration is not sufficient and we have to resort to formal modelling, which is the subject of the next section.

## 3. A MODEL OF OPTIMAL EXTREMISM AND RADICALIZATION

Let $y$ be the net per capita income of the political cooperative's members, which the cooperative seeks to maximize. Production of this income depends on two factors: members' labor $L$ and the degree of extremism $E$, and an exogenous "success" parameter $S$ which describes

---

[11] Thus "fellow travelers," "middle-of-the-roaders," the national bourgeoisie, the progressive intelligentsia, the middle peasantry, and other such figures were in principle right to take their chances and – in many, not all instances – support the communist revolution. Our model of mature extremism thus satisfies the requirement, set forth in the Introduction, that actors in the political market be *ex-ante* rational.

the politico-economic environment. No production is possible without labor while extremism is a cooperating factor. As usual, the technology exhibits diminishing returns to both factors. Each factor's effect on income, however, is nonmonotonic. Holding $L$ constant, increasing $E$ initially increases, but beyond some point begins to decrease, income; that is, at some point $E$ turns from a "good" to a "bad" from the organization's point of view, embodying the infantile extremism hypothesis. Similarly, holding $E$ constant, increasing $L$ initially increases and then begins to decrease per capita income. So there exists a level of employment and a level of extremism, respectively, which maximize income given the other factor. If extremism were not a choice variable (formally, if it were a fixed factor) as in the textbook LMF model, the cooperative would always set its membership at the income-maximizing level, where $\partial y / \partial L = 0$. There is no reason for this to be the case here, however, as maximization is taken over both factors. Thus the organization's objective function is:

$$y = y(L, E, S) \qquad \text{with } \frac{\partial y}{\partial L}, \frac{\partial y}{\partial E} \text{ first} > 0 \text{ then} < 0$$

$$\frac{\partial^2 y}{\partial L^2}, \frac{\partial^2 y}{\partial E^2} < 0; \frac{\partial y}{\partial S} > 0; y(0, E, S) = 0 \tag{1}$$

The organization is constrained by a market-clearing condition. Being a monopsonist, the cooperative faces the whole market supply of political labor, whose supply price $w$ is assumed to be increasing and convex in both $L$ and $E$. The inverse labor supply function is:

$$w = w(L, E) \qquad \text{with } \frac{\partial w}{\partial L}, \frac{\partial w}{\partial E} > 0; \frac{\partial^2 w}{\partial L^2}, \frac{\partial^2 w}{\partial E^2} \geq 0 \tag{2}$$

This formulation captures the disutility effect of extremism, that is, the assumption that increasing $E$, given $L$, invariably makes effort harder to the workers: other things equal, increasing extremism turns workers away from the firm and therefore requires additional compensation. If extremism were not a choice variable, the cooperative would either set employment at the income-maximizing level (unless it was rationed) irrespective of labor supply, as in the textbook model, or, assuming as we do that merger or collusion is always profitable, it would take all applicants in and end up at a free-access equilibrium as dictated by labor supply with a lower income. It can achieve a superior outcome, however, by optimally choosing $E$ together with $L$: a market-clearing equilibrium where per capita income is maximized subject to the condition that income exactly equal the supply price of labor for the chosen levels of extremism and membership.

Then for any given state of the environment (S) the cooperative solves the problem:

$$\max_{L,E} y(L, E, S) \quad \text{subject to} \quad y(L, E, S) = w(L, E) \tag{3}$$

The first-order conditions for this problem yield:

$$\frac{\dfrac{\partial w}{\partial L}}{\dfrac{\partial w}{\partial E}} = \frac{\dfrac{\partial y}{\partial L}}{\dfrac{\partial y}{\partial E}} \tag{4}$$

and

$$y(L, E, S) = w(L, E) \tag{5}$$

Equation (4) says that the factors' marginal supply prices ratio equals their marginal per capita productivities ratio. As the LHS of equation (4) is greater than zero by assumption, this shows that at the equilibrium $\partial y/\partial L$ and $\partial y/\partial E$ must have the same sign, either positive or negative; that is, the levels of both factors must be either below or above the levels that separately maximize income. Which sign will in fact obtain of course depends on how tight the labor supply constraint is. If this constraint is tight enough the cooperative will be forced to settle where both $L$ and $E$ are still productive. If labor supply to the cooperative is plentiful, an equilibrium with "excess" employment and extremism will still be superior to a free-access outcome which, under our hypotheses, would obtain if extremism were not optimally chosen. The two possibilities are illustrated by equilibrium point A in Figures 9.2(a) and (b), where the $w$ and $y$ curves are drawn as a function of $L$. It is easy to see why in equilibrium the two partial derivatives of the objective function must have the same sign. If for example factor levels were such that $\partial y/\partial L < 0$ and $\partial y/\partial E > 0$ (as in the example shown in Figure 9.1 above), it would be profitable to increase extremism, thus shifting up the income curve for all levels of employment and at the same time reducing labor supply and thereby moving backward and up on the new income curve; the advantage of doing so would be fully exploited only when $\partial y/\partial E$ turned negative as well.[12]

---

[12] The second-order conditions (not reported here) indicate that for the solution described by equations (4) and (5) to be a maximum, it must be the case that $(\partial y/\partial E) < (\partial w/\partial E)$ and $(\partial y/\partial L) < (\partial w/\partial L)$ and, if $\partial y//\partial E$ and $\partial y/\partial L$ are negative, that they be not both inordinately large in absolute value. Within these limits, the equilibrium may have $\partial y/\partial E$ and $\partial y/\partial L$ taking on any sign and magnitude.

(a)

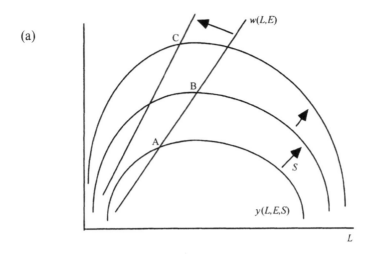

(b)

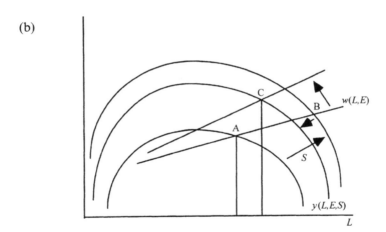

Figure 9.2 The general case: radicalization as optimal response to success ("mature extremism"). (a) Positive returns to extremism; (b) negative returns to extremism

In order formally to address the questions of mature and senile extremism, we want to ascertain how the equilibrium described above is changed by an exogenous shift in the success parameter $S$. For example, if a revolutionary party succeeds in conquering state power (a big increase in $S$), will it react by increasing or decreasing its equilibrium degree of extremism, and concomitantly, its membership level? To answer such questions we must perform a comparative statics analysis of our model by totally differentiating equilibrium conditions (4) and (5) with respect to $S$, $E$, and $L$ and investigating the signs of the total derivatives $dE/dS$ and $dL/dS$. With some simplifying assumptions[13] this exercise reveals, first of all, that $dE/dS$ and $dL/dS$ cannot be both negative: success will not drive the coop to reduce usage of both inputs. Furthermore, either of these derivatives can be negative only if either $\partial y/\partial E$ or $\partial y/\partial L$, respectively, are not just negative but large enough in absolute value (compared to $\partial w/\partial E$ and $\partial w/\partial L$ respectively) as to drive the sign of the total expressions (and provided marginal disutilities of both labor and extremism are strictly increasing).[14]

A very strongly negative value of $\partial y/\partial E$ (but not of $\partial y/\partial L$) implies that at the equilibrium there is a strong "excess" of extremism, which is, however, optimal because workers demand little additional compensation for increased extremism ($\partial w/\partial E$ small); that is, more extreme effort can be bought at little additional cost to the firm whereas additional units of labor are expensive ($\partial w/\partial L$ high). In such a case one would expect that success enables the firm to curtail some of the surplus extremism and substitute additional labor for it. A symmetric situation obtains for a very strongly negative value of $\partial y/\partial L$ (but not of $\partial y/\partial E$).[15] Between these two polar cases, for a broad range of positive or mildly negative equilibrium values of factor productivities, $\partial y/\partial E$ and $\partial y/\partial L$, success will drive the cooperative to increase employment of both factors; therefore $dE/dS > 0$ and $dL/dS > 0$. Of course, the magnitude of these positive reactions to success will be the greater, the larger the value of factor productivities and the larger the factors' marginal disutilities to their suppliers, the workers. Thus if success hits an initial equilibrium where, due to a tight labor supply constraint, marginal productivities are still positive and/or the required wage is steeply increasing in both the amount of labor and the degree of extremism, then the extremist reaction to success will not only be certain to occur but the largest possible in mag-

---

[13] For simplicity we set the second-order cross partials of both the income and the labor supply functions equal to zero, that is, $(\partial^2 y)/(\partial L \partial E) = (\partial^2 y)/(\partial E \partial L) = 0$ and $(\partial^2 w)/(\partial L \partial E) = (\partial^2 w)/(\partial E \partial L) = 0$. Also, for want of a strong intuition to the contrary, we neutrally assume that success has no direct effect on the marginal productivity of extremism, that is $(\partial^2 y)/(\partial E \partial S) = 0$. Mathematical proof of what follows is available from the author upon request.

[14] A countervailing factor would be $(\partial^2 y)/(\partial L \partial S) > 0$ and large enough. This would mean that success by itself has a very strong, direct positive effect on the marginal productivity of political labor, which seems rather implausible.

[15] This implies that the equilibrium features a strong "excess" employment, which is, however, optimal because workers demand little additional compensation for increased units of labor ($\partial w/\partial L$ small) whereas additional extremism is costly to the firm ($\partial w/\partial E$ high). In such a case one would expect the firm to exploit its success to curtail excess employment and increase its degree of extremism.

nitude.[16] We can then summarize our comparative statics results in the following proposition and corollary.

**Proposition 1.** Consider a standard setup in which the direct effect of success on labor's marginal product $[(\partial^2 y)/(\partial L \partial S)]$ is not inordinately large and the labor supply function is strictly convex in both arguments $[(\partial^2 w)/(\partial L^2)$ and $(\partial^2 w)/(\partial E^2) > 0])$. Then we have three cases.

*Case 1*: the general case. $dE/dS > 0$, $dL/dS > 0$ when either (a) $\partial y/\partial E$ and $(\partial y)/(\partial L) > 0$ or (b) $\partial y/\partial E$ and $(\partial y)/(\partial L) < 0$ but small in absolute value and/or $\partial w/\partial E$ and $\partial w/\partial L$ are relatively large.

*Case 2*: surplus extremism. $dE/dS < 0$, $dL/dS > 0$ when $\partial y/\partial E$ and $(\partial y)/(\partial L) < 0$ but $|\partial y/\partial L|$ small and $|\partial y/\partial E|$ large and/or $\partial w/\partial L$ large and $\partial w/\partial E$ small.

*Case 3*: surplus labor. $dE/dS > 0$, $dL/dS < 0$ when $\partial y/\partial E$ and $(\partial y)/(\partial L) < 0$ but $|\partial y/\partial L|$ large and $|\partial y/\partial E|$ small and/or $\partial w/\partial L$ small and $\partial w/\partial E$ large.

**Corollary.** In the standard setup, success will bring political radicalization (the mature extremism syndrome) unless there was a large surplus of extremism to begin with, that is, strongly negative marginal returns to extremism and/or a low marginal disutility of extremism.

The various cases of Proposition 1 are illustrated by Figures 9.2 and 9.3. In each the firm starts at equilibrium point A with an optimal choice of $(L, E)$, then the shock of success $S$ shifts up the revenue curve and, if $E$ is held fixed, brings about a free-access solution at B with "too many" members for those values of $S$ and $E$. Optimal adjustment of extremism upward or downward, through appropriate shifts of the revenue and labor supply curves, achieves in all cases a superior equilibrium at C. The $w(L, E)$ curve shifts to the left as $E$ is increased and vice versa. Figure 9.2 depicts the general case, where radicalization is the optimal response to success. In Figure 9.2(a) (Case 1(a) of Proposition 1) extremism is still productive and its increase shifts up both curves. In

---

[16] One should not be misled by a positive sign of $dL/dS$: it means that membership optimally increases as a response to success compared to the *initial* equilibrium, but it really shrinks compared to what it would have been absent the extremist reaction, that is, in the free-access equilibrium. The case $dL/dS < 0$ is rather extreme as it implies that employment is curtailed below the initial level. The real meaning of our results must be sought in the optimal reaction on extremism, that is, the sign of $dE/dS$.

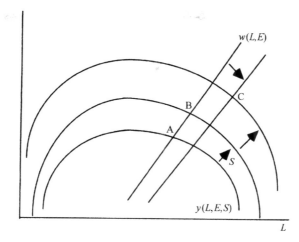

Figure 9.3 The surplus extremism case: moderation as optimal response to success

Figures 9.2(b) and 9.3 extremism's productivity is negative so its change shifts the two curves in opposite directions. Figure 9.2(b) (Case 1(b) of Proposition 1) shows increased extremism to be still profitable, with employment ending up above its initial level but below the free-access level.[17] Figure 9.3 (Case 2 of Proposition 1) shows moderation to be profitable, with employment of course larger than in the free-access position. These outcomes are due to different magnitudes of the curves' shifts in accordance with the different magnitudes of partial effects as specified in each case of Proposition 1.

## 4. SOME EVIDENCE FROM REVOLUTIONARY REGIMES

A number of real-world examples were provided in Section 2 to illustrate the working of infantile extremism. This section is devoted to supply some evidence to substantiate our analysis of the mature extremism syndrome and, as a side product, to illustrate the more infrequent and perplexing phenomenon of senile extremism. The cases surveyed below are all drawn from the multi-faceted world of successful revolutionary politics: our concern will be to see if and when the victorious organization turns extremist upon taking over the government, and with what consequences.

---

[17] Case 3 of Proposition 1 ("surplus labor") would be represented by a figure wholly analogous to Figure 9.2(b) except that point C would be to the left of point A. As it is a limit case (see footnote 16 above), difficult to distinguish empirically from the general case (Case 1), we will not consider it any further in what follows.

The first class of cases includes the successful revolutionary regimes which did not turn extremist, or even turned moderate and conciliatory. Four cases[18] spring readily to mind: the fascist regimes that rose to power in Italy in 1922 and shortly afterwards in Portugal and Spain, the short-lived anarchist regime that ruled over Catalonia from 1936 to 1939, the Sandinista regime that conquered power in Nicaragua in 1979, and the African National Congress that, led by Nelson Mandela, rose to power in post-*apartheid* South Africa. Whatever programs or policies had carried these movements to power, they were not radicalized in the wake of victory; the regimes did not resort to broad revolutionary terror and purges within their ranks, did not suppress their allies, and did not develop the institutions and policies of totalitarianism. As a result, in each case the ruling organization was large and remained relatively open and non-monolithic, enjoying widespread, though selective, popular support until the end and sometimes beyond.[19]

Why did just these regimes eschew the extremist drift? The specific reasons are different in each case but they are all instances of Case 2 of Proposition 1, the surplus extremism case (Figure 9.3), which implies $\partial y/\partial E \ll 0$ (very strongly negative returns to extremism on the margin) and/or a low $\partial w/\partial E$ (low marginal disutility of extremism). In the case of the Catalonian anarchists, it was their perpetual extremism that made mature extremism not worth the while.[20]

The fascist case may be rationalized by thinking of fascism as a form of capital dictatorship. In all three cases fascism was brought to power

---

[18] On the Spanish anarchists see the references cited in footnote 1 above, and in addition Joll (1979) and Hobsbawm (1971). On the fascist regimes see the comprehensive historical account by Payne (1995). On the Sandinista revolution see O'Kane (1991, ch. 8) and Ferrero (1995) for discussion and references. On the South African case see *The Economist*'s survey (1995).

[19] Witness the enduring underground popularity that surrounded the Spanish anarchists through much of the Franco era, the broad acceptance and good recollections of fascism by the Italian people up through the outbreak of World War II, and the excellent showings of the Sandinista front in the free 1990 election in Nicaragua, with a 40 percent vote share, and of the ANC in the South African election of 1994, with a 63 percent share.

[20] See the discussion in note 1 above. The equilibrium level of extremism achieved before the conquest of power – in everyday anarchist practice, as it were – was already very high, and this in turn was because the negative reaction of volunteer supply to increased extremism was (in absolute value) very small over the whole policy range due to the peculiar anarchist device of compensating increased disutility of political labor with total individual freedom of action. A very extremist starting point implies that we are far down the range of negative marginal returns to extremism. These factors together imply that further radicalization once in power would have caused a catastrophic fall in support and resources and a modest reduction in membership, compared to the free-access outcome.

by the great fear of communism. It also answered, especially in Italy, working-class demands for economic security, but in a way that did not threaten the propertied classes. A radicalization of the regime once established would have implied more extensive interference with the market, property rights, and the distribution of wealth, that is, a direct clash with the special interests that lay behind its accession to power and hence a substantial fall in support and resources; at the same time, due to fascism's "socialization" ideology, increased extremism would have driven away only few activists. The barrier to mature extremism here arose from the fact that fascism was a class dictatorship of the "wrong" kind from a totalitarian point of view, supported by property-holders but acted out by little people.

The unique feature that set the Nicaraguan case apart from all other Marxist revolutions was the inordinate degree of concentration of wealth directly in the hands of the Somoza dictatorship: when the dictator and his cronies fled the country, they left behind huge vacant properties for the Sandinistas to seize that put the government in control of about 40 percent of GNP without having to expropriate anybody. With the big property-holders gone, an extremist shift would have pitted the regime upfront against small ownership and the middle class and would therefore have been very damaging to the economy and popular support, while the party's rank-and-file would have resented it very little after long years of clandestine struggle. Unlike most other revolutionaries, the Sandinista regime was blessed at its inception by a bequest of such magnitude as to render mature extremism just too costly.

Finally, in South Africa there were powerful sectors within the ANC pushing for reverse discrimination and retaliatory policies against the whites; but a break with its liberal white allies and the institution of a "black dictatorship," in a country whose financial, physical and human capital was overwhelmingly in whites' hands, would have implied such a catastrophic fall in the regime's available resources as to make the prospect unattractive. Mature extremism was prevented here by the fact that the blacks in South Africa were the "wrong" race to be made the social base of a racial dictatorship: big numbers but no capital resources.

Next we examine the class of revolutionary organizations which did turn extremist after the conquest of power. They all belong in the general Case 1 of Proposition 1 (Figure 9.2), which implies $\partial y/\partial E$ positive or mildly negative and/or $\partial w/\partial E$ high, and their prevalence substantiates the corollary. A good, visible indicator of such a mature extremist drift is the resort to widespread repression, revolutionary terror, and political purges by these regimes, all usually conducted in a campaign-like fashion, that is, by promoting mass mobilization directed from above.[21] These are good indicators of extremism because the "enemies" against whom repression and purges are directed are themselves a product of the regime's policies and a function of its radicalism. Now under many circumstances repression and terror, coupled with tightened central control on resources, have a feedback effect well known to students of totalitarianism: they *increase* the supply of political labor to the regime because by reducing the range of alternative opportunities open to individuals, they increase the cost of remaining outside and put a premium on conformity and opportunism; formally, repression lowers the reservation wage and therefore curve $w(L, E)$ slides downward. Thus there are not just one but two effects of the first extremist shift, in successive stages: first it squeezes out excess membership, as it was meant to, and then it swells it up again by virtue of a *totalitarian reaction*. The latter in turn, if conditions permit, makes room for further radicalization. For this totalitarian reaction to occur three conditions must be met: first, the economic structure must be such as to permit centralized control of responsible positions and managerial jobs for the regime to allocate rewards to loyal supporters; second, selection or self-selection for political office must not be made conditional on prior credentials acquired outside the political realm; third, there must be no alternative course open to the people other than volunteering political service to the regime. If the first condition does not hold, then there is no incentive for the people to offer loyal services to the regime; if the second or the third conditions are not met, then opportunistic entry prompted by the regime's radicalization is foreclosed or unnecessary. The Jacobin dictatorship, to be examined below, is one example in which the first condition was not satisfied, whereas Iran's Islamic republic and Cuba's communist regime are two examples which do not satisfy the second and third conditions respectively. In all these cases the totalitarian reaction of labor supply to extremism did not materialize.

The Iranian revolution[22] clearly turned extremist after victory, even though, like the Sandinistas, it was blessed by the bequest of the huge fortunes left behind by the fleeing Shah, amounting to 20 percent of total assets of all private firms in the country. However, after the first wave of repression and purges, the regime did not continue to escalate

---

[21] On revolutionary dictatorships and totalitarian regimes the classic works are Arendt (1973) and Friedrich and Brzezinski (1965). For a political economist's approach, and especially for analysis of the relationship between repression, terror, and loyalty, see Wintrobe (1998). See also the recent works by O'Kane (1991, 1996) on revolutionary terror and terrorist regimes, which also provide a useful selection of case studies.

[22] O'Kane (1991, ch. 11) is a useful compendium of information on the Iranian regime.

radicalization and terror but, despite continued infighting within the ruling elite, seemed to settle into a fairly stable pattern of policies and institutions. A key to understanding both features is suggested by the religious nature of the regime's extremism. On the one hand, this offers an avenue to redistribution other than encroaching on private property rights, that is, charitable giving ordained by the faith and managed by the clergy, something that was not available to the Sandinistas. On the other hand, in a theocratic polity political service may not be offered directly to the regime but must first pass through the bottleneck of religious service, which prevents the totalitarian reaction of political labor supply to extremism. This rules out one powerful motive for further radicalization, as typically observed in the totalitarian regimes to be examined below.

The Cuban revolution[23] underwent dramatic radicalization after 1959, rapidly turning the country into a Soviet-type system and stamping out any social or political unrest aroused in the process. However, in contrast to communist precedents, mature extremism did not trigger further radicalization and successive waves of revolution and purges: by the end of the 1960s the regime had settled into a pattern of institutions and policies that have remained more or less unchanged to this day, and the party has remained a comparatively broad, participatory organization. Why? An answer is suggested by the special technique employed by the Cubans to dispose of undesirable or uncooperative people: instead of being deported to labor camps as in the Soviet Union or to the countryside to undergo reeducation as in China, or of being exterminated as in Nazi Germany, they were let free to leave for the United States and indeed shown to the door. This implies that political service to the party was, to a degree, optional rather than compulsory, undermining the basis for a totalitarian reaction and thus avoiding the need for further extremist shifts.

Classic communist regimes and Nazi Germany comprise the range of cases in which the above-stated conditions were all fulfilled and the totalitarian reaction did occur. These regimes had mixed feelings toward the totalitarian reaction: on the one hand the latter was evidence that their radical policies were effective in curbing opposition and removing potential competitors for the regime's monopoly of power, on the other hand the increased labor supply diluted per capita incomes and brought back the problem which the extremist shift was intended to address in the first place. Then a second extremist shift could be a rational response to the

---

[23] On the Cuban regime see the discussion in Ferrero (1994, 1995) and the references cited therein.

totalitarian reaction to the first shift.[24] In turn if this second shift had a substantial negative impact on resources and popularity, it might temporarily be relaxed and give in to a period of moderation and recovery until the stage was set for the next wave of attack; if, on the other hand, the effect of the second shift on productivity was negligible or even positive, then no alternate phases of "advance" and "consolidation" were needed and the regime could continue on its course of ever-increasing radicalization till the end.

The Soviet Union up to the Khruschev era and communist China at least up to the end of the Maoist period[25] are the prototype cases in which successive "revolutions from above" alternated with periods of liberalization and recovery. Starting without any substantial bequest from heaven, as in Nicaragua, these regimes had to turn at once to confiscation and collectivization, thus parting company with their previous "fellow travelers" and setting up the "dictatorship of the proletariat;" the negative reaction of political labor supply to the extremist shift was magnified by foreclosing any avenues of escape, Cuban-style, which made them more perfected totalitarian systems. For the same reason, as the totalitarian reaction, that is, the opportunistic flocking to the regime's service, developed, it was profitable to effect a second extremist shift. Since each time the economy and the bureaucracy were disrupted by the new outburst of "class struggle" (as if by a fall in $S$ in our model), a moderate turn was ushered in to let them recover, again with mixed effects on political labor supply (moderation first increases labor supply then, by relaxing totalitarian control, it decreases it), until the regime was ready for the next turn of the screw. This wavelike pattern of radicalization and moderation is, from our perspective, entirely due to the fact that each successive extremist shift was both profitable in the short run and damaging in the longer run as it curtailed resources and support to the regime.[26]

---

[24] It is a straightforward exercise to show that the optimal response of the political organization to the totalitarian reaction, that is, to the induced increase in labor supply, is entirely analogous to its response to success, under the same conditions as spelled out in Proposition 1. As with the first extremist shift in response to success, also the second shift in response to the totalitarian reaction will be more likely to be profitable if it has a positive, or a small negative effect on productivity and a relatively large effect on labor supply.

[25] The literature here is of course enormous. For a guide to selected references and discussion see Ferrero (1994) and, on the Soviet Union, the works cited in note 21 above.

[26] Remarkably, in both the Soviet Union and China the last moderate turn was the re-enfranchisement of the victims of terror (the Gulag's surviving inmates and the victims of the Cultural Revolution), a move that prompted the purging of the Stalinists and the Maoists respectively to make room for the newcomers, giving the regimes, under Khruschev and Deng Xiao Ping respectively, some more steam to carry on. Such an opportunity for horse-switching would not be available to the Cubans, who practiced the exit option, or to the Nazis, who practiced the extermination option to dispose of their victims.

As a contrast, consider Nazi Germany, perhaps the paragon of the totalitarian syndrome.[27] Unlike the communist dictatorships, the Nazi regime turned extremist right after 1933 and followed a steady course of continuing radicalization until the end, without any temporary relaxation, so much so that the impending military defeat was apparently not perceived as such until the very last months of the war, by which time no amount of moderation could save the regime. Nazism was many things at once, including aspects of the fascist regimes discussed above, but unlike them it was above all a racial dictatorship, and unlike the South African ANC, its race base was the "right" one from a totalitarian point of view. Now as radicalization centered on stepping up the policies of cleansing the German nation and the whole world of inferior races, this did little damage to the economy and indeed provided for cheap slave labor to boost the profits of German businesses and to support the war effort. Thus the totalitarian reaction of "volunteer" labor supply to the regime could be met with continuing escalation of these policies. Whereas the radicalization of class struggle under communism directly impinged on ownership rights and work incentives and thus necessitated breaks, the radicalization of race struggle could proceed uninterrupted to the verge of final collapse.

Another regime which, in its own terms, went to historically unmatched extremes is the Pol Pot regime[28] in Cambodia, 1975–79. Seen in historical perspective, the Khmer Rouge played out basically the same policy ingredients as the Soviets and the Chinese had before; what is unique to their regime is that they managed to go so far so fast, as evidenced by the appalling human toll, without lapses or retreats. The key to this frenzy was probably a level of agricultural productivity so abysmally low at takeover (because of the devastation of war) that extremism could not do much harm provided the human cost was not counted in: forced labor in the rice fields and irrigation projects could for the time being extract additional resources for the regime to use as long as skill and output quality were unimportant and one did not mind executing or starving to death over 20 percent of the population in three years. The totalitarian reaction undoubtedly ensued, with new recruits, especially very young boys, rushing to volunteer for political service, and it was met with sweeping purges in the party and the military, ever more radical collectivization of all facets of life, and increased armed confrontation

---

[27] The interpretation offered in the text is based on Burleigh and Wippermann (1991). See also the discussion and information contained in the works cited in note 21 above.

[28] The best selection I could make of the scanty scholarly literature that exists on the Pol Pot regime includes Etcheson (1984), Jackson (1989), and Kiernan (1996). See also the discussion in O'Kane (1996).

at the borders up until the regime's overthrow at the hands of the Vietnamese in early 1979. Thereafter Pol Pot retreated to the jungle with a substantial following of young guerrillas who were able to engage the new government's forces for years to come, which suggests that had it not been overturned, the regime could have held on for many more years.

As will be recalled, the extremist shift in response to success as well as in response to the totalitarian reaction will not only be certain to occur but the largest possible in magnitude when it has a positive effect on productivity. Thus the enormity and steadfastness of extremism in the Nazi and Cambodian episodes are explained by the fact that these regimes, unlike the Soviet and the Chinese, started out and remained through their life in the range of positive returns to extremism; that is, they belong in Case 1(a) of Proposition 1 (Figure 9.2(a)) whereas the Soviet and the Chinese belong in Case 1(b) (Figure 9.2(b)). Recall that here extremism had not been pushed further up because of the labor supply constraint. If now the revenue curve shifts outward, the participation constraint is relaxed and the firm can afford to increase extremism because it is productive. This picture seems to fit the case of a political organization that labors under especially adverse circumstances, and that is blessed with a sudden, unexpected strike of luck: then it can draw on an unexploited "reserve" of extremism to its advantage. Thus revolutionaries who succeed in a conquest of power that appeared most unlikely beforehand are particularly prone to large doses of extremism, and therefore are not likely to find allies and fellow travelers along the way because these people rationally expect the revolutionaries soon to turn against them and their policies to be very harsh indeed. This characterization seems to accord well with the meteoric rise to power of Adolf Hitler and with the strange case of Cambodia's Khmer Rouge, a lonely, hard-fighting group whose unexpected victory in 1975 was entirely due to the fall of the American-backed regime in nearby Vietnam.

Another famously extreme regime – indeed, the archetypal example of radicalization of a successful revolution – was the Jacobin dictatorship in the French revolution.[29] It may be likened to Pol Pot's in that, although the Jacobins accomplished no more and no less than the other "bourgeois" revolutions before and after, they did it with an amazing speed and ruthlessness. Unlike Hitler's and Pol Pot's, however, the Jacobin regime eventually collapsed because it thinned out its own ranks to the point of running out of militant volunteers at the crucial juncture. Our model suggests that the first feature may be due to continuing positive returns

---

[29] On the French revolution and the Jacobin terror the literature is again unmanageably large. For useful overviews from the point of view adopted in this chapter see O'Kane (1991, ch. 4) and Skocpol (1979).

to extremism (Case 1(a) again), under not just one but a whole chain of exogenous successes, while the second is evidence of the absence of a totalitarian reaction to extremism. Indeed, the whole course of the French revolution could be retold as the story of a young, broad, fairly amorphous coalition which suddenly found itself in control of the state at a very moderate starting point; as events unfolded, experience showed that further radicalization continued to pay back and consolidate the revolutionaries' hold on power. On the other hand, the absence of the totalitarian reaction means the absence of a countervailing force to the drift toward an extremist corner that the escalation of extremism, in response to each new round of political success, necessarily entails.[30] Thus the totalitarian reaction helped Pol Pot and Hitler to end up at an interior solution, whereas its absence pushed Robespierre toward a left-hand corner where his political organization shrank to such a tiny size as to finally collapse.

If success often brings political radicalization, one should think that hardships and failures symmetrically bring moderation. Along these lines one could perhaps rationalize the onset of economic reforms in China, Vietnam, and the Soviet Union under Gorbachev. Sometimes, however, we observe radicalization as a response to strain, and in particular, radicalization by dying or doomed political regimes – what we have called senile extremism.

Two current instances may be North Korea and Cuba in the 1990s, which reacted to the disintegration of the communist bloc, with the ensuing drying up of Soviet or Chinese aid and trade, by tightening ranks and remaining basically unreformed. As the situation of those regimes is precarious at the time of this writing, we will single out as an illustration

---

[30] The French revolution's radicalization consisted essentially of defending its democratic achievements against counterrevolution from within and without. In turn, successfully waging a series of civil and foreign wars required squeezing supplies and conscripts out of a reluctant countryside to feed the cities and the armies. Given the economic structure of the time, this did not, and could not, involve central control of production but simply requisitioning and commandeering private producers and traders, military style. At least for the time being, and for the purpose at hand, this technique worked and proved capable of broadening and strengthening the Jacobins' power base, while the terror (they invented the word!) struck at ever-closer rings of associates. But then just as victory on all fronts had been achieved and the revolutionary dictatorship seemed secure, Robespierre and his friends suddenly found themselves alone, were swiftly overthrown and brought to the guillotine without leaving behind any significant trace. A case of bad miscalculation? Maybe, but our approach suggests a different rationale: Robespierre's fatal weakness lay in instituting terror without totalitarianism. The absence of centralized control of the economy meant that the Jacobins had it the easy way, but it also meant that the totalitarian reaction of labor supply to each successive dose of extremism did not take place.

of senile extremism the Republic of Salò, a renewed fascist regime set up by the German army in North-Central Italy in September 1943, which was, however, already doomed at birth because war prospects were hopeless by then.[31] Instead of yielding to moderation and compromise, Salò reacted to failure by steadily radicalizing its policies till the end. Why? In our model this can only happen when returns to extremism are very strongly negative at the margin ($\partial y/\partial E \ll 0$), that is, in Case 2 of Proposition 1: here success brings moderation (see the non-extremist regimes discussed above) and conversely, failure brings radicalization and reduces optimal membership. Therefore, the Salò case may be rationalized as a fascist version of our model working backward: as in a capitalist dictatorship marginal returns to extremism are strongly negative to begin with, success dictates moderation as in the 1920s whereas failure dictates radicalization as in the 1940s. Being widely regarded as a puppet of the Nazis, the regime had to face widespread desertion from the previous fascist party and an acute shortage of volunteers, but for the very same reason a broad application of mobilization, coercion and terror turned out to be productive and increase available resources per capita at least in the short run (which was the regime's horizon anyway) because membership contracted more than total income. Furthermore, the negative shock was repeated (in terms of the model, $S$ fell continuously): the military defeat only went from bad to worse until the end. To this the regime responded by continued radicalization because there existed no totalitarian reaction to set a limit to the extremist drive under duress, as opting out, or even joining the anti-fascist partisans on the mountains, was a real possibility. And so it went on to meet its fate in less than two agonizing years.

However, a regime that keeps escalating extremism and shrinking its membership faces the threat of Robespierre's dreadful outcome, that is, a drift to a left-hand corner where the organization shrinks to extinction. To ward off this threat the Salò regime employed a technique of last resort: it successfully targeted propaganda and recruitment to the youth, and indeed the main force that came forward to the regime's support were not veterans but young, untested new volunteers. Our model can accommodate this observation by noting that the young have a lower reservation wage than the general population as far as political labor supply is concerned: when, other than in the final days of a totalitarian regime, may a teenager hope to become a small but powerful political boss? He may well undertake a successful political career after the regime's downfall, but *by then* he will no longer be a teenager. This implies that his best alternative

---

[31] The fullest treatment in English is Deakin (1966).

opportunities rank very low compared to political activism here and now. Shifting recruitment toward the young is tantamount to a parametric fall in the reservation wage which increases labor supply, thereby giving the regime more room to satisfy the labor supply constraint while pushing extremism to the utmost – a policy that obviously made sense only in the direst straits.

Salò, then, is the paragon of senile extremism: a sinister story in which, paradoxically enough, the regime buys time by allowing ever more extreme policies to be pushed forward by militant youngsters as the catastrophe draws nearer. For *them*, however, it is just the rational thing to do.

## 5. CONCLUSION

By making the political enterprise and its policy choice the center of analysis, this chapter has tried to make sense of the different facets of extremist political behavior in the real world. Its main contribution has been to show that because a political firm engaged in long-term operation may be meaningfully interpreted as a form of producer cooperative, its tendency to curtail its membership when faced with an increase in revenue provides a mechanism that explains the otherwise puzzling phenomenon of mature extremism, that is, the extremist reaction to political success such as the conquest of power. While such an explanation stands or falls with the appropriateness of the labor-managed firm model to describe the working of a political organization, the comparative statics predictions generated by the model have been tested on a broad sample of cases of revolutionary regimes. While doing justice to the complexity of each historical case is obviously beyond the scope of this chapter, it turns out that despite its high level of abstraction, our model fits reasonably well the broad comparative picture of radicalization (or lack of it) in these regimes, and is therefore a promising starting point for further study.

### REFERENCES

Arendt, H. 1973. *The origins of totalitarianism*, Harcourt Brace, New York.

Bergmann, U. et al. 1968. *Die Rebellion der Studenten oder Die neue Opposition*, Rowohlt, Hamburg.

Bonin, J. and L. Putterman. 1987. *Economics of cooperation and the labor-managed economy*, New York.

Burleigh, M. and W. Wippermann. 1991. *The racial state: Germany 1933–1945*, Cambridge University Press, Cambridge.

Deakin, F. 1966. *The six hundred days of Mussolini*, Anchor Books, Garden City (NY).

Debray, R. 1967. *Revolution in the revolution? Armed struggle and political struggle in Latin America*, Monthly Review Press, New York.

*The Economist.* 1995. A survey of South Africa, vol. 335, May 20.

Etcheson, C. 1984. *The rise and demise of Democratic Kampuchea*, Westview Press, Boulder.

Fanon, F. 1963. *The wretched of the earth*, Grove Press, New York.

Ferrero, M. 1994. "Bureaucrats versus Red Guards: A politico-economic model of the stability of communist regimes," in R. W. Campbell, ed., *The postcommunist economic transformation. Essays in honor of Gregory Grossman*, Westview Press, Boulder, 281–316.

Ferrero, M. 1995. The economics of socialist nationalism: Evidence and theory, in A. Breton et al., eds., *Nationalism and rationality*, Cambridge University Press, Cambridge.

Ferrero, M. 1999. A model of the political enterprise, Working Paper no. 9, Department of Public Policy and Public Choice (POLIS), University of Eastern Piedmont.

Friedrich, C. and Z. Brzezinski. 1965. *Totalitarian dictatorship and autocracy*, Harvard University Press, Cambridge (Mass).

Hobsbawm, E. 1971. "The Andalusian anarchists," in *Primitive rebels*, Manchester University Press, Manchester, 74–92.

Hobsbawm, E. 1973. "The Spanish background" and "Reflections on anarchism," in *Revolutionaries*, Pantheon Books, New York, 71–81 and 82–91.

Ireland, N. and P. Law. 1982. *The economics of labor-managed enterprises*, St. Martin's Press, New York.

Jackson, K. 1989. *Cambodia 1975–1978: Rendezvous with death*, Princeton University Press, Princeton.

Joll, J. 1979. *The anarchists*, Methuen, London.

Kiernan, B. 1996. *The Pol Pot regime*, Yale University Press, New Haven.

Lenin, V. I. 1920. " 'Left-wing' communism, an infantile disorder," in R. C. Tucker, ed., *The Lenin anthology*, Norton & Co., New York 1975, 550–618.

Lowenthal, R. 1970. "Development vs. utopia in communist policy," in C. Johnson, ed., *Change in communist systems*, Stanford University Press, Stanford, 33–116.

Menchik, P. and B. Weisbrod. 1987. "Volunteer labor supply," *Journal of Public Economics*, 32, 159–83.

O'Kane, R. 1991. *The revolutionary reign of terror: The role of violence in political change*, Edward Elgar, Aldershot.

O'Kane, R. 1996. *Terror, force and states*, Edward Elgar, Cheltenham.

Orwell, G. 1952. *Homage to Catalonia*, Harcourt Brace, New York.

Payne, S., 1995, *A history of fascism, 1914–1945*, University of Wisconsin Press, Madison.

Skocpol, T. 1979. *States and social revolutions: A comparative analysis of France, Russia and China*, Cambridge University Press, New York.

Wintrobe, R. 1998. *The political economy of dictatorship*, Cambridge University Press, Cambridge.

# 10

# Rationally Violent Tactics: Evidence from Modern Islamic Fundamentalism

*Luisa Giuriato and Maria Cristina Molinari*

## 1. INTRODUCTION

The "clash of civilization" is one of the most recent intellectual ghosts haunting the imagination of Western peoples. The expression has been coined by the political scientist Samuel Huntington (1993), who sees the impending danger of a world conflict in the clash of two opposing cultures, the Western and the Islamic. Evidence for this theory is found in the increasing consensus that accompanies the Islam-inspired political movements that have spread in the Arab–Islamic countries since the 1970s. These movements are named "Islamic fundamentalism," a synonym for fanaticism, intolerance, and extremism (Mimouni 1996). Islamic fundamentalism is thus considered an atemporal phenomenon, devoid of historical, social or economic context, with a single illiberal, dangerous face: this deforming lens is today the common key of interpretation of the Arab–Islamic world.[1]

The stereotype of Islamic fundamentalism[2] prevents us from recognizing, instead, a definite historical phenomenon, born in Egypt in 1928 with the first modern Islamist movement, the Muslim Brotherhood, which was characterized by the rigorous respect for the Koran law and by anti-colonialism. The movement's founder, Hasan al-Banna, said in 1939:

---

[1] There are more than 935 million Muslims in the world: of these, 612 million live in Asia (of whom about 200 million in the Middle East, including 50 million Turks and 52 million Iranians) and 265 million in Africa. For reasons of numerical importance, therefore, it is not correct to identify Islam with the situation of the Arabs in the Middle East nor of the Palestinians in Israel.

[2] Fundamentalism and integralism are often used as synonyms, but they indicate different phenomena. Both refuse any change to their traditional religious forms, but integralism refers to a radicalization inside Catholicism, based on the official doctrine of the Church and on the ecclesiastical hierarchy. Fundamentalism, on the other hand, has as its main characteristic the reference to a holy text which is considered infallible and inaccessible by critical interpretation.

We, the Muslim Brothers, believe that the laws of Islam and its universal teachings integrate everything that concerns the human being in this world and in the
future one; on the contrary, those who believe that these teachings concern only
the religious and spiritual sphere, are mistaken. Islam is faith and worship,
country and citizenship, religion and State, spirituality and action, Book and
sword.[3]

In 1948 the movement was charged with anti-government demonstrations and closed; its leaders were exiled and took refuge in the Maghreb
countries, Syria and Jordan, where the movement was welcomed with
enthusiasm. The reasons for its rapid spread stemmed from the complex situation of the Arab–Islamic countries after the colonial period,
when the new national governments introduced Western (capitalist or
socialist) programs of social and economic modernization that margin-
alized the Muslim culture, divested it of its ancient primacy, excluded
it from the public sphere and banished it to the area of worship and
private morals. In Section 2 we shall analyze how these lacerations in
the identity of the Muslim countries, together with the political
mistakes, the anti-democratic repression, the economic crisis and
the foreign influence, explains the success of the fundamental
re-Islamization projects.

In these projects, politics is of essential importance, as fundamentalism
aims at the recovery of the preeminence of religious laws over the human
positive laws and questions the bases of the State through the examination of the ethical ties and of the ultimate foundations of society. Its
conclusion is that the political community that takes form in the State
must be grounded on a pact of religious brotherhood (Pace and Guolo
1998). In the expression of its political projects, fundamentalism shows a
radical character. This radicalism has many sources: according to the
different interpretations, it stems from the utopia of the ethical State
(Choueiri 1990, Guolo 1994a, Roy 1992), or from the reaction to modernity, or from the attempt to "avenge" religion against the laicism of the
State (Kepel 1991). However, radicalism and political confrontation with
the governments are not sufficient conditions for Islamist movements to
choose violence. Here, what Hardin says about conflicts of interest
applies: "norms of difference and exclusion can establish in and out
groups and thereby ground a conflict of interest between the groups.
Having a conflict of interest is not, however, sufficient for producing
violence".[4] Thus, we distinguish radicalism and extremism and say that
the passage from the first to the second is not direct and unavoidable: the
outbreak of violence and extremism which, in some countries (Algeria

---

[3] Quoted in Pace and Guolo (1998), p. 134 (our translation).
[4] Hardin (1995), p. 142.

and Egypt in particular) has accompanied the rise of Islamic fundamentalism, is more a product of political circumstances than an inevitable consequence of the Islamic revival and of its attempt to implement a religious ideal (Jabri 1994, Burgat 1996).

Extremism is, indeed, a strategy of political struggle that is sometimes adopted when democratic confrontation, dialogue, or compromise are deemed impossible or useless.[5] In this sense, extremism is not a special feature of some particular country, group or party: in the twentieth century, religious extremism spread from India to Northern Ireland, while Europe was torn by pure political extremism in the 1970s. In the Arab–Islamic world, not all the movements of radical political Islam preach violence, but some of them have chosen extremism when the governments' safeguard of the economic and political status quo has prevented the dynamics of political opposition, democratic decision making and the regeneration of political regimes.

Besides, extremism has sometimes been the strategy the governments employed to overcome the opposition movements: it is what Jabri calls "l'extrémisme à rebours."[6] State extremism is the consequence of the fact that most governments in the Arab–Islamic countries are authoritarian democracies (Huntington 1995). Although they try to give themselves a democratic face, they refuse the principle of alternating parties, oppress minorities, control freedom of expression, suppress political debate, persecute their opponents. Since the end of the colonial period, these illiberal democracies have been dominant: they have fossilized the élite in power, established single-party regimes and made large use of repression. This has caused a radicalization of the social and political confrontation with the movements of radical political Islam and has prepared the ground for the development of tensions and the formation of armed opposition groups. The French scholar F. Burgat summarizes the situation as follows:

[5] As a means of political struggle, extremism may be used to claim legitimate rights denied by the social and economic system, and it may also employ peaceful means. Gandhi and Martin Luther King were considered extremists and indeed they were, although their claims were legitimate and their struggle non-violent. For example: at the campaign for civil disobedience in Birmingham (Ala.) in 1963, Martin Luther King declared: "This attitude is called extremist. I admit that, at first, this definition disappointed me. But, thinking about it, I began to be pleased to be called an extremist. Jesus was an extremist of love. Luther was an extremist. T. Jefferson was an extremist. Then, the question is not, if we are extremists, but which type of extremists are we? Will we be extremists for a perpetual injustice – or extremists for the service of justice?" (quoted in Zitelman, 1997, p. 92, our translation).

[6] "L'extrémisme n'a pas seulement existé hors du pouvoir politique ou contre lui. L'Etat est en effet éminemment susceptible de dériver vers un type d'exercice du pouvoir n'ayant d'ature finalité que sa propre préservation ou l'exploitation du poivoir au profit de ses dirigeants ou des clans et clients qui lui sont liés" (Jabri 1994, p. 31).

Un pluralisme de façade, accepté comme tel par l'environnement occidental avec une parfaite complaisance, sert à masquer un verrouillage du système institutionel qui requiert un niveau particulièrement élevé de répression. De l'impasse politique ainsi verrouillée, qui nourrit et légitime toutes les formes de radicalisation, débouche inévitablement un certain coefficient de radicalisme idéologique et de contre-violence politique. Cet épouvantail intégriste permet alors au régime d'entretenir la confusion entre les pratiques de la frange de ses opposant qu'il a lui même contribué à radicaliser et l'ensemble de l'opposition légaliste, justifiant ainsi aux yeux de ses partenaires européens le report éternel de toute ouverture démocratique qui est la clef de sa survie.[7]

The fragility of democracy opposes no institutional barrier to the outbreak of violence: from Algeria to Syria, repression and extremism are the outcomes of a political conflict which has not been solved by institutional means and which leads both governments and Islamists to preemptive strikes. "On a Hobbesian view of political life [says Hardin] without institutions to help us stay orderly, we take a view of all conflicts. Self-defense against possible (not even actual) attack suffices to motivate murderous conflict."[8]

In order to examine the political background of extremism in the Arab–Islamic countries, we shall try to single out the actors and the causes of violence, identifying the conditions that influence the probability that, in an authoritarian democracy, the government's refusal to accept dialogue with fundamentalism gives rise to a violent escalation. In Section 3 we analyze a game-theory model of extremism related to the class of conflict resolution games (Bueno de Mesquita, Morrow, and Zorick 1997, Zagare and Kilgour 1993 and reference therein). The game is based on three considerations which are translated into corresponding hypotheses. The first hypothesis concerns the identification of the two main parties of the extremist confrontation in the Arab–Islamic countries: the radical Islamic movements and the government forces defended by the army. Their political confrontation can either be peaceful or escalate to violence when the Islamic movements' request for political participation is opposed by the governments and the army or some of the most radical Islamic groups resort to extremism as a means of political struggle. With this hypothesis, we implicitly take into account two facts. First, we discriminate between the limited cases of extremist violence and the more widespread phenomenon of Islamic revival. Second, we assume that Islamic extremism is directed against an internal enemy, the government in power, and not against an external one, be it the Western world, Christianity or capitalism, as is sometimes believed (Lewis 1994).

---

[7] Burgat (1996), pp. 264–5.
[8] Hardin (1995), p. 143.

The second hypothesis is that the strategies of both parties include the possibility of a non-violent outcome. The Islamists choose between claiming a share of power and accepting the status quo; the army, on the other hand, chooses between opposition and acceptance of the Islamists' claim. This range of possibilities takes into account the fact that resorting to extremism is not an unavoidable choice for radical Islamic movements; it is rather the outcome of an exacerbated political confrontation that is not solved through democratic rules (Burgat 1996).

The third hypothesis is that, even when the army's reaction is opposition, there remains the possibility that the confrontation does not degenerate into extremism but ends, instead, in a compromise.

A key element of the model is the assumption that both parties are uncertain about the payoffs associated to the extremist strategy and that their strategic decisions depend on two elements: the comparative advantage, in terms of popular support, of the Islamic party with respect to the government; and the degree of radicalism. While the consensus is an observable element, the level of radicalism is *ex ante* private information of each party.

In Section 4 we present the main results of the game and we use them to identify some common features in the dynamics of extremism in the history of the Arab–Islamic countries. In particular, the cases of Tunisia, Turkey, Algeria, and Egypt are examined in Section 5, as they illustrate our main outcomes: Tunisia is an example of the status quo outcome, Turkey of the compromise outcome, while Algeria and Egypt represent the extremist result.

In Tunisia the weak popular support for the Islamic parties and the strength of the government have prevented open political conflict for decades and now the Islamists do not hope for a share of power. In other countries, the Islamic party has gained a growing popular support met by the government's opposition; even so, however, the outcome is not necessarily a violent conflict. In Turkey, for example, when the Islamic party demanded a share of the power on the basis of its favorable electoral results, the army objected by institutional means and has so far avoided an extremist escalation. On the contrary, the political crisis degenerates in extremism when, as in Egypt, well-supported Islamic movements ask for a larger participation in power and the army opposes them with repression: the high level of extremism of both parties leads to a violent escalation. The same happens when, as in Algeria, the Islamic party obtains a strong electoral result that justifies its claim to the government of the country but the army decides to oppose it: the weakness of the institutional framework and the parties' radicalism spark off violence.

Finally, Section 6 presents the conclusions and some proposals: the way out of extremism is identified in a process of liberalization and democratization that takes into consideration all the components of the civil society, primarily the Islamic one.

## 2. THE RADICAL POLITICAL ISLAM

"Islamic fundamentalism"[9] indicates those currents in modern and contemporary Islam that aim at the restoration of a social and political order consistent with the rules of the Islamic law (Burgat 1995 and 1996, Etienne 1988, Du Pasquier 1990, Lewis 1991, Choueiri 1990, Guolo 1994a and b). The main currents are labelled "Islamic revival," "reformism," and "radicalism" (or fundamentalism). Their political principles all derive from the Koran, but their conclusions are different. The Islamic revival began at the end of the eighteenth century with renewal movements aiming at the establishment, in the Muslim world, of an Islamic state based on strict conformity with the "pure" Islamic law and on the refusal of every innovation contrary to it. The first movement, the "Wahhabite movement" (from its founder Muhammad Abd al-Wahhab, 1705–87), started in Central Arabia; the present Saudi Arabia was built on its doctrine.

The "reformist movement" arose in the nineteenth century and spread throughout the whole Islamic world, dividing itself into different currents. The most famous one was the Egyptian "Salafiyya," whose two major leaders, Jamal al-Din al-Afghani and Muhammad Abduh, ascribed the decadence of the Muslim world and its backwardness with respect to the West to the fact that the believers' community (Umma) had increasingly moved away from God. Only the return to God could allow the establishment of the Islamic unity and the defeat of the colonial powers. Some of the reformist political goals have been resumed by the most recent radical movements (the Algerian GIA, for example), in particular the restoration of the Islamic caliphate, which was abolished after the fall of the Ottoman empire.

The "radical" or "fundamentalist movement" arose from the reformist movement when the Ottoman empire fell and new nationalist or socialist ideologies spread in the Arab–Islamic world. The first movement, the Muslim Brothers, was founded in Egypt by Hasan al-Banna: its ideology was further developed by Sayyd Qutb (1906–66), who defined

---

[9] As the term "fundamentalism" is strictly connected to a particular Western religious phenomenon, expressions like "radical political Islam" or "Islamic revival" are preferable. The label "fundamentalism" comes from a precise historical context, the United States at the end of the nineteenth century: it identifies a theological current of the Protestant Church that opposed the liberal theology and the use of new historical and critical instruments in the interpretation of biblical texts. As Lewis (1991) explains, the word "fundamentalism" is inappropriate with reference to Islam.

the theoretical foundations of radicalism. The radical movement affirmed Islam as a universal reference: all questions concerning human life and society must be regulated according to the Koran's principles. The fundamentalists proposed the model of a perfect political system, where laws, justice, and distribution of wealth are regulated by Islam: the form of government is less important than the enforcement of the *shari'a* and the implentation of social justice. The materialistic and secular view of mankind and human relations, which is proposed by both capitalism and socialism, is rejected.

There are many explanations of the rise of radical Islamic movements in this century: first of all, the failure of the economic and social policies implemented after the end of the colonial regime and the "de-Islamization" processes imposed by governments. After achieving political independence, the winning nationalist movements tried to start the economic development of their countries. In this effort, they adopted the values of modernity of the Western countries: "la modernisation s'écrit en français ou en englais bien plus qu'en arabe," writes a French scholar, F. Burgat, who continues, "plus explicitement encore qu'avant les indépendences, modernisation rime avec déislamisation".[10] The society was built on the modern and secular values of the Western world, while the traditional and religious values were put aside as "anti-modern" and the Islamic movements that supported them were excluded from power. It is remarkable that the most extreme instances of "de-Islamization" took place immediately after independence; for example, the closing of the University of Tunis (Zitouna) or the prohibition on teaching Islamic theology in Algeria.

However, since the beginning of the 1970s, the results of these modernization programs have been disappointing: with the exception of some Gulf countries, the Arab–Islamic countries are still underdeveloped and subject to economic neocolonialism; their population is impoverished and suffers from high rates of unemployment, uncontrolled urbanization, and widespread corruption. The Islamic opposition is an answer to the weakness of economic development and the high degree of inequality. Westernization has enlarged the gap between rich and poor and broken the net of solidarity between them: it has created wide-scale opportunities to consume and made the poor more conscious of their poverty and of the wealth of their neighbours. These inequalities greatly contributed to the alienation and rage that fueled the Islamic opposition (Lewis 1991).

Nevertheless, the economic and social failure of the reforms imposed after independence is not sufficient to explain the Islamic revival. In this sense:

[10] Burgat (1996), p. 74.

Ne lire la poussée islamiste qu'à travers la grille de la faillite des équipes au pouvoir risque de nous empêcher de percer le secret de sa capacité de mobilisation et de nous priver de comprendre pourquoi, même confinée au monde arabe, cette rumeur islamiste est si pénible à nos oreilles occidentales. Une fois attesté l'échec économique ou politique des régimes arabes, encore faut-il expliquer pourquoi ce sont les islamistes et eux seuls, ou presque, qui parviennent à l'exploiter, pourquoi ce ne sont pas des courantes de gauche ou laïques ou libéraux qui remplissent les urnes arabes, pourquoi, sur la rive sud de la Méditerranée, si on fait aujourd'hui de la politique, on n'a peu près aucune chance de remporter les élections à moins de mettre . . . un I, commee Islam, dans le sigle de son parti.[11]

Islamic revival is neither simply an economic phenomenon nor a religious one: it is instead an endogenous process of recovery of an identity that Western models have discredited. This process of "re-traditionalization after an excess of modernity" (Guolo 1994a) turned to religious values (Colombo 1991, Etienne 1988, Leveau 1994): the refusal of Western models, the dismissal of the post-colonial experience, and the search for a new identity are more effective when they resort to a symbolic system and to a traditional language uncontaminated by external influences (Burgat 1996).

The push towards the recovery of an Islamic identity was also encouraged by the complex history of the southern shore of the Mediterranean Sea. Many scholars identify in the Six Days' War of 1967 and in the ensuing Israeli victory the beginning of the process of Islamic radicalization. With the Iranian revolution of 1979, the radical political Islam showed its resolute refusal of Western models: Iman Khomeini's strong influence on the Islamic world spread the fear of Islamic fundamentalism in the Western world.

Even if it is difficult to summarize the causes of the Islamic revival, an Italian scholar, A. Riccardi, gives an effective interpretation suggesting the image of "a great '68 of the Islamic world":

Islamism plays the same role that Marxism of '68 played among the young European and American generations in '68. It's a climate more than an ideology, a hope and a vehicle for protest. The young generations, between social marginalization and frustration, rediscover reasons of identity and struggle in the Islamic heritage. Their fight is essentially against the establishment, often against omnivorous and corrupt States, like those created by the Arab socialism. The responsibility for decadence and crisis is ascribed to the establishment.[12]

Faced by the Islamic challenge, governments tried to stop it and in the 1980s began to repress the fundamentalist groups that contested their power; meanwhile, they assimilated some of the Islamists' topics, hop-

---

[11] Ibid., p. 69.
[12] Riccardi (1997), p. 204 (our translation).

ing to recover some legitimacy and the approval of the population and of the more moderate religious groups.[13] The State introduced an Islamic language into official declarations, religious programs were broadcasted, legislation began to make open reference to the *Shari'a*, in Algeria Friday became an official day of holiday, and it became compulsory to teach the Koran at school in Turkey. The process of re-Islamization touched to a lesser extent the kingdoms of Morocco and Jordan, which had remained closer to the religious traditional values and had succeeded in integrating the Islamic movements without making any particular concessions. However, due to their weak credibility, the governments' strategy to recover a religious identity did not succeed in stopping Islamic movements that, free of compromise with the party in power, set themselves up as a new uncorrupted opposition and effectively exploited the religious language and the nationalist rhetoric.

### 3. A MODEL OF EXTREMISM

In the Arab–Islamic countries, attempts to participate in the political process by the Islamists are often seen as a challenge to the establishment and as a threat to the secularism of the State. The escalation that these attempts may initiate are not much different from those familiar in international crisis: therefore, models of the resolution of international conflicts can be fruitfully applied to the study of extremism. Indeed, the claims of political participation by Islamic movements can be compared with the challenge a nation sets when it lays a claim (an ultimatum, for example) and is prepared to defend it with force.

Borrowing from Bueno de Mesquita et al. (1997), as amended by Molinari (1998), we model the political system as a game with two players, the Islamic party and the Army, which struggle over the division of power. The Army represents the interests of those in power: its aim is to preserve the status quo and to avoid religious influences on the political process. The Islamic party, on the other hand, wants a share of the power in order to introduce laws aimed at reinforcing the religious values of Islam in the society.

The game begins after both players have learned the extent of the support the Islamic party enjoys, either through an election or through some other public event. We let $\varphi \in [-1, 1]$ be a measure of the Islamic party's popular or electoral support with respect to the government[14] and

---

[13] Among the Islamic countries with a written Constitution, only Turkey and Lebanon do not have a state religion; the others accord a more or less important role to Islam.

[14] When $\varphi$ is negative the government has a popular or electoral advantage over the Islamic party.

we assume that a party with a larger relative advantage has a higher probability of seizing power in the event that a civil war breaks out.

The Islamic party's popular support $\varphi$ is not the only element that influences the probability of success in a civil war. The latter also depends on each player's level of radicalism, that is on the will and determination that a player has to pursue power through violence. We denote the level of radicalism of player $i = I, A$ by $\theta_i \in [0, 1]$ and we assume that the Army can win the civil war if and only if his determination exceeds the sum of the Islamic party's electoral support and level of radicalism, that is, if $\theta_A > \theta_I + \varphi$.

A crucial assumption of the model is player $i$'s level of radicalism is not known to his opponent, who thinks that it is uniformly distributed in $[0, 1]$ and that $\theta_I$ and $\theta_A$ are independent. The electoral support $\varphi$, on the other hand, is common knowledge. The game, therefore, is one of two-sided incomplete information. This assumption is justified by the fact that more moderate currents usually coexist with radical ones, both in the Army and in the Islamic party; under these circumstances, the actual level of radicalism $\theta_i$ will depend on which of the many different orientations will prevail and this is, understandably, private information known only to the insiders.

In order to account for the diversity of the Arab–Islamic countries' politics, we assume that there are three different ways in which power can be allocated. First, either player can voluntarily forego power; second, a violent and extremist conflict, such as a civil war, can decide who will be in office; and, third, power can be shared through political compromise. To allow for the possibility of a negotiated settlement is important because, as the example of Turkey shows, there are often institutional channels through which challenges to the status quo can be confronted; striking a balance between opposite interests is not only a desirable but also a possible political outcome.

More precisely, we model the political process as follows: at the beginning of the game the Islamic party can choose between claiming a share of the power or not; in the latter case the status quo prevails and the power remains with the Army simply because the Islamic party did not even challenge it. If, instead, the Islamic party demands a larger political role, the Army can either accept the Islamic party's request or oppose it. When the Army acquiesces, the Islamic party gets all the power and an Islamic government is formed. When, on the other hand, the Army opposes the Islamic party's claim, a confrontation begins that can either lead to a compromise or to an outbreak of violence. We model this stage as a simultaneous move game in which each player decides either to compromise or to turn to extremism and violence. If both players choose to compromise they end up sharing the power; if at least one decides not to, the game results in violence. Therefore, opposition is not necessarily carried out through military action. Modeling the confrontation phase as a simultaneous move game is justified by the fact that the weakness of the Arabic–Islamic countries' democracies makes commitment to cooperation and respect for the Constitution virtually impossible; thereore, preemptive motives are to be expected (Hardin 1995).

The timing of the game and the results associated with each combination of actions are illustrated in Figure 10.1, where *I* stands for Islamic party and *A* stands for the Army. At the first node, labeled **I.1**, if the Islamic party does not request a share of the power (*NR*), the game results results in the status quo (*SQ*). If, instead, a request is made, node **A.2** is reached and the Army can either decide not to oppose (*NO*) the Islamists' claims, in which case an Islamic government (*IG*) would form, or it can oppose it (*O*). If it does, the Islamic party and the Army reach node **I.3** and they simultaneously choose either to turn to extremism (*E*) or not (*NE*). A compromise solution, labelled *C*, can be reached only if both players choose to; otherwise the game results in violence (*V*).[15]

To complete the description of the game we need to specify the players' preferences. As we said at the beginning of this section, the matter of contention in this game is power, whose value is normalized to one. Therefore, we can simply assume that a player's payoff reflects the share of power he can seize in a particular outcome. In the status quo the Army has all the power; its payoff is equal to one and the Islamic

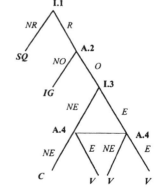

Figure 10.1 The timing and outcomes of the game

---

[15] Notice that the tree of Figure 10.1 does not represent the game we are modeling. In fact, it does not include the players' incomplete information.

party's payoff is zero. The reverse holds when an Islamic government is formed; the Army gets zero and the Islamic party gets one. To allow for the fact that a compromise is usually reached by finding ways to "enlarge the pie" to be divided, we assume that a compromise solution corresponds to an equal division of $1 + 2a$ between the two parties, where $a > 0$. Finally, because a civil war ends with either one of the two players winning the power, we let the winner get one and the loser get zero; however, to account for the difference that exists between gaining the power through the institutional channels provided for by the Constitution and a possibly bloody war, we assume that whenever violence is used a cost of $c \in (0, 1/2)$ is paid by both parties. Notice that the cost of violence is not too high, so that, when $a$ is small, the players would rather fight a war and win it than compromise. The payoffs are summarized in Table 10.1.[16]

Before moving to a description of the equilibria, it is useful to analyze further the possible strategies the Army and the Islamic party have. Since player $i$'s likelihood of winning a war depends, among other things, on his level of radicalism $\theta_i$, player $i$'s best course of action may change with $\theta_i$. For example, it could be the case that a not very determined Army yields to the Islamic party's requests but it opposes them if its determination is high. When this is the case, the Army's behavior can be described by a threshold value $t_A$: if the value of $\theta_A$ is below $t_A$ the Army does not oppose; if it is above $t_A$ the Army rejects the request and then chooses extremism. Similarly, we shall denote by $t_I$ a strategy according to which the Islamic party does not make a request if its radicalism is below the threshold value $t_I$ and it makes a request and chooses extremism when its radicalism is above the threshold value $t_I$.

Notice that even if each player does not know its opponent's level of radicalism, it can draw inferences on it. For example, if the Islamic party employs a threshold strategy $t_I$, the Army can infer, after observing that the Islamic party has asked for a share of power, that the Islamic party's level of radicalism is above $t_I$. In other words, the Islamic party conveys

**Table 10.1 The payoffs of the game**

| PLAYER | OUTCOME | | | | |
|---|---|---|---|---|---|
| | $SQ$ | $IG$ | $C$ | $V$ and $I$ wins | $V$ and $A$ wins |
| Islamic party | 0 | 1 | $1/2 + a$ | $1 - c$ | $-c$ |
| Army | 1 | 0 | $1/2 + a$ | $-c$ | $1 - c$ |

[16] Our results do not depend qualitatively on this very stylized assumption on payoffs.

information to the Army through its behavior. The equilibrium notion we use accounts for such updating of information and postulates that decisions are optimal based on the updated information.[17]

## 4. THE EQUILIBRIA OF THE GAME

In this section we analyze the pattern of equilibrium behavior as a function of the parameters $\varphi$, $c$ and $a$. Propositions are proved in the Appendix. Our first result shows that radicalism does not entail the use of violence.

**Proposition 1** *In equilibrium violence never occurs with certainty.*

This proposition says that violence is not a necessary result of the Islamic revival. Extremism is, instead, to be understood as a strategy of political struggle employed by either the Army or the Islamic party, when the institutional channels to power cannot be used. Violence is used by the parties as a means to signal to one's opponent that there is a strong will to pursue power. Such a signal is costly and, therefore, it is never used indiscriminately.

Proposition 1 leaves open the question of how likely violence is to occur as a function of the underlying parameters. In order to address this question we first analyze the game for $a = 0$.

**Proposition 2** *Suppose that $a = 0$.*

 (i) *For $\varphi \in [-1, c - 1]$ there is an equilibrium in which the Islamic party plays $(NR, NE)$ and the Army plays $(O, E)$. This equilibrium results in the status quo.*
 (ii) *For $\varphi \in [-1/(1 + c), c(1 - c)/(1 + c)]$ there is an equilibrium in which the Islamic party and the Army play, respectively, the threshold strategies $t_I$ and $t_A$, where $t_I = [c(1 - c) - \varphi(1 + c)]/(1 + c - c^2)$ and $t_A = [c(2 - c + \varphi)]/(1 + c - c^2)$.*
 (iii) *For $\varphi \in [-c^2/(1 + c), 1 - c]$ there is an equilibrium in which the Islamic party plays $(R, E)$ and the Army plays the threshold strategy $t_A$, where $t_A = \varphi + c$.*
 (iv) *For $\varphi \in [1 - c, 1]$ there is an equilibrium in which the Islamic party plays $(R, E)$ and the Army plays $(NO, E)$. This equilibrium results in an Islamic government.*

---

[17] For a precise definition of the strategies of the game and the equilibrium notion used, see the Appendix.

Of the four equilibria identified in Proposition 2, Equilibria (i) and (iv) do not lead to violence. These two equilibria correspond to values of $\varphi$ very skewed in favor of one of the two players. Since $\varphi$ is observable, the bias in the balance of power is known and there is no need to signal information through violence.

More precisely, in Equilibrium (i), the Islamic party's observable support $\varphi$ is very low; when this is the case, the party cannot hope for a share of power because the Army, knowing its advantage, would oppose any request and be willing to fight a war, regardless of its own determination. Therefore, no request is made and the status quo prevails.

At the opposite end we have Equilibrium (iv). In this equilibrium $\varphi$ is very large or, in other words, the Islamic party is known to be strongly supported and always ready to fight, no matter what its level of radicalism is. The Army, therefore, prefers not to oppose the Islamic party's requests and acquiesces in the formation of an Islamic government.

The equilibrium behavior for intermediate values of $\varphi$ is much richer in terms of information that is signaled. In fact, for moderate values of public support to the Islamic party, neither side has an observable advantage such as to induce the opponent spontaneously to forego power. Threshold strategies are then used and extremism becomes the device that either a strong Army or a radical Islamic party must use to signal its determination and strength.

In Equilibrium (ii), which exists for medium–low values of $\varphi$, both the Army and the Islamic party use threshold strategies: when the Islamic party has a low level of radicalism ($\theta_I < t_I$), it does not advance any request; when, instead, it has a high level of radicalism, it asks for a share of power and it is willing to fight it. Similarly, a weak Army ($\theta_A < t_A$) never opposes but a strong Army opposes and is willing to fight.

Finally, Equilibrium (iii) describes the behavior for medium–high values of $\varphi$. As one would expect, with a larger popular support the Islamic party has a more aggressive behavior than in Equilibrium (ii); accordingly, the party asks for a share of power and is willing to fight for it, regardless of its degree of radicalism. On the other hand, what is now a relatively disadvantaged Army opposes the Islamic party's requests only if it is extremely determined ($\theta_A \geq t_A$).

What kind of prediction about the effect that the Islamic revival has on political outcomes can we make on the basis of Proposition 2? As we said, when the Islamic party's support is either very large or very small, we can make the unambiguous prediction that violence does not occur. For intermediate values of $\varphi$, instead, the players use a threshold strategy and, as a result, the actual behavior depends on the degree of radicalism. Since this is ex ante unobservable, a deterministic forecast of the outcome cannot be made. For example, Equilibrium (ii) leads to either the status quo, an Islamic government or violence, depending on the level of the Army's and Islamic party's level of radicalism $\theta_A$ and $\theta_I$. Similarly, Equilibrium (iii) leads either to an Islamic government or to violence.[18]

The possible equilibrium outcomes as a function of $\varphi$ are illustrated in the upper part of Figure 10.2.[19] Moving from left to right we see that, for low values of $\varphi$, the status quo is the unique equilibrium outcome. As $\varphi$ gets larger, an Islamic government and an outbreak of violence are added to the possible outcomes but, as $\varphi$ gets even larger, the Islamic party's support becomes too strong for the status quo to survive as a possible result. Finally, on the extreme right of the range of values of $\varphi$, only an Islamic government is a possible occurrence.

As the upper part of Figure 10.2 shows, for intermediate values of $\varphi$ we cannot make a deterministic forecast. Nevertheless, we can predict the expected equilibrium outcome. The ex ante probability of an outbreak of violence is plotted in the lower part of Figure 10.2.[20] Such a probability is positive only for intermediate values of $\varphi$. Also, as one would expect, it is larger for values of $\varphi$ around zero. In fact, when $\varphi = 0$, neither player has an overwhelming observable advantage; this implies that the players' uncertainty about who would win a confrontation is maximum. When this is the case, an outbreak of violence is very likely because each party is taking a chance to show its superiority.

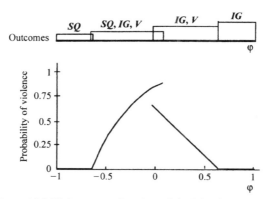

Figure 10.2 Violence as a function of the Islamic party's support, $\varphi$

---

[18] Another reason that prevents us from making deterministic predictions is the multiplicity of equilibria for some values of the parameters $\varphi$ and $c$.

[19] The size of the intervals corresponds to $c = 0.25$. When the cost of violence gets larger, the range of values of $\varphi$ for which Equilibria (i) and (iv) exist gets larger.

[20] The ex ante probability of violence is $(1 - t_I)(1 - t_A)$ and $(1 - t_A)$ for Equilibria (ii) and (iii) respectively.

In the results presented so far political compromise seems to play no role. It turns out that this depends on having looked only at the case $a = 0$.

## Proposition 3

(i) *If $a = 0$, a compromise is never reached in equilibrium.*

(ii) *Suppose $a > 1/2 - c$. If $\varphi \in [1/2 - a - c, -1/2 + a + c]$, there is an equilibrium in which the Islamic party plays $(R, NE)$ and the Army plays $(O, NE)$. This equilibrium results in a compromise. Also, violence cannot be an equilibrium outcome.*

If the allocation of power is a constant sum game, that is $a = 0$, a compromise solution is never possible. In fact, by assumption, each player prefers to fight a war and win it when $a = 0$. Therefore, compromise can only arise if either the Army or the Islamic party (or both) uses a threshold strategy that calls for compromise for low levels of radicalism and extremism otherwise. However, it turns out that the updating of information that such strategies allow makes the players more aggressive, so that compromise cannot be sustained as an equilibrium outcome.

The result can be illustrated with an example. Suppose that the Islamic party, after a request for a share of power, chooses to compromise when scarcely radicalized but prefers extremism otherwise. When the Army decides whether to compromise or not, it is only interested in the level of radicalization of the Islamic party when the latter is willing to compromise. This is so because, if the Islamic party chooses extremism, violence would ensue no matter what the Army did. Therefore, the fact that the Islamic party uses the threshold strategy above is, for the Army, good news because such a strategy says that compromise is the choice of a scarcely determined Islamic party. Since the Army is more likely to win when the Islamic party is not very determined, the updating of information makes the Army more aggressive and, overall, less willing to compromise. In other words, the propensity to compromise of one party unravels the willingness to join in the compromise of the other.

It turns out that the unraveling of compromise due to updating is complete when $a = 0$, so that compromise is only made possible by increasing $a$. In particular, by rewriting the condition $a > 1/2 - c$ of Proposition 3(ii) as $2(a + c) > 1$, we see that, in order to sustain compromise as the equilibrium outcome, the total surplus to be gained by switching from a violent outcome to a compromise must be greater than the utility of being in power. This is bad news because it makes the compromise outcome difficult to achieve. On the other hand, when such a condition is satisfied the players will be able to coordinate on the compromise solution and avoid the costly and inefficient violent outcome for sure, despite the asymmetry of information.

According to Proposition 3, in order to interpret the political reaction of the Arabic–Islamic countries to the Islamic revival, it is important to understand under what condition $a$ is large, that is when the allocation of power is not a constant sum game. One element that is likely to affect $a$ is the ideological distance between the Army and the Islamic movements. In fact, when this distance is small, it is easier for the players to envisage profitable ways to share power; when, instead, this distance is too large, cohabitation may become impossible. Notice that the distance is small either because the Islamic movements' aims are not too extreme or because the Army is not too secularized. Therefore, we can say that $a$ is likely to be larger the more homogeneous the society is. Notice , however, that having a larger $a$ is not necessarily a positive fact for a country. In fact, the most obvious way to raise $a$ is to increase political corruption. However, in the long run corruption undermines the political system and is often a source of conflicts.

Before moving to the empirical evidence supporting the model, we would like to summarize our main findings. The first main result says that violence is never an unavoidable consequence of an increase in the Islamic movements' support and that the presence of radical Islamic movements alone is insufficient to generate extremism. As a matter of fact, as illustrated in Figure 10.2, the increase in the Islamists' political activity is associated with various possible outcomes: depending on the support to the Islamists and on the level of radicalism of both the Islamic party and the Army, either the status quo is maintained or an Islamic government is formed or extremist violence erupts. We can thus explain the fact that in the Arab–Islamic countries the presence of radical Islamic movements has manifold expressions, diverse attitudes towards the government, and different consequences for political life.

The second main result of the chapter suggests that, in order to explain the different consequences of the Islamic revival in the various Arab–Islamic countries, it may be necessary to consider exogenous elements. In fact, there are values of the parameters for which multiple equilibria exist. These are represented by the overlapping intervals in Figure 10.2. In such intervals, the outcome of the game may depend on elements such as cultural and political traditions or the presence of a charismatic leader, that determine which equilibrium will prevail. This fact would explain why countries with seemingly similar situations sometimes exhibit contrasting outcomes.

Finally, according to our model, compromise is possible if (and only if) it can guarantee a sufficiently high gain for both the Army and the Islamic movements. As Proposition 3 shows, when $a$ is large and the support to the Islamic party reaches intermediate values, compromise becomes the best response for both parties. The value of $a$ expresses the payoff from cooperation; its value depends, negatively and positively, on many elements, among which we can list the propensity to political exchange, the level of polarization of the society, and the presence of constitutional guarantees that make preemptive moves useless and enhance trust. According to this result, the greater the homogeneity of the society and the strength of the democracy, the larger the scope for compromise. Therefore, one way to raise the payoff of compromise is to reinforce the democratic system by making the principle of alternating parties and the respect for the rules of democracy accepted principles. This would imply that, while the secular parties should accept the Islamists movements in political competition, the latter should commit themselves to the respect of the Constitution and the secular character of the State. This two-sided commitment could help the parties act in a cooperative way, thus avoiding the Army's opposition to the Islamists' claims to political participation and the escalation to extremism.

## 5. AN INTERPRETATION OF ARAB–ISLAMIC COUNTRIES' POLITICS

In this section we present some important facts about the last fifty years' history of Tunisia, Turkey, Egypt, and Algeria and we interpret them in terms of the results of our game-theory model. Before looking at each country individually, we summarize some political features of the nine Arab countries in the Mediterranean area. Of these, Algeria, Egypt, Lebanon, Syria, Tunisia, and Turkey are republics, Jordan and Morocco are kingdoms, and Libya is ruled by a military dictatorship. Together with their geographical position, all of them share some common political features:

1. In all of them power is firmly in the hands of a single political party, despite the diversity of political systems that, at least on paper, have democratic features.
2. All of them have experienced an increase of the Islamist movements' political activity.

Notwithstanding these common features, however, their political situations are extremely diversified: they all have active Islamist movements but these enjoy varying support and engage in extremism and violence to different degrees. In order to better understand the main political characteristics of these nine countries, we summarize some data in Table 10.2. In particular, for each country we give the name of the Islamist party and its electoral support at the last election, if available, and we observe whether Islamic extremist groups are active.

As Table 10.2 shows, the countries can be divided into three groups according to their political situation. In the first group, formed by Jordan, Morocco, and Tunisia, an authoritarian regime which enjoys a strong consensus has managed to exclude the Islamist movements from political competition without triggering any extremist reaction. These correspond to the situation we labeled

**Table 10.2 Arab–Islamic countries' political situation**

| Country | Political system | Islamists' electoral support at the most recent political election for which they could run | | | Islamic extremist groups |
| | | Party's name | Year | % votes | |
| --- | --- | --- | --- | --- | --- |
| Jordan | Parl. monarchy | Front of Islamic Action | 1997 | absent | no |
| Morocco | Const. monarchy | Reform and Renewal | 1997 | absent[a] | no |
| Tunisia | Pres. republic | Al-Nahda | 1989 | 13% | no |
| Lebanon | Parl. republic | Hizbullah | 1996 | [b] | yes |
| Turkey | Parl. republic | Refah | 1995 | 21% | yes |
| Algeria | Pres. republic | FIS | 1991 | 47.27% | yes |
| Egypt | Pres. republic | Muslim Brothers | 1996 | illegal | yes |
| Libya | Military regime | Muslim Brothers | – | illegal | yes |
| Syria | Pres. republic[c] | Nat. Front of Salvation | 1994 | illegal | no |

[a] In Morocco the political parties' activity is limited by the extensive powers of the king, who decides the government formation and its conduct. Some leaders of the Islamic movement Reform and Renewal support a party, the Constitutional Democratic Popular Movement. In the local elections of June 1997 some of the Islamic leaders were elected.

[b] Under Syrian pressure, Hizbullah formed a list with the other Shia party, Amal, as in the previous election of 1992. Their candidates won overwhelmingly in Southern Lebanon.

[c] Syria is a socialist presidential republic: political activity is monopolized by the main party, Baath, which has been in power since 1963.

*Source*: Stato del mondo (1993–98).

status quo. As the results of Section 3 show, this situation is compatible with either weak electoral support to the Islamic movements (low $\varphi$), as in Tunisia, or with a situation in which the Islamic movements have a limited determination to pursue power through violence combined with a medium–low popular consensus (low $\theta_I$ and medium–low $\varphi$), as in Morocco and Jordan. Islamic movements in Morocco and Jordan are no negligible presence, but they are cautious in the expression of their claims, thereby accepting the status quo: the charismatic leadership of King Hassan II in Morocco and of King Hussein in Jordan have certainly contributed to this result.

In the second group, formed by Lebanon and Turkey, Islamic parties are allowed to participate in the elections and they get good electoral results. In both countries a compromise solution prevails in which the Islamic parties participate in the political decision-making process. However, while Turkey fits our model, Lebanon presents a different situation. Turkey has experienced in different ways an enlargement of the social and political "pie," which in the model corresponds to $a$ larger than zero: this has been possible because of the widespread laicity of the society and because the main Islamist party, Refah, is not very different from the other political parties and shares their propensity for political exchanges and mutual favors. Lebanon is, instead, the stronghold of Syria, that controls the economic and political life of the country. The main Islamic movement, Hizbullah, is a Shia militia whose principal aim is armed resistance to Israeli occupation in the south. Since 1989, when the Taif Agreement ended the civil war between Christians and Muslims, the movement has made itself more Lebanese, shedding its Iranian roots and trying to enter mainstream politics. Hizbullah's main enemy is thus an external one, as it is allowed political participation in Lebanon even if under Syria's control.

Finally, the third group, to which Algeria, Egypt, Libya, and Syria belong, is made up of countries where a strong authoritarian regime clashes with very active Islamic movements: this situation leads to political extremism and violence. Despite the fact that the Islamic parties' electoral support can only be documented for Algeria, due to the legal restraints to open political competition that exist in the other countries of the group, it is a matter of fact that the Islamists enjoy widespread popular support and that they have shown an extreme determination to use violence (high $\theta_I$ and high $\varphi$). In these countries the inability of the regime in power to facilitate the integration of the Islamist fringe, by keeping the allocation of power as a constant sum game, has determined the impossibility of a compromise equilibrium.

A more detailed analysis of the recent history of some of these countries can help to explain the reasons for extremism and the outcomes of the model.

## 5.1   The status quo outcome: Tunisia

Tunisia belongs to the group of countries where the status quo has been preserved for decades thanks to the lack of an aggressive and strongly supported Islamic opposition and to the widespread consensus that the regime enjoys. Tunisia, a French protectorate since 1881, gained independence in 1956 and from then to 1987 was led by Habib Bourguiba, a secular autocrat with a French background, who decided to modernize the country. He promoted economic development, technological innovation, law and educational reforms; he introduced the new civil code, which replaced the *Shari'a*, suppressed the Islamic courts and took over the Islamic welfare centres and schools. Unlike the Turkish leader Ataturk, Bourgiba never made open declarations of secularism, but he tried to be on good terms with Islam; for example, in 1959 he declared Islam to be the state religion and he introduced a law according to which only a Muslim could become the President of the Republic. Despite these acts, Islam has never become the unifying symbol of the Tunisian nation, mainly because secular education has established a Western lifestyle.

Fundamentalist movements in Tunisia have always been fragmented and for a long time they have preferred to avoid open confrontation with the government, even during the popular protests against the recurring economic crises that took place in Tunis in 1978, in Gafsa in 1980 and during the bread uprising of 1984. The Islamic movements tried, instead, to oppose the government by expressing their criticisms through a lively literary and journalistic production.

In 1987 Bourgiba was removed from power and substituted by the former Chief of the Security Forces, Zayn al-Abidin Ben Ali, who is still President. One of the first moves that Ben Ali made, once in power, was to release the militants of the radical Islamic Tendency Movement (MTI) from jail: their leader, Rachid Ghanouchi, then decided to participate in the drafting of a National Pact to rule the political life of the country. To circumvent the law that forbids political parties from having religious ties, the MTI was renamed Renascence Party (*al-Nahda*) and under this name it backed independent lists in the elections of 1989, getting 13 percent of the vote nationally and 30 percent in Tunis. However, *al-Nahda* accused the government of electoral fraud and tried to stir up a popular reaction to which the government, backed by popular support, responded with a resolute repression, suppressing the *al-Nahda* party and controlling the press and the trade unions. The weak and divided opposition gave in to the impositions[21] and Ben Ali's grip on power became stronger:

Most Tunisians seem prepared to put with such restrictions in return for stability and economic growth. The idea of an Islamist takeover terrifies Tunisia's liberal-minded middle-class, which eschews veils and beards. A generous welfare system wins over many of the poor. People grumble openly about corruption and rising prices as subsidies disappear and, at the moment, such pressure has no legal outlet.[22]

The large popular support enjoyed by Ben Ali corresponds to a very low $\varphi$ in the model: this gives the Islamic party no hope of sharing power (Proposition 2(i)). Besides, as in the model, extremism is always the Army's best response: the Tunisian Islamists learnt this and after initial protests against the government, they have accepted the status quo.

### 5.2   The equilibria with extremism: Algeria and Egypt

In Algeria and Egypt the conflict between the government and the Islamic movements has degenerated into extremism. In both countries the regime has proved unable to find common ground to make a compromise possible, both because the distance from the Islamic movements is very large and because the governments have shown a complete closure towards the opposition. No compromise has been possible as the allocation of power has been maintained as a constant sum game.

#### 5.2.1  Egypt

Egypt gained independence from the United Kingdom in 1922, although Britain maintained its control over the army and foreign policy as long as King Faruk was in power. British interference was opposed by both the nationalist movement, represented by the *Wafd* party, and by the Muslim Brothers. The latter wanted not only independence but also the establishment of an Islamic social and political system. In 1952 a coup overthrew the monarchy and brought G.A. Nasser to power, who, despite his socialist policies, did not manage to attenuate the deep inequalities in Egyptian society. Nasser did not reject Islam and, in the beginning, he actually used it to strengthen his power. However, when in 1954 the confrontation with the Muslim Brothers became too heated, the regime employed harsh repressive measures and the movement was outlawed. The bid for an Islamic redemption became greater in 1967, when Nasser lost the war against Israel.

---

[21] The opposition parties are in the minority: in the elections of 1994, their total share of the votes was 2.27 percent.

[22] *The Economist*, January 21, 1998, p. 47.

In 1970 A. Sadat succeeded Nasser without being able to improve the relationship with the Islamic movements or the state of the Egypt society (Kepel, 1984). The despotism and unfairness of the State and the treason of the peace with the eternal enemy, Israel, induced an Islamic radicalization that led to Sadat's killing in 1981. Things did not get any better with his successor H. Moubarak, who continued the politics of absolute closure towards the Islamists:

Certes, l'opposition islamique comporte une composante fermée et intolérante. Mais son influence tient surtout à la politique du régime: en discréditant les attitudes légalistes et participationnistes, celui-ci renforce et légitime la posture de refus de cette composante extrémiste . . . Sous l'effet d'une répression souvent trés préventive, ce durcissement produit lui-même inéluctablement un certain coefficient de contre-violence. Le régime, qui craint moins en fait les quelques bombes de la péripherie extrémiste de son opposition que les millions de bulletins de vote de son centre, brandit alors cette violence pour justifier – notamment aux yeux de ses bailleurs de fonds internationaux – l'absolu verrouillage du système qui seul lui permet de survivre.[23]

The reinstatement of political pluralism in 1977 started a period of democratic openings: however, the implementation of the principle of alternating parties has not yet been attained, as getting into Parliament is very difficult.[24] The National Democratic Party, the party in power, has managed to withdraw 75 percent of parliamentary seats from electoral competition: today, it holds 417 seats out of 444. The electoral lists have not been updated since 1956 and include less than 15 percent of the potential electorate: electoral participation is usually no more than 10 percent. There are also frequent restrictions and threats to the opposition parties, especially the Labour Party, which includes some leaders of the Islamic opposition.

The consensus in favor of the Muslim Brothers is high: evidence of this is in fact that, whenever democratic decisions are possible (for example, in the elections of the representatives of professional associations or trade unions), the Islamists gain a net advantage over the party in power and the other political formations. However, as the law forbids parties with a religious background, the Muslim Brothers have never achieved legal status, although they have applied for it 45 times.

Since the 1970s, some Islamic groups have chosen armed confrontation with power, criticising the Muslim Brothers' policy for being too accommodating. The two main organizations, *al-Jihad al-islami* and

---

[23] Burgat (1996), p. 142.

[24] To get into Parliament, a political party must pass a selection test and obtain the approval of a "Court for political parties," which has the authority to grant or refuse legal status.

*Jama'at al-islamiya*, aim at overthrowing the government and are responsible for attacks against state representatives and foreign tourists. Although the Muslim Brothers condemn terrorism, the government usually charges them with the extremist activity of the armed groups: "They are all the same . . . all of a kind" declared Moubarak.[25] The army's repression is harsh and employs torture and the taking of hostages: there were about 50 000 political prisoners in 1995. This repression meets with international support.

The campaign, successful so far, by Egypt's army and security services to eradicate the militarist Gama'a has tacit blessing in the West, which sees Egypt as a bulwark against an Islamic fundamentalist wave coursing irresistibly across the region. This latest recycling of the domino theory, originally adduced to combat communism in South-East Asia and then to justify intervention against left-wing rebellion in Central America, has attractions in the Middle East and North Africa too: regimes facing revolt or unrest find the spectre of fundamentalism a useful lever in extracting military and financial aid from a frightened West.[26]

Egypt's case corresponds to Proposition 2(ii) where $\varphi$ has intermediate values and extremism is the outcome when the Islamic parties have a high level of radicalism and the Army strongly opposes them. Although the lack of free elections makes it impossible to quantify the consensus in favor of the Egyptian Islamic movement, its popular support is quite wide. This and a high level of radicalism had initially given rise to demand for a larger political participation: the government refused and both parties chose an extremist strategy.

### 5.2.2 Algeria

Algeria freed itself from French domination through an independence struggle (1954–62) led by the Front de Libération Nationale (FLN). Independence was followed by a period of increasing authoritarianism, where the FLN imposed itself as the only party, excluding the Islamic and the democratic currents, whose leaders were forced into silence or sent into exile. In 1965 President Ben Bella was deposed by the army and a Revolution Council was formed: the former Defence Minister, Houari Boumedienne, became the country's arbitrator. He started a program of "authoritarian socialism," which promoted economic development through heavy industrialization and gave the State a central role in the direction and financing of the economy. The results of these policies were impressive: from 1965 to 1980 the average annual

---

[25] Interview to *The Financial Times*, May 15, 1995.
[26] *The Financial Times*, May 15, 1995.

growth rate was 7.5 percent and that of industrial production was 8.1 percent.

The socialist experiment ended in 1979, when Boumedienne died and the army backed Chadli Bendjedid as the sole candidate in the presidential elections.[27] Bendjedid reduced the state presence in economic and social life, started new free trade policies and opened Algeria up to economic and diplomatic contacts with the West and with France in particular. The new policy obtained modest results and did not eliminate the widespread corruption. The *laissez-faire* strategies hit the poorest part of the population and caused the first protests, which culminated in the demonstration of October 6, 1988. The government's response was harsh: the army fired at the crowd and a state of siege was declared and kept until, unexpectedly, President Bendjedid announced new important political and economic reforms, the end of the FLN's monopoly, and the birth of political pluralism.

In 1989 a new Constitution, which took the French one as a model, was approved by 73.4 percent of the population. Political pluralism, human rights, and the courts' independence were guaranteed. Sixty new political parties were formed and recognized: "c'est l'Algérie toute entière qui entre en ébullition, exprimant, pour la première fois, son irréductible pluralité."[28] The Islamic Salvation Front (FIS) cultivated its electoral base in the working-class neighborhoods, where it created assistance centers for the poor and often became the only reference point in areas where the State was absent.

The old National Assembly was still working when the first local elections were held in June 1990: the FIS obtained 54.25 percent of the votes, while the FLN obtained only 28.1 percent. In the following parliamentary elections, in December 1991, the FIS obtained the relative majority at the first ballot (47.27 percent), while the FLN got only 23.38 percent. The second electoral ballot did not take place as the army, frightened by the FIS's success, decided to close the National Assembly and to force President Bendjedid to resign. He was replaced by the Haut Conseil de Sécurité (HCE), led by Mohamed Boudiaf: the HCE, which was not provided for by the Constitution, decided to suppress the FIS. As a reaction to the repression, the FIS separated into many independent movements and, although some continued their struggle mostly on political grounds, others, such as the Armed Islamic Movement (MIA) and the Armed Islamic Group (GIA),

---

[27] On recent years see Impagliazzo and Giro (1997) and Stone (1997).
[28] *Le Monde*, November 16, 1995.

decided for an extremist reaction. The conflict has become increasingly violent and bloody, with about 80 000 victims since 1992. So L. Addi comments:

Cette sanglante évolution était inscrite dans l'annulation des élections de janvier 1992: un régime autoritaire n'a pas les moyens de combattre le terrorisme, car il ne peut s'appuyer sur la population. De quelle légitimité peut se parer un régime qui a truqué tous les scrutins qui se sont déroulés, notamment ceux, législatif et municipal, de 1997? Faute de permettre l'expression des aspirations des Algériens, comment ce pouvoir tournant le dos à la démocratie pourrait-il isoler une violence terroriste née précisément d'un blocage politique?[29]

Algeria's case falls in Proposition 2(iii), where $\varphi$ is larger, the Islamic party's radicalism is high and extremism results if the Army is determined to oppose any Islamic claim to power. The electoral victories in 1990 and 1991 granted the FIS, the main Islamic party, large popular support: this led to a claim for greater participation in power. However, the claim was not accepted, because the more radical wing prevailed inside the army, giving rise to a coup and to the armed repression of the Islamic movements. The outcome has been a widespread armed conflict.

### 5.3 The compromise outcome: Turkey

Turkey is an example of the compromise outcome: the Islamic party's claim to political participation was followed by the army's opposition. However, some features of the Turkish society and of the political system helped to avoid the extremist escalation.

After the collapse of the Ottoman Empire, Turkey became a parliamentary republic. Kemal Ataturk, the first president, had as his highest priority the modernization of the country and the establishment of a secular republic; among other things, he introduced the Western alphabet and he outlawed religious schools and any interference of religion with politics.

In Turkey, the army is viewed as the most trustworthy institution by the majority of the population, despite the fact that it has been involved in three coups in the last 37 years: it is considered as the true guardian of the unity of the State, of its secularism and democracy.[30] In the 1960s and 1970s the army started opening to Islam as an antidote to Marxism,

---

[29] *Le Monde Diplomatique*, February 1998.
[30] In an interview to *The Financial Times* (May 22, 1997) General I. Karadayi said: "The armed forces would ensure that Turkey remains a democratic and secular State based on the rule of the law. The armed forces are dedicated to Ataturk's nationalism and are the untiring guardians of his reforms and principles." No different were the expressions of a left-wing Member of Parliament, M. Soysal: "The army is the founder of the State. The Republic has military blood. This is not an ordinary Republic, it is a Jacobin Republic."

making schools and religious confraternities legal. At the beginning of the 1990s some members of the Islamic groups began taking up positions in the army, in public office, and in the police. The elections of December 1995 saw the Islamic party, the *Refah*, gain 21 percent of the votes, thus winning the relative majority. In second and third place came the right-wing secular parties Motherland Party (ANAP), with 19.7 percent of the votes, and True Path Party (DYP), with 19.6 percent. *Refah*'s victory is usually ascribed to the divisions among the secular parties and is interpreted more as a vote of protest than as an ideological vote. In July 1996, after the attempts to form a centre-right coalition had failed, an alliance between *Refah* and DYP gave birth to a government led by *Refah*'s leader, Necmettin Erbakan: this was the first religiously inspired government of the Turkish Republic.

This initial success of the Islamists has, since then, been challenged by a reaction of the army, although Mr Erbakan never began to implement his Islamist agenda. In February 1997 the National Council of Security (MGK), an institutional agency through which the army controls the State, warned Erbakan not to pass Islamic laws and forced him to limit the introduction of Islamic and Arab influences on education. The army also obtained the exclusion of some strongly pro-Islam officers and asked the government to "boycott" some companies accused of reactionary activities but, in fact, only guilty of financing the building of mosques and Islamic schools. In June 1997, Erbakan's government resigned and was replaced by a coalition government led by Mesut Yilmaz. In January 1998, by strictly applying the principle of the Constitution that forbids any activity contrary to the secular character of the State, *Refah* was suppressed and its leader, Erbakan, was sentenced to political exile for five years. No violence was exercised by the army against *Refah*'s members, and Erbakan, on his side, invited his supporters to abide by the law and appealed to the European Court of Justice.

Radicalism is not widespread in *Refah*. The Turkish Islamists did not even oppose an agreement between Turkey and the traditional enemy of the Islamists, Israel. Ferrari, an Italian journalist, comments:

If the Algerian Islamic extremists are first of all Islamic, then Algerian, the Turkish extremists are first Turkish, then Islamic. They are Turks, proud of belonging to a country which has never been colonised, they are proud of their Ottoman past, they are mingled in hundreds of trades that have nothing to do with the "pureness" preached by Islamic fundamentalists . . . They are used to the periodical suppression of their parties, knowing that the following day they will be able to start them again.[31]

---

[31] Ferrari, *Corriere della Sera*, January 18, 1998 (our translation).

As a matter of fact, *Refah* was immediately replaced by the Virtue Party, now the biggest party in Parliament. The more accommodating attitude of the Turkish Islamists is explained by the process of secularization, which has reached deeply into Turkish society and seems hardly reversible, and also, according to some commentators, by the widespread use of corruption and the exchange of political favors.

Turkey needs to reform, if it is to evolve into a fully modern state. However, democracy has till now proved vital. The country has avoided unrest, despite the army's resumption of a direct role in politics and the country's history of creeping political violence. Besides, in spite of an abundance of controls and restrictions on free speech, public opinion is lively, as was proved by the recent protests against corruption and by the peaceful demonstrations demanding more democratization. All these observations are compatible with a high level of parameter *a* in our analysis: as Proposition 3 shows, this is necessary for a compromise equilibrium to exist.

### 5.4 The Islamic government outcome

None of the Islamic countries we analyzed has ever reached the outcome of the game we labeled Islamic government. The only case where an Islamic regime has come to power is Iran, which, however, does not exactly fit the model: the Islamic radical movements took power via a revolution,[32] and not via a transfer of power within the same political system, as the model foresees for the *IG* equilibrium.

### 6. CONCLUSIONS

Our analysis of extremism in the Arab–Islamic countries shows the effects of the radicalization of the confrontation between Islamists and the governments in power. It is natural to ask ourselves if there is a way out of this situation. Suggestions can be drawn from the model of Section 3, which shows that the compromise solution is possible when the Islamic party obtains a limited success and somehow it is possible to enlarge the political "pie." One way to achieve this is by deepening and strengthening democracy, compelling the political parties to respect democratic rules and the principle of alternating parties. This would imply that, while the secular parties should accept Islamist movements in political competition, the latter should commit themselves to respect for the Constitution and for the secular character of the State. These two-sided commitments could help the parties to act in a cooperative way, avoiding the Army's opposition to the Islamists'

---

[32] See Gresh and Vidal (1991).

claim of political participation and the extremist escalation. In this sense, Addi believes that in Algeria, "si l'engrenage de la violence n'a pu être évité, c'est aussi du fait de l'absence, avant les élections, d'un contrat national garantissant aussi bien les droits de l'individu que ceux de l'opposition en cas de victorie islamiste."[33] Guarantees and commitments that reassure the opponent could be useful to introduce a gradual democratization of political life in the Arab–Islamic countries.

At this point, inevitably the question arises that Burgat calls "l'impossible débat," that is if Islam is compatible with democracy (Botiveau 1994). The question is complex, given the wide range of statements of the Islamic leaders. On one hand, great Muslim thinkers affirm that democracy is not in contradiction with Islam,

because, giving sovereignty to the people, democracy does not exclude Allah's sovereignty. . . . According to this current, the principles of democracy already exist in Islam and the assumption of other countries' models is not in contradiction with Islam, as the Muslim will take what is in accordance with their religion.[34]

Islam's political category nearest to democracy is consultation, which was introduced by the Prophet himself, who asked for the believers' advice when taking important decisions. Some Islamic leaders make reference to it to show that democracy had already been anticipated by Mohammed in the seventh century. The principle is compatible with both an electoral system and a party structure: for example, the Algerian FIS employed it.

On the other hand, Islamic political ideals are often far from Western ones: "the Koran is our Constitution," "the sovereignty belongs to God," declare the radical political wings. However, it should be remembered that this detachment from the democratic system is used by Islamic rhetoric to distinguish itself from Western culture.[35] Besides,

---

[33] Addi, *Le Monde Diplomatique*, February 1998.

[34] Benantar (1994), p. 60.

[35] "Lorsque elle dénonce l'univers démocratique, la revendication islamiste n'entend pas nécessairement supprimer toute espace d'intervention autonome de la volonté humaine, proscrire toute possibilité de régler par des lois profanes les modes de dévolution, de transmission et d'exercice du pouvoir ou encore moins sonner le glas des minorités. Bon nombre des concepts de cette pensée ont en fait perdu leur portée technique pour n'être plus que des marques identitaires fonctionnant surtout sur le mode réactionnel: 'Je suis contre leur démocratie, donc je commence à exister'. Les références étrangères a la culture locale demeurent en effet largement tributaires du sens acquis dans le contexte de leur irruption en terre musulmane" (Burgat, 1996, pp. 191–2).

the poor implementation of democracy in recent decades has reduced the credibility of Western political systems. Moreover, cultural differences make the transposition of Western political categories harder: for example, State and Nation are concepts foreign to Islam, the distinction between political and religious authorities does not exist, and in classic Arabic there are no pairs of words to translate the dichotomies secular and religious, or spiritual and temporal (Lewis 1991). The sense of identity in Islam comes from the political–religious community, not from the nation, the ethnic group or territorial belonging. "A Muslim country is the place where the holy law of Islam is applied," as the Great Vizier of the Ottoman Empire said in 1917.

The complex question of the democratic potential of Islam does not give grounds for concluding that changes in the political conduct of the Arab–Islamic countries towards a larger pluralism are impossible. If this pluralism is not democracy *stricto sensu* (Huntington 1995), it is however a positive step to abandon fossilized systems of power and avoid the radicalization of political conflicts. The opening up to pluralism and tolerance must obviously also include the Islamic movements:

Parce qu'ils sont une des composantes intrinsèques, la participation des islamistes apparaît comme la condition *sine qua non* d'une véritable transition démocratique: celle-ci perdrait toute signification en l'absence – et *a fortiori* contre – de toute une génération politique.[36]

Notwithstanding the fear that the Islamic parties will not respect the rules of a liberal system, the alternative cannot be repression, which inevitably leads to extremism and violence. Islamism is a deep historical current and, therefore,

il est illusoire d'imaginer la démocratisation, ou au moins, le retour à la paix civile, sans le concours de l'ensemble des forces politiques, y compris les fondamentalistes musulmans. L'essentiel n'est pas de chercher un consensus autour d'un projet de société, car chaque courante a le sien propre et il y tient. L'important est de s'entendre sur les modalités d'accession au pouvoir et la légitimité de l'opposition, en clair sur un *pacte* civique minimum.[37]

The "pacte civique minimum" could overcome the present logic of warlike confrontation we have sketched in our model and begin a time in which disputes among the different political parties are settled peacefully.

---

[36] Burgat (1996), p. 209.
[37] Addi, *Le Monde*, January 12, 1995.

## APPENDIX

The strategies $t_I$ and $t_A$ are described as follows:

$$t_I = \begin{cases} NR, NE & \theta_1 < t_I \\ R, E & \theta_I \geq t_I \end{cases}$$

$$t_A = \begin{cases} NO, NE & \theta_A < t_A \\ O, E & \theta_A \geq t_A \end{cases}$$

We denote by $B_i^n$ player $i$'s belief in his opponent's type at information set $n$, where the numbering of the information sets corresponds to the numbering of the nodes in Figure 10.1. Also, we let $b_i^n(\theta_i)$ be player $i$'s behavior strategy at the information set $n$. The equilibrium notion used is perfect Bayesian equilibrium.

### Proof of Proposition 1

Suppose that for all $(\theta_I, \theta_A)$ the game outcome is $V$. Then $b_I^1(\theta_I) = R$ and $b_A^2(\theta_A) = O$ for all $(\theta_I, \theta_A)$, beliefs $B_I^3$ and $B_A^4$ are uniformly distributed on $[0, 1]$ and the expected equilibrium payoffs in the simultaneous move subgame for type $\theta_I$ and $\theta_A$ are, respectively, $\theta_I + \varphi - c$ and $\theta_A - \varphi - c$.

Since $b_A^2(\theta_A) = O$ for all $\theta_A$, by sequential rationality $\theta_A - \varphi - c \geq 0$ for all $\theta_A$, which implies $\varphi + c \leq 0$. But then, in equilibrium types $\theta_I \in [0, 2c]$ get $\theta_I + \varphi - c = \theta_I + (\varphi + c) - 2c \leq \theta_I - 2c < 0$ and would rather deviate to $NR$ and get 0.                                    Q.E.D.

In the proof of Propositions 2 and 3(ii) we complete the description of the equilibrium by giving the beliefs and we then prove sequential rationality by backwards induction, from information set **A.4** to information set **I.1**.

### Proof of Proposition 2(i)

By Bayes' rule beliefs $B_I^1$ and $B_I^3$ are uniform on $[0, 1]$. Bayes' rule cannot be applied for $B_A^2$ and $B_I^4$, so we arbitrarily choose them to be degenerate on $\theta_I = 0$.

Sequential rationality. **A.4**: type $\theta_A$ gets $1/2$ by playing $NE$ and $\mathrm{Prob}\{0 \leq \theta_A - \varphi\} - c$ by playing $E$. Since in the interval given, $\varphi < 0$, we know that $\theta_A - \varphi > 0$ and, therefore, $\mathrm{Prob}\{0 \leq \theta_A - \varphi\} - c = 1 - c > 1/2$. **I.3**: since $A$ plays $E$, any action is sequentially rational. **A.2**: by playing $NO$, $A$ gets 0 and by playing $O$ gets $1 - c > 0$. **I.1**: by playing $NR$, $I$ gets 0 and by playing $R$ it gets $\theta_I + \varphi - c \leq \theta_I - 1 \leq 0$.                                    Q.E.D.

### Proof of Proposition 2(ii)

First notice that, for the equilibrium to be properly defined, we need $t_I \in [0, 1]$ and $t_A \in [0, 1]$. One can check that the condition $\varphi \leq c(1 - c)/$

$(1 + c)$ guarantees that $t_I > 0$ and that the condition $\varphi \geq -1/(1 + c)$ guarantees that $t_A < 1$. When these two conditions are satisfied, $t_A \in [0, 1]$. By Bayes' rule belief $B_I^1$ is uniform on $[0, 1]$, $B_I^3$ is uniform on $[t_A, 1]$ and $B_A^2$ and $B_A^4$ are uniform on $[t_I, 1]$.

Sequential rationality. **A.4**: since $A$ expects all $\theta_I$ in this node to play $E$, any action is sequentially rational. **I.3**: since $I$ expects all $\theta_A$ in this now to play $E$, any action is sequentially rational. **A.2**: by playing $NO$, $A$ gets 0 and by playing $O$, he gets $-c$ if $\theta_A \leq t_I + \varphi$ and $\theta_A - \varphi - t_I/1 - t_I$ otherwise. Then, type $\theta_a = t_A$ is indifferent between $NO$ and $O$. **I.1**: by playing $NR$, $I$ gets 0 and by playing $R$, he gets $t_A - c(1 - t_A)$ if $\theta_A < t_A - \varphi$ and $(\theta_I + \varphi - c)(1 - t_A)$ othewise. Then, type $\theta_I = t_I$ is indifferent between $NR$ and $R$. Q.E.D.

### Proof of Proposition 2(iii)

First notice that $\varphi < 1 - c$ guarantees that $t_A \leq 1$. By Bayes' rule belief $B_I^1$ is uniform on $[0, 1]$, $B_I^3$ is uniform on $[t_A, 1]$ and $B_A^2$ and $B_i^4$ are uniform on $[0, 1]$.

Sequential rationality. **A.4** and **I.3** as in the proof of Proposition 2(ii). **A.2**: by playing $NO$, $A$ gets 0 and by playing $O$ he gets $\theta_A - \varphi - c$. Then type $\theta_A = t_A$ is indifferent between $NO$ and $O$. **I.1**: by playing $NR$, $I$ gets 0 and by playing $R$, he gets $t_A - c(1 - t_A)$ if $\theta_I < t_A - \varphi$ and $\theta_I + \varphi - c(1 - t_A)$ otherwise. Therefore sequential rationality for types $\theta_I < t_A - \varphi$ follows from $t_A - c(1 - t_A) = t_A(1 + c) - c = \varphi(1 + c) + c^2 \leq -c^2 + c^2 = 0$ and for types $\theta_I > t_A - \varphi$ from $\theta_I + \varphi - c(1 - t_A) \leq t_a - c(1 - t_A)$. Q.E.D.

### Proof of Proposition 2(iv)

By Bayes' rule beliefs $B_I^1$, $B_A^2$ and $B_i^4$ are uniform on $[0, 1]$. Belief $B_I^3$ is arbitrarily chosen to be degenerate on $\theta_A = 0$.

Sequential rationality. **A.4**: since $I$ plays $E$, any action is sequentially rational. **I.3**: type $\theta_I$ gets $1/2$ by playing $NE$ and $\text{Prob}\{0 \leq \theta_I + \varphi\} - c$ by playing $E$. Since in the interval given $\varphi > 0$, it follows that $\theta_I + \varphi > 0$ and $\text{Prob}\{0 \leq \theta_I + \varphi\} - c = 1 - c > 1/2$. **A.2**: by playing $NO$, $A$ gets 0 and by playing $O$ he gets $\text{Prob}\{\theta_I \leq \theta_A - \varphi\} - c = \theta_A - \varphi - c \leq \theta_A - 1 \leq 0$ for all $\theta_A$. **I.1**: by playing $NR$, $I$ gets 0 and by playing $R$ he gets 1. Q.E.D.

### Proof of Proposition 3(i)

The proof is given in Molinari (1998) as Proof of Proposition 1.

### Proof of Proposition 3(ii)

Given $a + c > 1/2$, the interval of values of $\varphi$ is well defined. By Bayes' rule, all beliefs are uniformly distributed on $[0, 1]$.

Sequential rationality: **A.4**: type $\theta_A$ gets $1/2 + a$ by playing $NE$ and $\text{Prob}\{\theta_I \leq \theta_A - \varphi\} - c = \theta_A - \varphi - c \leq 1 - \varphi - c \leq 1 - 1/2 + a + c - c = a + 1/2$ by playing $E$. **I.3**: type $\theta_I$ gets $1/2 + a$ by playing $NE$ and $\text{Prob}\{\theta_a \leq \theta_I + \varphi\} - c = \theta_I + \varphi - c \leq 1 + \varphi - c \leq 1 - 1/2 + a + c - c = a + 1/2$ by playing $E$. **A.2**: by playing $NO$, $A$ gets 0 and by playing $O$ it gets $1/2 + a > 0$. **I.1**: by playing $NR$, $I$ gets 0 and by playing $R$ he gets $1/2 + a > 0$.

To prove that violence cannot be an equilibrium outcome an argument analogous to the one in Proposition 3(i) can be used to show that there is no equilibrium in which $V$ occurs with probability strictly between 0 and 1. We also know, by Proposition 1, that in equilibrium $V$ never occurs with probability one. The conclusion follows. Q.E.D.

## REFERENCES

Benantar, A. 1994. "La traide di fine secolo: Islam, islamismo e democrazia," *Limes*, no. 2, 55–64.

Botiveau, B. 1994. " 'Charia' et démocratie, les aléas d'une comparaison," in *L'Islamisme*, La Découverte, Paris.

Bueno de Mesquita, B., Morrow, J. D. and Zorick, B. R. 1997. "Capabilites, perception and escalation," *American Political Science Review* **91**, 15–27.

Burgat, F. 1995. *Il fondamentalismo Islamico: Algeria, Tunisia, Marocco, Libia*, SEI, Torino.

Burgat, F. 1996. *L'Islamisme en face*, La Découverte, Paris.

Choueiri, Y. M. 1990. *Islamic Fundamentalism*, Pinter Publishers Ltd, London (Italian trans., Il Mulino, Bologna, 1993).

Colombo, A. 1991. "Islamismo e deoccidentalizzazione in Medio Oriente," in Santoro, C. M. (ed.), *Il mosaico mediterraneo*, Il Mulino, Bologna.

Du Pasquier, R. 1990. *Il risveglio dell'Islam*, Ed. S. Paolo, Milano.

Etienne, B. 1988. *L'islamismo radicale*, Rizzoli, Milano.

Gresh, A. and Vidal, D. 1991. *Guida storico-politica del Medio Oriente*, Edizioni Associate, Roma.

Guolo, R. 1994a. *Il partito di Dio. L'Islam radicale contro l'Occidente*, Guerini e Associati, Milano.

Guolo, R. 1994b. "Geopolitica dell'islamismo," *Politica Internazionale*, no. 2, 71–82.

Hardin, R. 1995. *One for all. The logic of group conflict*, Princeton University Press, Princeton.

Huntington, S. P. 1993. "The clash of civilizations?," *Foreign Affairs* (summer), 22–49.

Huntington, S. P. 1995. *La terza ondata. I processi di democratizzazione alla fine del XX secolo*, Il Mulino, Bologna.

Impagliazzo, M. and Giro, M. 1997. *Algeria in ostaggio: tra esercito e fondamentalismo, storia di una pace difficile*, Guerini e Associati, Milano.

Jabri, M. A. 1994. "Extrémisme et attitude rationaliste dans la pensée arabo-islamique," in *L'Islamisme*, La Découverte, Paris.

Kepel, G. 1984. *Le Prophète et le Pharaon*, La Découverte, Paris.

Kepel, G. 1991. *La revanche de Dieu*, Seuil, Paris.

Leveau, R. 1994. *Vers une fonction tribunicienne?*, in *L'Islamisme*, La Découverte, Paris.

Lewis, B. 1991. *La riconquista Islamica*, Il Mulino, Bologna.

Lewis, B. 1994. "Musulmani, Cristiani ed Ebrei: coesistenza e laicità," in Riccardi, A. (ed.), *Il Mediterraneo nel Novecento*, Edizioni S. Paolo, Milano.

Mimouni, R. 1996. *Dentro l'integralismo. La testimonianza di uno scrittore algerino*, Einaudi, Torino.

Molinari, M. C. 1998. "Military capabilities and escalation: a comment on Bueno de Mesquita, Morrow and Zorick," mimeo.

Pace, E. 1990. *Il regime della verità: il fondamentalismo religioso contemporaneo*, Il Mulino, Bologna.

Pace, E. 1994. "I guardiani della causa di Dio: forza e debolezza dell'Islam politico," *Politica Internazionale* 2, 83–96.

Pace, E. and Guolo, R. 1998. *I fondamentalismi*, Editori Laterza, Bari.

Pasquinelli, C. (ed.). 1994. *Fondamentalismi*, Parolechiave, Donzelli Editore, Roma.

Riccardi, A. 1997. *Mediterraneo*, Guerini e Associati, Milano.

Roy, O. 1992. *L'échec de l'Islam politique*, Seuil, Paris.

*Stato del mondo. Annuario economico e geopolitico mondiale*, Il Saggiatore, Milano, anni 1993–98.

Stone, M. 1997. *The agony of Algeria*, Hurst & Co., London.

Zagare, F. and Kilgour, D. M. 1993. "Asymmetric Deterrence," *International Studies Quarterly* 37, 1–27.

Zitelman, A., 1997. *Vita di Martin Luther King*, Feltrinelli, Milano.

# 11

# De Bello Omnium$_i$ Contra Omnes$_j$

*Guido Ortona*

## 1. INTRODUCTION

The subject of this chapter is mass ethnic violence. Mass ethnic violence is fortunately quite rare; but, shamefully, not so rare as to be considered exceptional. And, as it is not exceptional, it deserves a theoretical explanation. A theory actually exists, but it admits non-rational behavior (see Wintrobe, 1995; more on this in Section 2). In this chapter I will suggest a theory of mass ethnic violence produced by fully rational subjects. The argument is based on the theory of nationalism and xenophobia developed mostly by Breton and Wintrobe (see Breton, 1964; Breton and Breton, 1995; Wintrobe, 1995), and on the theory of conventions (see for instance Sugden, 1986). A definition of mass ethnic violence is provided in this section. Section 2 summarizes the state-of-the-art economic theory of nationalism and xenophobia. The basic model of the chapter is described in Sections 3 to 6. A couple of extensions are discussed in sections 7 and in the Appendix. Some general and concluding remarks are in Sections 8 and 9.

I define a state of mass ethnic violence, from now on "V-State," as a situation in which

$$\hat{p}(iAj) > z_i^*, \quad \hat{p}(jAi) > z_j^* \tag{1}$$

$$\hat{p}(iAj)/\hat{p}(iAi) > y_i^*, \quad \hat{p}(jAi)/\hat{p}(jAj) > y_j^* \tag{2}$$

where $aAb$ stands for "subject $a$ assaults subject $b$," $i$ and $j$ are subjects belonging to ethnic groups $I$ and $J$ respectively, $\hat{p}(aAb)$ is the average probability across subjects $a$ of assaulting subjects $b$, and $z^*$ and $y^*$ are numerical values to be determined (elsewhere, and possibly case by case) by empirical inquiry.

In other words, there is a V-State when a member of ethnic group $I(J)$ is sufficiently likely to assault a member of ethnic group $J(I)$, while he[1] is much less likely to assault a member of his own group. Of course, condition (1) is sufficient to define *mass* violence; condition (2) restricts the definition to *mass ethnic* violence, as it rules out the cases where the probability of inter-ethnic aggression is not that different from that of intra-ethnic aggression.

The meaning of "to assault" is that provided by dictionaries, something like "to try to produce an injury to someone." To avoid unnecessary complications with expected values, I suppose for simplicity (but see footnote 5) that an assault is necessarily successful. This does not amount to saying that aggression is costless, but simply that if the assault takes place, the injury to the victim will be serious enough to prevent a retaliation. The definition of $A$ is consequently $aAb$ if $a$ makes it physically impossible for $b$ to produce any significant harm to $a$.

Note that the definition of mass ethnic violence, and hence the level of $p(aAb)$ that individuates a V-State, implies that ordinary people take part in assaults. Consequently, the definition does not apply, for instance, to the Israeli–Palestinian conflict or to Irish terrorism. In both cases only a few, specialized subjects provide the aggression; the average probability across subjects of an aggression is relatively low. Actually, in both cases the potential victims try to keep on with their ordinary way of living, differently from the examples quoted below. Nor does it apply to Hobbes's *Bellum omnium contra omnes*, as the assault must be against a given subset of the *omnes* (whence the title of the chapter). It applies instead to the events in Bosnia and Central Africa in recent years. Evidence of other cases may easily be found, for instance in Horowitz (1985).

For reasons to be explained below, it is useful to distinguish between V-States in which xenophobia is low and V-States in which xenophobia is high. I label the former ones T-States (for Tolerance), and the latter X-States (for Xenophobia). According to the definition, we have a T-State when $\hat{X} < x'*$, while we have an X-State when $\hat{X} > x'$; where $\hat{X}$ stands for the average level of xenophobia, and $x^*$ and $x'$ are specific values.[2]

## 2. THE ROLE OF ETHNIC CAPITAL

The theory of nationalism and xenophobia among rational subjects is quite well established. Most papers in Breton et al. (1995), for instance, employ it. Essentially the same theory is pivotal for Landa (1995). I will label this theory, admittedly imprecisely, the Breton–Wintrobe Model, or BWM. It may be summarized as follows, on the basis of Breton and Breton (1995) and Wintrobe (1995). There is an "ethnic capital," mostly

---

[1] Empirical evidence suggests that "he" is more appropriate than "she" in this context.

[2] According to Breton and Breton (1995: 110) "xenophobia is a continuous variable, which, properly measured, could be normalized to vary between zero and one."

made up of ethnic relationships, whose role in production is to reduce transaction costs. This capital is not transferable; hence, groups successfully endowed with it are visible and envied. Ethnic capital is accumulated through education, and it is managed by "ethnic entrepreneurs," whose characteristics vary according to the setting. The existence of ethnic capital introduces a sort of custom duty among groups, and consequently restricts the market and creates inefficiency. The reduction of transaction costs may more than compensate for such inefficiency, but only for subjects endowed with ethnic capital. If this is the case, we will have in equilibrium a positive level of "nationalism." We may roughly define nationalism as a preference for having relations of any kind with members of the same ethnic group.

A weakness of former versions of BWM (see Breton, 1964) was the explanation of xenophobia. Empirically, xenophobia is strongly linked with nationalism; the only explanation for it offered within the context of the BWM thus far described is the mix of envy and contempt produced by successful use of ethnic capital. Breton and Breton admit that this explanation is not convincing, and in their 1995 paper they provide a more compelling one. The argument may be summarized as follows. Ethnic entrepreneurs aim at maximizing the return on ethnic capital. They consequently have an interest in hindering inter-ethnic links. In many societies, including Western and Soviet-type ones, this is hardly possible on a legal basis: hence the resort to cultural weapons. Xenophobia, in other terms, raises the productivity of ethnic capital: "Xenophobia, then, increases the rate of return on investments in cultural nationalism and, because of the relationship . . . between political and cultural nationalism, on investments in political nationalism as well" (Breton and Breton, 1995: 111); "The capital formed by investing in cultural nationalism is . . . more or less like the "ethnic capital" analysed . . . elsewhere in this book" (p. 102). To be more faithful to Breton's terminology, the xenophobia of the masses is produced by ethnic élites, who mostly stand to gain from the use of ethnic capital. It is important to observe that xenophobia may be, and normally is, produced through manipulation of information; thus it is not necessary to postulate a "taste for xenophobia" *à la Becker*[3].

---

[3] BWM was developed mostly looking at Canada, but it aims to be general, and it is. For example, Lemarchand (1993) writes about Burundi that "The Hutu–Tutsi conflict is a recent phenomenon, rooted in part in the process of social change introduced by the colonial state, in part in the rapid mobilization of ethnic identities under the pressure of electoral competition" (p. 153); "The polarization of ethnic feelings did not just happen: it came about as the result of a deliberate, organized and sustained effort of the part of ethnic entrepreneurs to mobilize a substantial ethnic following" (p. 157). With reference to newly independent states, Horowitz (1985: 97) notes that "the very élites who were

*(continued overleaf)*

Next, we move from xenophobia to mass ethnic violence. According to Wintrobe, the return on ethnic capital is especially high when "other mechanisms which can enforce trade, such as legal enforcement, are weak, and vice versa" (1995: 62). It follows that resorting to ethnic capital is particularly useful in economic, and hence social, crises. As a crisis deepens, however, the return on ethnic capital diminishes, while its stock is high and, presumably, group and family pressure to obey ethnic engagements grows. In this situation, Wintrobe asks,

> what can the individual do? I suggest that individuals in this position are particularly likely to develop prejudices against members of other ethnic groups, and have the potential to engage in conflict with them . . . in order to raise the yield on ethnic capital. To buttress this assertion, I will try to show that the constellation of returns just described is consistent with the peculiar syndrome described in the classic work by Adorno and others, *The Authoritarian Personality* (1950).

This is accomplished convincingly in the pages following the quotation. Thereafter Wintrobe concludes (p. 64) that "the extremity of some ethnic conflicts, such as the behavior of the Nazis, and perhaps the contemporary conflict between Serbs and Croatians, is difficult to explain with a strictly rational approach, and can be explained with the approach suggested here."[4] Mass ethnic violence, in other words, is a consequence of the outburst of the authoritarian personality, owing to the stress produced by the conflict between the low return of ethnic capital and the necessity of paying for it.

## 3. THE ETHNIC GAME

The limitation of this model is that it cannot explain the existence of T-States, that is, of mass ethnic violence when xenophobia is low. According to the model, we may expect, before the unleashing of mass ethnic violence, a long-lasting (at least a generation-long, in Wintrobe's version) accumulation of ethnic capital, nationalism and xenophobia. This is surely not the case, for instance, of Bosnia-Herzegovina before the civil war. There was one language, dialects were not ethnic but local, people "were among the least religious people in the world," and they

---

*(continued from previous page)*
thought to be leading their peoples away from ethnic affiliations were commonly found to be in the forefront of ethnic conflict;" and with reference to former Yugoslavia, Hardin (1995b: 31) argues that "Only certain leaders may have improved their lot and their prospects. Oddly, these leaders have improved their lot not by raising the level of welfare for their groups, but through individually specific rewards of leadership."

[4] The quotation has been slightly modified for convenience of insertion.

were "heavily intermarried;" and more generally there is no evidence of large-scale nationalism and xenophobia (Hardin, 1995: 157–8).

BWM may consequently explain only some cases of mass ethnic violence; let us admit that it may explain X-States, but not T-States. We need, then, a theory for T-States; better, we need a unified theory for both T-States and X-States. In addition, as X-States are more common than T-States, the theory should also suggest an explanation for this feature. This is what the model presented in this chapter aims to do. It moves from a "folk conjecture" made by many, for instance by Hardin: "Why violence? . . . On a Hobbesian view of political life, without institutions to help us stay orderly we take a preemptive view of all conflicts. . . . Self-defence against possible (not even actual) attack suffices to motivate murderous conflict" (1995b: 30). This suggestion is useful, but in these terms it is hampered by two serious limitations. First, it lacks an explanation of why the conflict occurs only against aliens, and not against *omnes*. The second limitation will be discussed further below.

Suppose an economy (a society, if you prefer) with two ethnic groups, labeled $I$ and $J$. The interaction of interest between a typical subject belonging to $I$, $i$, and a typical subject belonging to $J$, $j$, is defined by a symmetrical two-person, two-strategy game, where the strategies are simply 'to assault," $a$, and "not to assault," $n$;[5] note that $a$ and $n$ form a partition. The game is the following:

|   |   | $j$ | |
|---|---|---|---|
|   |   | $n$ | $a$ |
| $i$ | $n$ | $nn, nn$ | $na, an$ |
|   | $a$ | $an, na$ | $aa, aa$ |

Payoffs are identified by the strategies chosen by the relevant player (first letter) and by the opponent (second letter). For instance, *an* means "payoff of a player adopting $a$ against an opponent adopting $n$." In the following, I will label this game "*the ethnic game.*" In the setting of the

---

[5] I admit discrete strategies only for the sake of simplicity. The whole discussion could easily be made in terms of continuous strategies. In this case, we should admit "aggressiveness" to be a continuous function, as we did for xenophobia; "assault" would correspond to values of "aggressiveness" beyond a given threshold. A further, plausible complication is to admit that an assault may be unsuccessful. In this case, payoffs become expected payoffs, without substantial changes in analysis.

ethnic game, a V-State corresponds to a probability sufficiently high that one subject (or both) chooses *a*.

I assume that:

(a) If there are enforceable legal and/or moral sanctions against aggression, the ranking of the payoffs is the following:

$$nn > an > na > aa$$

In other words, the worst outcome corresponds to a double aggression, and the best to the absence of aggression. In the case of one-sided aggression, the assailant ends up better than the assaulted.

(b) In the case of aggression, there exists a first-shot advantage. Consequently, if there are no enforceable sanctions, legal or moral,

$$aa > na.$$

(c) The ethnic affiliation of both subjects is (no cost) common knowledge.

(d) The existence of other ethnic groups is irrelevant.

(e) $nn > an$ even in the absence of sanctions. Hence, due to assumption (b), the complete rank of payoffs if there are no sanctions is $nn > an > aa > na$.

(f) The game is symmetrical.

(g) The game describes the situation *before* the start of the process leading to mass ethnic violence.

Assumptions (a) and (b) are technological, and it seems quite safe that they correspond to the state of the world in most societies. The others are not only simplifying. They generalize the case: there are only two ethnic groups, characterized only by the common knowledge of membership. Assumption (e) deserves some comment. It rules out the case of a positive payoff in assaulting, if there are no sanctions. This case has often been considered the most relevant for mass ethnic violence (see a review in Horowitz, 1985); actually, it is both trivial and uncommon. If there is a gain in assaulting there is no problem in explaining mass ethnic violence. But what we want to explain is precisely the outburst of mass ethnic violence when empirical evidence makes it clear, both to observers and (presumably) to the subjects involved, that there is no direct gain in assaulting the alien neighbor, if he is not likely to assault first. The proviso is ruled out by assumption (g). The absence of direct, non-preemptive gain in assaulting is patent in recent civil wars in Bosnia and Central Africa. I suggest that this is actually the case in most instances of mass ethnic violence in modern societies. Only in hunter–gatherer societies might robbing the neighbor be a rational strategy for the typical subject – and even for these societies the point is under debate.

In fact, the only purely simplifying assumption is (f). If payoffs are different, the overall result does not change, but we obtain a quite interesting particular case. As it is not central to the main argument, a discussion of it is postponed to the Appendix.

It is worth emphasizing that this model cannot be applied to situations characterized by the violation of one or more of assumptions (a)–(e). Most notably, this is the case of mass ethnic violence prompted by sudden mass immigration, as well as that of ethnic warfare in hunter–gatherer societies, as we noted. In both cases, assumption (e) may be violated.

For the sake of simplicity, we may employ a numerical example. Values are obviously arbitrary; however, the results we may read in it are general, as they depend only on the *order* of values. Let's suppose the ethnic game to be

|   |   | *j* | |
|---|---|-----|-----|
|   |   | *n* | *a* |
| *i* | *n* | 0, 0 | −20, −10 |
|   | *a* | −10, −20 | −23, −23 |

Some payoffs include several additive components. *an* consists of the (negative) payoff of the fighting and of a sanction. In the example, the value of both is −5. *aa* consists of a lesser physical damage than that of *na* (−13 instead of −20 in the example), of a sanction (−5), and of the fighting cost (−5).

The ethnic game is indefinitely repeated. Both players may be embodied by different couples of physical subjects. They develop a subjective probability for the choice of the opponent according to the history of the game. More precisely, I assume that the choice of a given strategy in repetition *t* by player *i(j)* increases the probability for the opponent that *i(j)* will choose that strategy in repetition *t* + 1.[6] In addition, I assume complete information. More simply, what the above amounts to is to assume that people may observe the behavior of the members

---

[6] This is the simplest form of the hypothesis about the nature of expectations commonly adopted in the literature about conventions. See for instance Hargreaves Heap and Varoufakis (1995), ch. 7.

of the other group, and that their expectations are based on that observation.

## 4. COLLAPSING OF THE STATE

In this game $n$ is a dominant strategy for both players. We need some realistic hypotheses capable of explaining the shift to $a$. If we admit that aggression is normally sanctioned, a necessary condition is the non-enforceability of sanctions. In the real world, this happens when, and only when, there is a serious institutional crisis, to the point that the state cannot accomplish its most fundamental duty, the exertion of coercion. I will label this situation the "collapsing of the state," according to the following definition: "there is collapsing of the state when legal sanctions are ineffective in determining the choice between $a$ and $n$." Clearly, this is the limiting case of a continuum of possibilities, with the certainty of sanctions at the other end; I adopt this "extreme" definition only for sake of simplicity.

If there is collapsing of the state, the ethnic game becomes:

|   |   | $j$ | |
|---|---|---|---|
|   |   | $n$ | $a$ |
| $i$ | $n$ | $nn, nn$ | $na^*, a^*n$ |
|   | $a$ | $a^*n, na^*$ | $a^*a^*, a^*a^*$ |

where $a^*(.)$ is the new, sanction-free, payoff of an aggressor. Due to our assumption,

$$nn > a^*n, nn > a^*a^* \text{ and } a^*a^* > na^*.$$

In the example,

|   |   | $j$ | |
|---|---|---|---|
|   |   | $n$ | $a$ |
| $i$ | $n$ | $0, 0$ | $-20, -5$ |
|   | $a$ | $-5, -20$ | $-18, -18$ |

Now $n$ is no longer dominant. The best response strategy to $a$ is $a$. Actually, there are two Nash equilibria, $[n, n]$ and $[a, a]$. However, $[n, n]$ is efficient: the game is a coordination game, there is no reason to choose the inefficient equilibrium.[7] It follows that the collapsing of the state is not sufficient to explain mass ethnic violence. This is the second error of the common argument accepted by Hardin. Hardin admits that in social crises $i(j)$ is bound to attack in order to prevent an act of aggression by $j(i)$. But what remains, and needs, to be explained is why in non-trivial settings $j(i)$ should attack $i(j)$ at first. The reason may be only to prevent an act of aggression by $i(j)$, and so on. The argument is circular; the circularity may be broken only if somewhere there is a reason to assault different from prevention. The preemptive argument can explain why mass ethnic violence is self-fueling once it has started, but cannot explain why it starts in the first place. Actually, in the very general model outlined so far, the subjective probability of $i(j)$ of being assaulted by $j(i)$ is positive only due to irrational or trembling-hand behavior. Consequently, we need further assumptions. They must be as few and as simple as possible, following Occam, and realistic. Before proceeding, note that as soon as $a$ becomes dominant, the probability of aggression will start rapidly to shift towards unity; unless something stops the process, condition (1) of Section 1 will assuredly be observed, and this implies that condition (2) will be too, provided that the probability of intra-ethnic aggression (that remains unchanged) is sufficiently low.

## 5. EXOGENOUS AND NORMAL SUBJECTS

More formally: for $a$ to be dominant it is necessary that

$$p(aa) + (1 - p)(an) > p(na) + (1 - p)nn \tag{4}$$

if there is no collapsing of the state, or that

$$p(a^*a^*) + (1 - p)(a^*n) > p(na^*) + (1 - p)nn \tag{4'}$$

if there is; where $p$ is the probability that the opponent chooses $a$. The additional assumption we are looking for – one is sufficient, as we will see – must produce an increase in $p$, to the point that condition (4) or (4') is respected. This result may be obtained if there are exogenous subjects who gain from normal subjects being assaulted. The terms "exogenous" and "normal" identify subjects who respectively do not and do play the ethnic game. More simply, normal subjects are typical members of the two ethnic groups, while exogenous subjects are not – as they have a different preference for violence. Exogenous subjects act as mobilizing agents, somehow *à la* Olson (see Olson, 1965). They may be religious or ethnic fanatics, weapons traders, alien agents, revenge seekers, mad, any mix of these, or whatever else. They may act as provokers, assaulting

---

[7] For experimental evidence that efficient Nash equilibria are actually attractors, see for instance Cooper et al. (1990).

$i(j)$ and pretending to be $j(i)$; or as instigators, manipulating the information of $i(j)$ in order to increase hate and fear towards $j(i)$; or as extorters,
forcing $i(j)$ to assault $j(i)$;[8] or in a mixed way. In any case, if $i(j)$ cannot distinguish perfectly between these subjects and $j(i)$, their activities
produce an increase in $p$. I will collectively label these subjects $A$, for
*agitators*.

Condition (4) cannot be fulfilled, as

$$(1 - p)an < (1 - p)nn \quad \text{and} \quad p(aa) < p(na).$$

This corresponds to what we already know: if sanctions are enforceable, a
V-State cannot be produced. Consequently, I will consider only (4′); that
is, I will suppose the state to have collapsed.

Condition (4′) may be reduced to

$$p(nn - na^* - a^*n + a^*a^*) > nn - a^*n \tag{5}$$

The term in brackets is positive, so the condition becomes

$$p > (nn - a^*n)/(nn - na^* - a^*n + a^*a^*) \tag{5′}$$

so that

$$p^* = (nn - a^*n)/(nn - na^* - a^*n + a^*a^*) \tag{6}$$

is the threshold value of $p$.

Condition (5′) determines the result of the activity of $A$. $A$ produces
$p$; and we may quite safely assume that the total cost of $p$ increases
with $p$.[9] It follows that $p^*$ will be produced if, and only if, the profit for
$A$ is positive at that value of $p$. In other words, agitators may make
people fear being assaulted by the members of the other ethnic group,
thus making rational the preemptive war suggested by Hardin. In still
other, and more suggestive, words, the preemptive war cannot be produced among rational subjects unless there are agitators, as defined
above. Equation (6) states more than the existence of a threshold
value of $p$, above which it is preferable to assault. It results that the
threshold value is positively related to $nn$, the payoff related to ethnic
peace. This produces a further, and relevant, result: *ceteris paribus*, if
ethnic peace is not that useful, the activity of agitators is particularly
likely to ignite mass ethnic violence. Note that ethnic peace is likely to

---

[8] Hardin (1995b: 35) quotes the statement of a Croatian militiaman in Bosnia: "I really
don't hate Muslims, but because of the situation I want to kill them all;" and he adds: "He
[the militiaman] had either to leave his community altogether or to identify with it altogether."

[9] $A$ draws a utility from the existence of a regime of violence; in order to promote the advent
of this regime, $A$ must do something – murdering, bombing, kidnapping, or whatever. As
these activities are costly, we may speak of a cost of $p$.

be of little use when economic links between ethnic groups are feeble, or when they become feeble due to any sort of social and/or economic crisis.

## 6. PROPENSITY TO ASSAULT

The ethnic game of the previous sections may be played by any couple made up of a member of ethnic group *I* and a member of ethnic group *J*. The values of the payoffs may be very different across the players. In this section I will argue that this feature does not harm the validity of the model.

We abandon the assumption of symmetry in the game, but retain all the other ones. Consequently, the cardinal value of the payoffs is specific for any player, while the ordinal one is the same. The propensity to assault changes accordingly. Suppose, for instance, a young male, karate-trained, a former special troops member, facing an old single lady: whatever the activity of agitators, his subjective probability of being assaulted is very unlikely to bypass the critical threshold. Consequently, he will not assault her; and knowing this, she will not assault him. But if the first subject faces someone similar to him, the fight is very easy to instigate.

The point is that even if the payoffs, and consequently the violence thresholds, are specific, the activity of agitators will increase subjective probabilities for *any* game worth such an investment. Consequently, the *average* propensity among subjects to assault will grow, possibly to the point that conditions (1) and (2) of Section 1 are satisfied.

## 7. THE ROLE OF XENOPHOBIA

Next, let us consider why X-States are more frequent than T-States. There are two reasons. First, according to BWM xenophobia is most likely to develop where there is an ethnic divide, return on ethnic capital is high, and return on "normal" capital is uncertain. These features are typical of poor economies facing changes; these economies also provide most cases of mass ethnic violence. In other words, in economies apt to develop into a V-State the presence of a high level of xenophobia is simply more likely than its absence. The second reason is less obvious. As we know, nationalistic élites produce xenophobia. However, the aim of the élites is to maximize the return on their assets. The maximum is very unlikely to be reached in a V-State, and more generally in a state of serious social unrest. We may consequently expect the élite not to be *A*. But in so far as the élites produce xenophobia, they reduce the cost of the aggression. Moral sanctions decrease (possibly to the point that their sign changes), and presumably legal ones too. This makes it easier for $p^*$ to correspond to a positive profit for $A$. More simply, if xenophobia is high $p^*$ is much more likely to be sufficiently cheap for $A$ to be reached.

Bosnia-Herzegovina is a very good case in point. Xenophobia, as was noted, was very low. The outburst of a V-State was impossible, unless costs for agitators were exceptionally low, and/or rewards exceptionally high. Both conditions were unfortunately satisfied, as many or most agitators were financed, protected, and rewarded by relatively powerful foreign governments.

In our example, it is preferable to assault if

$$0(1 - p) - 20p < -5(1 - p) - 18p$$

that is, if

$$p > 0.71$$

A V-State will result only if a *typical* subject $i(j)$ supposes that the probability of being attacked by subject $j(i)$ is greater than 0.71; that is, only if agitators find it worthy to produce $p$ up to this point. Note again that as soon as $p^*$ is reached for $i(j)$, $p$ will start to shift towards 1 for both players. In the jargon of the theory of conventions, the convention "live in peace" is displaced by the convention "assault your neighbor."[10]

## 8.  SUMMARY AND CONCLUSIONS

To sum up, five conditions are required for a V-State to break out:

(a) an initial divide of the population, such that any relevant subject may easily be assigned to a given group;
(b) the collapsing of the state, as defined above;
(c) a first-shot advantage in case of aggression;
(d) the existence of agitators, as described above;
(e) a payoff matrix such that the attainment of the threshold probability $p^*$ is worthwhile for the agitators.

Note that the outburst of the V-State results without any direct gain for a typical subject adopting $a$; as we noted, this feature is largely confirmed by empirical evidence in many cases of mass ethnic violence, and it often intrigued the observers.[11]

The presence of conditions (a) to (d) is relatively easy to assess. The initial divide either exists or not; the repressive apparatus of the state either crashed or not; the first-shot advantage, as was argued, is an

---

[10] As for Burundi, "Recourse to violence has become institutionalised in an almost routine-like mode of behavior [. . .] A new tradition has taken root which makes recourse to violence the norm, and compromise the exception" (Lemarchand, 1993: 168).

[11] As an instance among many, see Lloyd (1974), quoted in Horowitz (1985).

"always true," purely technological feature; finally, either there are agitators or not. It is true that the presence of agitators is a continuum, more than a yes–no variable; but whether the level of their activity is sufficient to produce a V-state pertains to condition (e). In a sense, conditions (a) to (d) are preliminary conditions: if they are present, and only if they are present, is there the possibility of mass ethnic violence. This possibility will turn into reality if condition (e) is satisfied too.

We can consider condition (e) as a "black box." The inputs are the first four conditions. The black box, if turned to "on," transforms these preconditions into mass ethnic violence. Condition (e) is made up of two requirements: the payoff for the agitators must be sufficiently high, and the probability threshold for the ordinary subjects must be sufficiently low. There is a trade-off between the two sub-conditions: if the payoff for the agitators is very high, they can succeed in promoting a V-State even in a very peaceful and well-off community; while if the community itself has a long-lasting tradition of violence and the gains from peace are low, even poor advantages for the agitators may produce the same result. As was suggested at the end of Section 5, the sub-condition related to the payoff of the typical subject may be approximated by the value of $nn$, the payoff of the peace; we may consequently think of a "frontier of mass ethnic violence." This frontier appears in Figure 11.1, where $P$ stands for the payoff of the agitators. The V-state will produce in the area above the curve.[12]

Figure 11.1 illustrates the empirical research program suggested by this chapter: to individuate the form and the position of the curve. The real problem is that of the payoffs of the typical subject. The "nature and cause" of the agitators are too contingent to specific situations and to historical features for a general model to make

Figure 11.1 The violence frontier

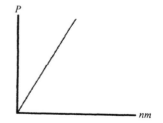

---

[12] The second derivative of the function is likely to be positive. Here it is graphed as a straight line to emphasize that to establish the real shape and location is a matter of empirical inquiry – see below.

sense, as was briefly suggested in Section 5. So we are left with just the one, yet gigantic, problem that may be described as follows: "to find out when the loss from the end of the ethnic peace is low for a typical subject dwelling in a state described by conditions (a) to (d) above." It is possible to suggest some factors that may contribute, even if this is mostly a matter for empirical research, as I have already stressed several times.

First, economic conditions (see again the end of Section 5). Ethnic integration promotes economic integration, hence *nn* is likely to be high in well-off communities. However, the value of *nn* may decline rapidly if the state collapses. In addition, work and business conflicts that are normal in normal conditions may add fuel to the fire if they can be aligned along the ethnic division.

Second, information. What is crucial is the *perception* of the threat for the typical subject. In the presence of a strong activity of agitators and of the collapsing of the state, the production of information may well be biased towards extremism and the production of panic-enhancing announcements.

Third, self-governing of the communities. If ethnic communities have sound traditions of ethnic leadership and self-governing, the ethnic violence may presumably be avoided more easily than in the opposite case. What is remarkable from this point of view is that mass ethnic violence would be more likely to result in modern ato-mized societies than in old, community-like ones – contrary to naive explanations based on ethnic hatred, but according to the evidence of the Bosnian war.

It is possible to think of other factors; however, those just mentioned are probably the most important. It must be stressed that what needs to be investigated is not how these characteristics (we may label them ethnic economic links, information and leadership) *are* in normal times, but how they *evolve* when the state collapses and agitators operate; in other words, how these institutions are *vulnerable* to these shocks. My suggestion is that they are more so than is commonly thought, and that this is the main reason why mass ethnic violence is so unexpected and so surprising in its features.

## 9. PREDICTIONS

The model allows us to make some predictions.

First, we will expect the absence of a V-State if at least one condition is not satisfied. In Israel and Northern Ireland (up to 1998), for instance, probably only (b) is missing, while in Italy and Canada only (a) and (c) are satisfied.

Of some interest is the case in which condition (b) is satisfied, but some other condition is not. We should observe in this case a very serious social and institutional crisis, but no mass ethnic violence. This case should be quite rare, given the pervasiveness of ethnic divides, the role of ethnic entrepreneurs and of xenophobia, and the increase of ethnic loyalty as the crisis deepens. A social crisis nurtures both the collapsing of the state and the ethnic conflict, as we have seen. Oddly enough, however, a case in point seems to have been taking place just when this chapter was begun (March 1997). This happened in Albania, where the state actually collapsed and there were divides in both language and religion, but a V-State did not ensue, presumably because condition (e) was not fulfilled.

Second, the initial divide does not need to be an ethnic one. In principle, a V-State is conceivable based on a non-ethnic clash. However, this should be a very rare case; I cannot quote an example. There are two reasons for this. First, ethnic division is pervasive, allows easy assignment of citizens to a group, and is particularly apt to produce agitators. Second, according to BWM, a division of an economy into two (or more) groups creates inefficiency. This inefficiency may be maintained only if the asset at the basis of it is not (easily) transferable. This is true for ethnic capital, but, very probably, only for it. In other words, while an initial fracture grounded on ethnic differences is likely to be deepened by ethnic entrepreneurs, other kinds of fracture are likely to be mended by market behaviors.

The most relevant predictions, however, are the following.

Third, the outburst of a V-State is impossible without agitators. The presence of agitators has often been considered a sort of by-product of mass ethnic violence. Instead, their activity may be a necessary condition for it.

Fourth, in settings where the model is relevant (see Sections 2 and 3), mass ethnic violence may occur without the breaking out of ancestral characters of mass psychology,[13] or of tribal *homo homini lupus* behavior.[14] These features may be absent, or relatively unimportant.

Fifth, according to the model, mass ethnic violence is essentially the result of mass greed for self-defence. This should be mirrored by per-

---

[13] For the sociobiological approach to ethnocentrism and xenophobia, see, for example, Van Der Dennen (1987); for the psychological one, see, for example, Brown (1985), ch. 15. Horowitz (1985: 180) writes: "It seems clear now that the Itsekiri, like the Sinhalese, the Hausa, the Malays, the Fijans, the Telanganas, the Assamese, and a good many other groups, were troubled by invidious group comparison with the 'dynamic' Urhobo in their midst . . . The Itsekiri were given to anxiety-laden perceptions – for that is precisely what their exaggeration and foreboding connote: they are textbook symptoms – and they were also inclined to conflict behavior based on their anxiety."

[14] For references, see Horowitz (1985), ch. 3.

ceived motivations of participants in violence;[15] to my knowledge, normally it is.

Finally, the outburst of mass ethnic violence should be a very rapid phenomenon; and it usually is. The reason is the following. Every subject has only two choices, to assault or not to assault. As soon as $p^*$ becomes sufficiently high for a given subject, he will change his strategy from not to assault to assault. But this will increase $p^*$ for other subjects too, and so on; in other words, the attainment of the threshold value of the probability of being aggressed is a self-propagating phenomenon, once it started.

Some words of conclusion may be useful. We saw that mass ethnic violence may arise in the absence of ethnic hatred. This does not amount to saying that mass ethnic violence does not produce hatred, nor that this hatred is unimportant. Hatred, as suggested above, fuels the convention of violence; it may also induce normal people to become agitators. If hatred is sufficiently high, it is obviously sufficient to induce mass ethnic violence. But where does hatred come from to begin with? If it is a product of mass ethnic violence, it cannot explain it. If it is not, this chapter suggests that hatred is unlikely to be so deep as to ignite mass ethnic violence, unless there are additional conditions. In a tragic setting, this is an encouraging result.

## APPENDIX

An interesting case arises if one of the players has a different hierarchy of payoffs.

Let us drop the assumption of symmetry. Two situations may result. First, the cardinal value of payoffs is different for the two players, but the order remains the same. This case is trivial. One of the typical subjects is more likely to be the first to move from $n$ to $a$, but as soon as this happens the probability of being assaulted starts moving towards 1 for the other one too, so we are again in the main model.

A more interesting result is obtained if we allow the order of payoffs to change for one of the subjects. In this case, we must verify (i) which orders of payoffs are plausible, (ii) if the resulting matrices are realistic, and (iii) which testable prediction(s) we obtain.

---

[15] See, for instance, Lemarchand (1993): "Tutsi apprehensions of a wholesale extermination by Hutu are indeed central to an understanding of the horrendous scale of the repressive measures triggered by the 1972 and 1988 uprisings (p. 158) . . . in 1988 the main perpetrators of anti-Tutsi violence were Hutu peasants, most of them panic-stricken at the thought that another 1972-style bloodbath was in the offing" (p. 165).

Some hierarchies of payoffs may be excluded *a priori*, due to plausible assumptions. More precisely, I assume that, whatever the hierarchy of payoffs, (a) $nn > aa$; (b) $an > aa$; (c) $nn > na$; and (d) $nn > an$. Assumptions (a) to (c) are "technological;" assumption (d) is required to avoid a trivial result.[16]

It is then simple, even if boring, to discover that only three profiles of payoffs may be acceptable, that is,

(1) $nn > an > aa > na$
(2) $nn > an > na > aa$
(3) $nn > na > an > aa$

Profile (1) is that of the chapter. So we are left with profiles (2) and (3).

Suppose that a player, $i$, has the payoff structure of the text, while $j$ has profile 2 or 3. For $j$, $n$ is dominant, so $j$ will never assault $i$ first. It follows that $i$ will not assault $j$, if the game is of complete information.[17] In addition, if $j$ is assaulted he prefers not assaulting to assaulting.

Are profiles (2) and/or (3) realistic? They correspond to a state of the world where the members of an ethnic group never assault first, and do not react if assaulted. This may be the case of an oppressed ethnic group in an un-collapsed state, whose members are punished if they assault, while members of the other group are not. Recent examples may be Blacks in the Southern United States or Jews in Germany. In this situation, *institutional* violence, as well as individual violence from fanatics or extremists, is presumably very high. However, the model predicts that there will *not* be *mass* ethnic violence. I suggest that this has actually been the case in both examples.

### REFERENCES

Breton, A. 1964. The Economics of Nationalism. *Journal of Political Economy* **72**, 4.

Breton, A. and Breton, M. 1995. Nationalism Revisited. In Breton et al. (1995).

Breton, A., Galeotti, G., Salmon, P. and Wintrobe, R. (eds, 1995). *Nationalism and Rationality*. Cambridge University Press.

Brown, R. 1985. *Social Psychology, the second edition*. The Free Press.

Cooper, R., DeJong, D., Forsythe, R. and Ross, T. (1990). Selection Criteria in Coordination Games. *American Economic Review* **80**.

Hardin, R. 1995. *One for All*. Princeton University Press.

[16] If $an > nn$, a player prefers to assault a non-hostile partner. This case is of no interest in this chapter, as discussed in Section 3.

[17] Note that the activity of agitators does not violate the hypothesis of complete information. Players know strategies and payoffs; what they ignore is *who* is assuming the role of their opponent.

Hardin, R. 1995b. Self-interest, Group Identity. In Breton et al. (1995).

Hargreaves Heap, S. P. and Varoufakis, Y. (1995). *Game Theory: a Critical Introduction*. Routledge.

Horowitz, D. L. 1985. *Ethnic Groups in Conflict*. University of California Press.

Landa, J. T. 1995. *Trust, ethnicity and identity: beyond the new institutional economics of ethnic trading networks, contract law and gift exchange*. University of Michigan Press.

Lemarchand, R. 1993. Burundi in Comparative Perspective, in McGarry, J. and O'Leary, B. (eds), *The Politics of Ethnic Conflict Regulation*. Routledge.

Lloyd, P. C. 1974. Ethnicity and the Structure of Inequality in a Nigerian Town in the Mid-1950s, in Cohen, A. (ed.), *Urban Ethnicity*. Tavistock.

Olson, M. 1965. *The Logic of Collective Action*. Harvard University Press.

Sugden, R. 1986. *The Economics of Rights, Cooperation and Welfare*. Basil Blackwell.

Van Der Dennen, J. M. G. 1987, ed. *The Sociobiology of Ethnocentrism*. Croom Helm.

Wintrobe, R. 1995. Some Economics of Ethnic Capital Formation and Conflict. In Breton et al. (1995).

# Index

Africa *see* Algeria; Burundi; Egypt;
Tunisia
African National Congress, 172, 173
agitators: in ethnic violence, 225–7,
228
Algeria: Islamic fundamentalism in,
63, 187, 191, 201, 202, 206–8
Americas *see* Cuba; Nicaragua;
United States
Amish: education restrictions, 20
anarchism, 156, 172
Arab-Islamic states: characteristics,
200–3; democracy in, 210–12;
Islamic fundamentalism in,
17–18, 190–1; *see also* Algeria;
Egypt; Iranian revolution;
Tunisia; Turkey
assimilation: ethnic, 9, 14–15
audience responsiveness: and terrorist
activity, 59–63
Australia: One Nation Party, 90
authoritarian democracy, 185–6
authoritarianism, 30
authority: and knowledge, 6–8
autonomy: potential for, 48–52, 55

belief: development of *see*
socialization; and fanatical
action, 15–16, 18–19; and
knowledge, 46; *see also* religious
beliefs

Bentham, Jeremy: on fanaticism, 3–4,
10
Bosnia: ethnic violence in, 17, 18–19,
220–1, 222, 226n, 228; *see also*
Yugoslavia
Bousquet, René: trial of, 84–5
brainwashing *see* socialization
bribery, 34–5
Burundi: ethnic violence in, 219–20n,
222, 228n, 232n
byproduct knowledge, 6, 7

Cambodia: Pol Pot regime, 177–8
campaign strategies: of political
parties, 106–7, 108–15
Catalonia *see* Spain
Central Africa *see* Burundi
centrism: efficiency of, 93–5
centrist co-location: breaking of,
95–100
centrist monomaniacs, 74, 78–9
charisma: and extremism, 101–3
China: policy choices in, 176, 178, 179
civil war: probabilities, 191–200,
213–15; *see also* ethnic violence;
violence
Civil War (UK), 129–30
coalitions, 74–81; non-responsibility
in, 81–2
collaboration: and patriotism, 83–4
communications gap *see* social holes

Printed in Great Britain
by Amazon